Restoration

THE FREE PRESS
A Division of Macmillan, Inc. · *New York*

MAXWELL MACMILLAN CANADA
Toronto

MAXWELL MACMILLAN INTERNATIONAL
New York · *Oxford* · *Singapore* · *Sydney*

GEORGE F. WILL

Restoration

CONGRESS, TERM LIMITS AND THE RECOVERY OF DELIBERATIVE DEMOCRACY

The Free Press
A Division of Macmillan, Inc.
866 Third Avenue, New York, N.Y. 10022

Maxwell Macmillan Canada, Inc.
1200 Eglinton Avenue East
Suite 200
Don Mills, Ontario M3C 3N1

Macmillan, Inc. is part of the Maxwell Communication
Group of Companies.

Printed in the United States of America

printing number
1   2   3   4   5   6   7   8   9   10

Designed by REM Studio, Inc.

Library of Congress Cataloging-in-Publication Data

Will, George F.
    Restoration : Congress, term limits and the recovery of
deliberative democracy / George F. Will.
        p.   cm.
    Includes bibliographical references and index.
    ISBN 0–02–934437–9
    1. United States.   Congress—Term of office.   I. Title.
JK1140.W55   1992
328.73'073—dc20   92–26005
                                                      CIP

To

Pat and Liz Moynihan

and

Jack and Sally Danforth

*Were more of the people who came to Washington like
these four, this book would not have been written.*

". . . yet we may safely pronounce, that the true test of a good government is its aptitude and tendency . . ."

—ALEXANDER HAMILTON
Federalist No. 68

Contents

ix

Introduction

On May 12, 1780, when the British siege of Charleston, South Carolina, succeeded and the town surrendered, American officers were at first permitted to keep their swords. However, the swords were soon demanded by British commanders who were annoyed by the Americans' defiant shouts of "long live Congress!"[1] Times have changed.

It has been some time since Americans felt an overmastering urge to shout their enthusiasm for Congress. But it also has been quite a spell since Americans so nearly unanimously spoke as disrespectfully of Congress as they do in this, the first decade of the Constitution's third century. Times have changed.

America's first two Congresses—the First and Second Continental Congresses of 1774 and 1775—were at best extralegal. They existed in defiance of, and were working to dissolve, the duly constituted authority in British North America, authority that emanated from Westminster in London. It is of course natural, and not alarming, that Congress does not now, in the 1990s, have a place in the affections of a secure and mature nation comparable to the place Congress occupied in 1780. Then the Congress was the sole focus of authority for, and the sole focus of patriotism in, an embryonic nation struggling to be born. Furthermore, nothing is more natural in a nation with America's intellectual pedigree than that Congress should come to be thought of, at best, ambivalently. Encoded in Americans' civic chromosomes, in their political DNA, is a deep—literally, congenital—suspicion of all government, and especially of that government that is most distant from them.

To be a politician in a democracy, and especially in the rough-and-tumble of American democracy, is to seek elevation while denying any desire to be special. Americans are always eager to reassure their politicians that no politician is immoderately reverenced. Making jokes at Congress's expense was an American tradition long before Mark Twain made his celebrated jape that America has no indigenous criminal class— other than Congress. Twain also said, suppose I am a crook; and suppose I am a congressman; but I repeat myself. For as long as there has been that distinct creature, the American, he has considered it good democratic fun to level the political people by leveling at them the guns of jest and disrespect.

But by the beginning of the 1990s the nation's jokes had an ugly bite, and the laughter had a bitter timbre. The condition of Congress, in its own estimation as well as that of its constituents, was worse than ever before. Opinion polls should be taken with no more than two grains of salt, but by the summer of 1992 some poll results were too extreme to ignore. To take but one example, an Associated Press poll found that just 1 percent of Americans (a sliver smaller than the poll's margin of error) said that they trusted Congress to do what is right "just about all the time." Now, that was, perhaps, a foolish formulation for a question, one designed to generate a memorable number. But a more revealing number from the same poll was that approximately one-third of the sample said they would almost never trust Congress to do the right thing.

By the beginning of the 1990s it was beginning to seem that Congress was not just going through another of its bad patches. Rather, Congress seemed to have settled into a deep trough, and it lacked the strength to lift itself out. More and more people, including many despairing—and departing— members of Congress, were convinced that this was not a mere bad patch to be got through, it was the future. Or it would be, unless something drastic were done. This book is written to give the rationale for one remedial measure, a limitation on the number of consecutive terms that members of legislatures can serve.

I have come slowly and reluctantly but firmly to acceptance of the need for this reform. My reflex is to recoil from proposals for constitutional change. However, under the accumulating weight of evidence I, like millions of other Americans, have been driven to the conclusion that something must be done to restore Congress to competence and respect, and that term limits can do it.

Americans today favor term limits by substantial margins. In every region and every demographic group, there is a substantial majority for term limits. This majority may have, as yet, only a shallow commitment to a reform that is only superficially understood. However, the more deeply Americans understand the philosophical justifications for term limits, and the probable consequences of limits, the more intense the support for limits should become. One lesson of American history is that when a majority of Americans have a strong and pro-tracted desire for something, they get it. This book is an at-tempt to nourish the intensity and staying power of the desire for term limits. My aim is to help transform this desire from a lightly held preference into a deeply felt, because fully com-prehended, conviction.

My passage from opposition to mere skepticism, through quickened interest, and on to conviction, was the result of revisiting some of the ideas and controversies that shaped America in the founding era, when the Republic was wax soft to the touch of strong, sharp thinking. That thinking concerned such ideas as deliberative democracy and classical republican-ism.

Term limits were included among the fifteen resolutions of the Virginia Plan submitted to the Constitutional Convention in Philadelphia. But term limits were put aside and character-ized "as entering too much into detail for general proposi-tions."[2] It is interesting that what looks to Americans today like a matter of potentially large consequence looked in 1787 like a mere matter of "detail," a subject not sufficiently mo-mentous to merit the gravity of being addressed in the nation's fundamental law.

The judgment of the Constitutional Convention was cor-rect, in its context. Term limits limit choices, and hence are an excision, albeit small, from the sphere of civic freedom. No such excision should be made lightly or unnecessarily. How-ever, the Founders' rejection of term limits in 1789, although wise, was no wiser than adoption of term limits would be now. The Convention was wise to reject term limits because they were not clearly connected with correcting a large problem. Now they are.

To demonstrate why they are, this book will explore two realms that often are, but never should be, separate—the realms of thought and action. It will examine behavior and ideas—primarily the contemporary behavior of politicians and old ideas about politics. In doing this I am drawing upon three areas of my professional experience.

Journalism is the third, albeit much the longest, of my three careers. I am the son of a professor of philosophy and began my professional life as a professor of political philosophy. I anticipated a lifetime in academia. However, in my third year in academic life I was offered a position on the staff of a U.S. Senator. I accepted with alacrity and spent three stimulating and happy years on Capitol Hill, where I acquired a lasting love of the Congress. Then I became a columnist. So I have worked in the realms of thought (academia), of action (politics) and of thinking about action (journalistic commentary). I have come to an emphatic conclusion. It is that ideas matter.

My point is not just that ideas have consequences, but that only ideas have large and lasting consequences. When firmly held, ideas are motives for action. When important ideas are forgotten by a republic, the forgetting of them is the reason why the republic lists dangerously in one direction or another. The good news about the abundance of bad news concerning American politics and government right now is that bad news has concentrated the national mind. The decline of public confidence in government and the resurgent interest in term limits have got the nation thinking about fundamentals. And not a moment too soon.

Political philosophers have frequently argued that the civic health of a free people requires periodic reflection about first principles. America's crisis of confidence in government in the 1990s can be good for this Republic if it provokes such reflection. It appears to be doing that.

It may seem hyperbolic to say that America in the 1990s is in a crisis. Never has the nation's physical security from foreign attack been greater—never. True, there was at the beginning of the 1990s an unusually long economic recession, but it was not unusually deep, and business cycles are not crises unless they involve social convulsions like those of the Depression. However, the word "crisis" is not hyperbolic in the context of the early 1990s, because what is ailing the nation is the essence of the nation's significance. What is in crisis is the public's faith in that which most makes America matter: self-government. The acids of cynicism and contempt are corroding confidence in the institutions of collective action and are giving rise to fatalism about events that seem to be spinning out of control. There is national queasiness about the slow but perceptible and accelerating downward spiral of national vigor and standards. This queasiness is part of the most pronounced mood swing in the nation's history, one coming after a moment of almost giddy triumphalism.

Contemporary history seemed to have an almost magical tidiness to it when the Berlin Wall fell (November 9, 1989) just three weeks after the sixtieth anniversary of the stock market collapse (October 24, 1929) that plunged the United States into six strenuous decades of Depression, war and Cold War. The end of the Cold War was punctuated by an extraordinary assertion of American power in the suddenly unipolar world—Operation Desert Storm. But just when America seemed securely at the wheel of the world, Americans began to worry that the wheels were falling off their nation. In the astonishing fifteen months from the bombing of Baghdad to the burning of Los Angeles, Americans passed from a complacency tinged with hubris to an anxiety bordering on despair. There came upon the nation a sense of abandoned standards and waning supremacies, a conviction that other leaner, hungrier, better-governed nations are making America's prosperity and position in the world precarious.

What needs to be recovered is a certain understanding of American democracy. Note that I speak not of democracy generally but of our American variant. The idea of democracy, severed from the context of a particular civic culture and its history, is an airy abstraction. But the American democratic tradition, rich in turbulent arguments, has distinctive values, a characteristic tang, and many tangible manifestations unique to it. We have lost much of the original sense of the drama of our democracy. Some of that loss is understandable, indeed inevitable, and not really regrettable. After all, two hundred years ago democracy was an experiment, and we were a novelty. Still, our continentwide laboratory of liberty is still the most noble, exciting and important political undertaking in history. And the difficulties confronting it today are, in some ways, as challenging as those that tested the prudence of the founding generation.

At one level, the yearning for national recovery merely focuses on recovery from particular current distresses and anxieties such as economic sluggishness and educational laxity. But such recovery can best be achieved and made lasting (or at least as lasting as things are in social arrangements) by a broader, deeper recovery. What needs to be recovered is contact with the intellectual wellsprings of our politics.

Political theorists have often argued that maintaining a republic is more difficult than founding one. Lincoln may have had this in mind when, on February 11, 1861, bidding goodbye to neighbors at the beginning of his journey from Springfield to his Inauguration in Washington, he said, "I now leave . . . with a task before me greater than that which rested upon Washington."[3] Today's task of restoring competent government is hardly comparable to Lincoln's or Washington's, but it is big and it must begin with restoration of Congress to its proper prominence and dignity. This depends on restoring a sense of proportion to the political class, and thereby to government.

I must now turn directly to describing some of the shortcomings and overreachings that have recently been emblematic of Congress and of today's governing class generally. Because I must do this, I want to preface the next chapter with a declaration: I harbor no hostility toward government in general or Congress in particular. As will become abundantly clear, I favor term limits not as a punitive measure but as a way of strengthening Congress as a countervailing power in a government in which the executive branch has become swollen and disproportionate, and the judiciary has become more intrusive than is healthy for our society.

America's movement to revolution and independence began, particularly in Boston and Virginia, as a recoil against the overbearing executive power wielded by Royal Governors. The Continental Congress was America's first weapon against that. But executive power is a perennial problem, and Congress must be counted on to be the primary check upon it. An argument advanced against term limits is that they would lead to further augmentation of executive power. Were I convinced that that is true, I might still be back where I was a few years ago, among the opponents of term limits. However, it is highly likely that term limits will help restore a healthy balance between the legislative and executive branches, and also between the legislative and judicial branches.

A strong, and itself sufficient, reason for term limits is that they would restore to the legislative branch the preeminence and luster that it rightly should have. There is a kind of scorched-earth, pillage-and-burn conservatism that is always at a rolling boil, and which boils down to a brute animus against government. Those who subscribe to this vigorous but unsubtle faith have had jolly fun in the early 1990s as public esteem for government, and especially for Congress, has plummeted. However, that is not my kind of conservatism. I do not fathom how any American who loves the nation can relish the spectacle of the central institutions of American democracy being degraded and despised. Patriotism properly understood simply is not compatible with contempt for the institutions that put American democracy on display.

Congressional supremacy is a traditional tenet of American conservatism. It had better be, because it also is a basic constitutional fact. The Constitution begins with a brisk fifty-two-word preamble about why we, the people, are constituting ourselves. Then the Constitution buckles down to business, the first item of which—Article I—defines the composition, duties and powers of the legislative branch.

It is altogether appropriate that the home of this branch, the Capitol, is the noblest public building in daily use anywhere in the world. And it is fitting that this building sits at the conjunction of the four quadrants of the Federal City. That setting symbolizes the fact that Congress is and ought to be the epicenter of the political expression of the nation's collective life. But in modern America, and in the context of today's Leviathan-like federal government, Congress can be entrusted with that centrality only if it is reformed by term limits. This is so because only term limits can break the nexus between legislative careerists and the capacity of the modern state to be bent to the service of their careerism.

This nexus, degrading to Congress and demoralizing to the country, is one reason why government performs so poorly and is therefore so disdained. Contemporary evidence confirms what reason suggests: A permanent class of career legislators is inherently inimical to limited government—government that is discriminating in its ends and modest in its methods. Interest in term limits has risen as government's record of practical achievements has become steadily less impressive.

Furthermore, any attempt to understand the waning of respect for government in general, and for the Congress in particular, should begin with this fact: As government has become more solicitous, it has not become more loved or respected. As government has become more determinedly

ameliorative, it has fallen in the esteem of the public whose
condition it toils to improve. There is a perverse correlation
between the increasing role of compassion in the rhetoric of
governance and the decreasing regard for government on the
part of the compassionated public. And there is a causal relation between many of the government's failures and the motives, attitudes and actions of legislative careerists. So to begin
the argument for term limits, let us turn to the behavior of
Congress that has imparted such momentum to the term limits
movement.

CHAPTER 1

From Bristol to Cobb County: The Decline of Representation and the Rise of Careerism

W hen the young Senator Henry Clay arrived in Washington in December, 1806, the nation's capital was a village lacking virtually every element of commodious living. "Pennsylvania Avenue, the city's main thoroughfare, was frequently so muddy as to be impassable."[1] When Clay's disciple, Abraham Lincoln, arrived fifty-five years later for his Inauguration, Washington was even worse than it was when the young Clay came to town, and worse than when Representative Lincoln had come in 1847. "Washington was a dirtier, ranker city than Lincoln remembered, with a plethora of livery stables and rancid saloons. Pigs rooted in the dirt streets slanting off from Pennsylvania Avenue, and sewage marshes lay at the foot of the President's park south of the old mansion. At the northern edge of the garbage-strewn Mall ran an open drainage ditch, 'floating with dead cats and all kinds of putridity,' said an observer, 'and reeking with pestilential odors.' Even now, in the early morning, a stench hung over the city worse than any Lincoln could recall."[2] In the nineteenth century accepting a job in Washington involved, for many people, accepting the discomfort of living in the cramped quarters of a boarding house. In February, 1869, while President-elect Grant was cobbling together a cabinet, "One lady, asked why she wished to speak to the general, told an aide (or perhaps a reporter) that she was calling to learn whom he had chosen, as she had rooms to rent."[3] Few people were drawn to the capital by any glitter, and few who came as congressmen could even bring comfort with them, or could afford to buy it in Washington.

That is one of several reasons why relatively few members of Congress—far fewer than today—made running for reelection the great constant of their lives. Perpetual incumbency was not the normal career aspiration for members of Congress. For a long time Washington was not a place where many people who had a choice chose to linger. People came to Congress for a while, then departed, either because they had other things they wanted to do—perhaps other political offices to seek—or because they were defeated. This mitigated the tendency—a timeless tendency in any political branch of any government—of Congress to become an insular ruling class, resented by a suspicious public.

That was then. This is now:

On autumn mornings in 1991, commuters driving into San Francisco on Interstate 80 had their eyes opened wide by billboards advertising a local morning TV news show. The billboard featured an image of the U.S. Capitol dome and these words: "Find out what they did to you last night."[4] The pronoun and the preposition were signs of the time. The sinister cabal denoted by the pronoun "they" were the representatives of the sovereign people who put "them" beneath the dome. The sovereign people, including the commuters, were being incited by anxiety about what was being done "to" them, not for them. The people were not feeling particularly sovereign and were not happy with the way American popular sovereignty was working. They were seething with resentment of a ruling class that was, infuriatingly and frustratingly, of their making. That class, the "they" beneath the Capitol dome, was resented both in spite of and because of its relentless attempts to ingratiate itself with the resentful public.

It was apparent at the dawn of this decade that Americans were entering a season of special discontent with the tone and substance of the nation's political life. Two disturbances—a movie and a man—were particularly vivid signs that 1992 was the year of the "outsider." Both Oliver Stone's movie "JFK" and the Ross Perot phenomenon were evidence of the pathologies to which a society is prey when it becomes extremely cynical about "insiders," meaning people operating within the constitutional institutions.

"JFK" was a pastiche of tendentious history, infantile paranoia and ideological fantasies, all purporting to prove that in 1963 Washington—all of it: the Vice President, the Chief Justice, the CIA, the FBI, the armed services, congressional leaders and everyone and everything else important—was completely controlled by a criminal, indeed treasonous, conspiracy. Furthermore, Stone implied, the fact that this conspiracy has not been unmasked (other than by his movie) proves that nothing much has changed in 29 years.

Ross Perot's promise to "buy" the presidency for "the people" was received rapturously by millions of people who knew next to nothing about his political ideas. They even seemed to like the fact that he had few ideas and that the few he had

proved that he knew next to nothing about America's Constitution, budget or recent political history. That seemed to rec-
ommend him as the outside-most outsider, someone outside the
mundane realm of information.

"JFK" was not jeered into instant oblivion. It was respect-
fully reviewed and treated as a serious contribution to understanding modern American history. And it made pots of money.
Perot, a political buccaneer, had his sails filled by just the sort
of gusts of popular passion that the Framers of the Constitution feared. But, then, his boast was that he had a relationship
of special immediacy with "the people." And he claimed he was
the kind of "can do" fellow who can do without the constitutional forms and mores that are supposed to shape the national
will and the relations between the people and the holders of
power. Or so the Framers thought. But what did they know,
that pack of eighteenth century "insiders"?

"JFK" and Perot were prominent among the 1992 symp-
toms of the severe distemper to which a republic is susceptible when people distrust their representatives. The movie
and the man were both fevers erupting in the context of col-
lapsing confidence in a political class composed primarily of
careerists.

Of course, complaining about the caliber and conduct of
politics is not only every American's birthright, it is also a
favorite recreation. And it is a reflection of national character,
for historical and philosophic reasons.

Our nation had a distinct founding moment featuring no-
tably reflective and eloquent statesmen. Hence ours is a nation
permanently poised for disillusionment. It is natural, if not
inevitable, for subsequent generations to measure their situation against the standards of a receding Golden Age that becomes more golden as it recedes. So it is natural for Americans
to decide that things are going to hell in a handcart. However,
the fact that a tilt toward pessimism about politics is built into

American history does not mean that pessimism is not some-times reasonable. It is today.

Furthermore, the broad outline of America's public phi-losophy inclines Americans toward disrespect regarding polit-ical people. That philosophy, in the form in which most Americans have internalized it, holds that government is a necessary evil. Or, to put the point more amiably, government is a useful nuisance. American history, from the Boston Tea Party (perhaps the earliest historical episode vivid to most Americans) through whatever contemporary tax or other gov-ernment act is most annoying at the moment, teaches Ameri-cans that government needs watching. Furthermore, today, as always, Americans have a lively thirst for scandal, as well as a journalism eager to slake that thirst. So there never has been a time when there were not heard discouraging words about politicians and their works. But differences of degree become differences of kind, and historians may one day conclude that in the autumn of 1991 American discontent became qualitatively different.

In that autumn interest in term limits reached the politi-cal equivalent of what nuclear physicists call "critical mass." As is often the case in the untidy politics of this large democ-racy, the large issue of term limits rose on the public's agenda because of an unplanned concatenation of small events, many of them manifestly trivial. Historians may one day conclude that Congress's slide into disrepute became especially steep on September 18, 1991, when the General Accounting Office released a report on the administration—or lack of adminis-tration—of the bank run for members of the House of Rep-resentatives. It was the first sputtering of the fuse that would lead, four months later, to the Big Bang of the check-bouncing debacle.

Debacle more than scandal. There probably was little pec-ulation of any sort involved, little conscious moneymaking from the calculated kiting of checks. Clearly, some members cynically exploited the chaotic conditions at the bank and used it as a source of interest-free loans. But many members simply had no idea that they were writing overdrafts, so badly was the bank administered. But for much of the public, shaky on the details but sound on intuitive judgment, maladministration was the symbolic truth, and that was enough: Those people in Congress did not know what they were doing. They couldn't run a little in-house check-cashing service called a bank without making a mess of things. Small wonder they can't run the country worth a damn. In time, and remarkably little time it was, a prairie fire of public disgust was raging. It was fueled by talk-radio, television newscasts and other media. The media at last had a subject small enough to wrap their comprehension around and simple enough to communicate with the concision of an uppercut.

Someday historians, pondering all this heat with the cool detachment conferred by distance in time, may marvel at the disproportion of American passions in the 1990s. Failures of government were manifold and manifest, but bouncing checks aroused more wrath than anything else. Why?

People became enraged by legislators' small abuses of a minor privilege because government is not using its power intelligently and competently regarding big problems. The small abuses are more comprehensible and more easily rectified than the big failures. What Stalin said about mass murder (one death is a tragedy, a million deaths is a statistic) is true, too, about politics in this democracy. A $400 billion deficit is a meaningless number. A few dozen checks bounced by a congressman at a bank that had no business being in business is an understandable focus for disgust. The bank debacle became a lightning rod, drawing down a lot of the gathered energy of anger that had been intensifying for years and was bound to be released, sooner or later, with an ear-splitting crack of thunder.

The basic question is why the public was so combustible. If you seek reasons, look around. They are everywhere. They are in the government's big policy failures—cities, schools, budgets, infrastructure—and also in its routine, mundane operations.

Speaking of the mundane, one day in November, 1991, Washington's scandal *du jour* posed a conceptual puzzle. Should something properly called a scandal be at least a little bit secret? Can a scandal be something done in plain view, with due process, by people who put out press releases boasting about what they have done?

Brooke Masters of the *Washington Post* revealed that beginning December 1, 1991, a one-plane commercial airline would get a substantial federal subsidy—more than half a million dollars a year—to fly mostly affluent business travelers to expense-account meetings at the posh Homestead resort in Hot Springs, Virginia.[5] Taxpayers from Harlem and Watts and everywhere else would pay more than $150 per passenger to reduce the price wealthy travelers would pay to get to their playground. This is part of a national program costing approximately $39 million a year. It is exquisitely titled Essential Air Service.

"Essential." To whom? "It's about jobs for the community," says an official of the airline. The congressman in whose district the Homestead sits says, "I consider [the subsidy] essential to keeping the hotel open."[6] Oh? The wealthy travelers (few from Harlem or Watts) taking tax-deductible trips (another subsidy) to a tony watering spot (three golf courses, stocked trout stream, skeet range, spa) will stay home and sulk unless taxpayers foot part of their travel bill? Most guests make the final leg of their trip by rented cars or limousines. The hotel has six hundred rooms. The plane has nineteen seats. In peak season it will make two round trips a day; the rest of the year, just one. It will average just six passengers per trip (although the subsidy will be paid even if the plane is empty). The hotel depends on this?

The Essential Air Service program is just another entitlement. Congress says many small communities are entitled to air service even if market realities make it unprofitable for commercial carriers to provide it. This is foolishness; it also is routine. It is a tiny part of an enormous pattern of federal activity. The *Post*'s Brooke Masters deserves accolades for excavating this story from the budget's fine print. But this subsidy, and thousands of other follies, are hardly hatched in secret. Thousands of such expenditures are supposed to be noticed by the direct beneficiaries but not by the likes of Masters, and certainly not by the 99.99 percent of the American people who have better things to do than browse through the budget. Such expenditures are among the means that members of Congress use to purchase perpetual incumbency. That is why America's spacious skies are dark with dollars flying hither and yon, doing thousands of things that are neither essential nor even defensible, while the deficit swells and the political culture curdles.

Today's national legislature lards the budget with spending for parochial projects and justifies this reelection ritual with solemn references to two values. One is a softhearted concern for "fairness." The other is a supposedly hardheaded, Hamiltonian concern for economic strength. The assumption about "fairness" is that everyone is entitled to partiality from the federal government in the allocation of special benefits. The economic assumption is that the maelstrom of political grasping that results from this entitlement mentality produces government activism that is conducive to national vigor.

Jeffersonians may have been dreamers, but their nightmare is today's normality—government as prize and prize-giver, politics as an endless auction. Can a practice so open and so common for so long be considered corrupt? We are back to the puzzle: Can something be a scandal if it does not scandalize? Or is that—the flaccid acceptance of things—the scandal?

If Americans accept the current mores of governance, they are accepting far more than the banal—and not itself dismaying—fact that government responds to interests. It always has; to some extent and in various ways it should. However, the word "respond" often gives too benign a description of what is going on. The modern state does not merely respond to interests, it generates them and even, in effect, organizes them. Many constituencies call for government programs. But some programs call forth constituencies. Consider, as just one of many possible examples, the mohair lobby.

What? You mean to say you think mohair is the hair of a mo? Not so. It comes from the Angora goat. In fact, from two million of them that frolic and grow and yield up their coats right here in America. Taxpayers should know that, because as fast as these goats are shorn, so are taxpayers. But if you buy a mohair coat, you are swathed in subsidies. Thus does government temper the wind to the shorn taxpayers.

Consider how this came to be, and how a government program achieves immortality.

In 1954 Eisenhower had been President for one year, Elvis had not yet become the King and the Angora goat, a shaggy creature with horns and dreadlocks, was discovered to be—or at least declared to be—a vital component in the nation's security planning. As Jonathan Rauch reconstructed the story,[7] the genesis of this subsidy was during World War II, when soldiers slogged to victory wearing heavy wool uniforms. The War Department, as it then was called, discovered that U.S. wool producers could deliver only about half the wool the military required and presumably would require again when next we fought a two-front world war in Europe and Asia.

The world has turned a few times since then. Today microchips and specialty metal alloys are strategic commodities.

Back then, wool was. Anyway, Congress decided that wool
production should be stimulated. And, oh, yes: To that end,
domestic wool producers should be protected from cheap foreign imports. Hence the 1954 National Wool Act. It paid farmers to grow wool. What did mohair have to do with this
supposed precaution against a possible sudden need for 12 million military uniforms? Nothing, really. Mohair was, Rauch
says, "just along for the ride." It has been some ride, long and
remarkably smooth.

As the world has turned, synthetic fibers have come upon
the scene. That is one reason why, in 1960, the Pentagon
dropped wool from its list of strategically critical materials. It
was good that it could do that, because the subsidy had failed:
Wool production had declined, steadily and a lot. And it continued to decline after 1960. Did this mean the death of the
wool subsidy or even of that hitchhiker, the mohair subsidy?
Are you kidding?

The Rockies may crumble, Gibraltar may tumble, they're
only made of clay, but federal programs are here to stay. Remember the great budget "summit" during the deficit "crisis"
of the autumn of 1990? Congressional and Bush administration
leaders, looking as somber as all get out, went to earth at
Andrews Air Force Base to wage a death-grapple with the
"runaway" budget deficit. There were more than four thousand
federal domestic spending programs when the grapple began.
And there were just as many when it ended. But I digress.

Defenders of the ongoing mohair subsidy, now nearing the
end of its fourth decade, say the subsidy is self-financing. They
say this for two reasons. First, almost all domestic spending
programs are said by their supporters to be self-financing.
(Public works? They put people to work, generate tax revenues, make the economy more efficient and—presto!—"pay for
themselves." Health care? Education? Spending programs in
these areas make people "more productive" and therefore "pay

for themselves." Such arguments can be true. They rarely are. But they always are enunciated.) Second, the mohair subsidy is said by its supporters to be self-financing because the money paid to mohair producers comes from receipts produced by a tariff on imported wool. But as Rauch notes, that merely means that the money paid to producers of mohair is from a wool tax paid by taxpayers who buy foreign sweaters. This is an example of Washington's notion of something that "costs nothing."

Another argument made by supporters of the subsidy is that other nations subsidize wool, so we should too. This crashing *non sequitur* rides on the usual rhetoric: "Wool and mohair, lamb and mutton, are an important industry for the United States that shouldn't be sacrificed to foreign competitors who are subsidizing their industry."[8] So says Representative Charles Stenholm (D., Texas). Stenholm is a leading light among congressional conservatives. He is among the most determined advocates of a constitutional amendment to require balanced budgets. But he is also, and foremost, chairman of the Agriculture Committee's Subcommittee on Livestock, Dairy and Poultry. Eighty-five percent of America's Angora goats reside in Texas. Stenholm's district ranks sixth in the nation in wool production.

His argument (about "sacrificing" an American industry to subsidized foreigners) is woolly. Australia and New Zealand are the major players in the world wool market. They account for 85 percent of the world's wool exports. Their subsidies account for a piddling 4 percent of their producers' receipts. U.S. subsidies account for a whopping 42 percent of U.S. producers' receipts. Also, Australian and New Zealand sheep are more productive than American sheep, producing twice as much wool per head.

But let's get back to the goat side of this subsidy saga. Mohair is a negligible part of the U.S. clothing market, amounting to no more than 1/100,000th of the fiber used. In fact, most

U.S. mohair is exported. That means the mohair subsidy is subsidizing European sweater-makers. They then send some of their sweaters to America, where Americans pay the tariffs that fund the mohair subsidy. Not to worry, say the subsidy's supporters, U.S. mohair exports contribute to a "positive balance of trade." But Americans are paying a subsidy of 387.3 percent to produce the mohair, probably the highest subsidy rate for any agricultural product. (In 1990 the average market price for mohair was 93 cents a pound; the federal mohair support price was $4.53 per pound.)

Actually, the subsidy is just another welfare program primarily for the wealthy, generating an entitlement mentality. Since 1954, 80 percent of the money has flowed to fewer than 6,000 producers, most of them doing quite nicely, thank you. By 1990 some producers were getting $200,000 checks for their subsidies. Rauch quotes "an industry source" as saying, "We're not proud of getting these checks. It's embarrassing."[9] Uh huh. And the producers will die in the last ditch fighting to defeat their senators and representatives if those legislators will not die fighting to preserve the producers' entitlement to those embarrassing checks.

In 1990 there actually was a fight. It was a mini-revolt led by a few of the representatives who represent the 99.99 percent of Americans who are losers from the mohair subsidy. The rebels suggested shrinking this lamb-and-goat socialism just a little bit by putting a $50,000 cap on annual payments to individual producers. Unfortunately the subsidy was defended more efficiently than wool and mohair are produced. (That is one perverse effect of modern government: Efficiency is elicited for the defense of the inefficient.) The subsidy has a stout defender in the House: Representative Kika de la Garza, Chairman of the Agriculture Committee. He is from Texas, naturally. In the Senate, the subsidy's strongest defenders—and they were more than sufficient—are Wyoming's two Republican Senators, Alan Simpson and Malcolm Wallop. They are both conservatives, or so they say. However, Wyoming is the second-ranking wool-producing state.

This subsidy is a perfect example of the Washington survivor. It is big enough for its beneficiaries to care about, passionately. But it is small enough (in 1990, $105 million, less than 2 percent of spending on farm programs) that it does not attract much attention. As Rauch says, the mohair subsidy has "the classic camouflage of a small boring farm program."[10] Almost no one knows about it. No one, that is, other than its beneficiaries and the politicians who benefit from the votes and financial contributions of their grateful constituents. Grateful producers are spread around. Every state has people producing wool. Such dispersal is useful—indeed, is irresistible—in congressional politics.

Some concentration also is useful: 60 percent of the combined wool and mohair subsidies go to Texas, a state with much muscle in Congress. So the wool and mohair lobby represents enough little beneficiaries to produce lots of plaintive letters urging Congress not to withdraw a subsidy on which "family farms" depend. And the lobby also represents enough big beneficiaries to fund potent Washington lobbying.

All the economic arguments for the subsidy are tendentious rubbish. They also are irrelevant to the subsidy's immortality. The subsidy has a political rationale: Some attentive and intense voters want it.

The price of mohair has fallen "disastrously." Which is to say, mohair supplies exceed demand. That is hardly a disaster for mohair consumers, but, again, we are now talking politics, not economics. This program, begun during the dark hours of the Cold War and in the name of national security, has been reborn as a "rural development program" to sustain a "treasured American way of life." But not the rural life that Jeffersonians celebrate. Put plainly, the mohair subsidy is one of

innumerable programs that sustain an urban way of life—the
life of career legislators, toiling, they hope for as long as they
like, smack in the center of the District of Columbia. By the
way, the District is the only one of the fifty-one political entities that cast electoral votes for the presidency that has no
agricultural interests at all.

Are mohair producers peculiar in their relationship to the
government? No such luck. Agriculture, which is supposed to
be a repository of the virtues Jefferson associated with sturdy
independence, is shot through with dependency. For example,
consider the busy bees. During World War II the government
got into the honey business. It decided to encourage—only
temporarily, of course; no war lasts forever—the production of
honey as a sugar substitute, and of beeswax for waterproofing
combat equipment. The war ended in 1945. The honey subsidy
was going strong in 1992, to the tune of an estimated $20
million.

In the early summer of 1992 Bill Clinton tried to use bees
to balance his image, if not the budget. He promised that as
president he would favor a $200 billion spending program for
public works. But he also said he would cut the budget, and he
singled out one wee $20 million subsidy from the more than $14
billion in agricultural subsidies, the price support for honey.
The beekeepers, all 2,000 of them, were as mad as hornets, but
not madder than Chairman Kika de la Garza who, according to
his staff, dislikes anyone targeting individual agricultural industries for cuts.[11] The policy is to cut all or none. Guess which
it will be.

Mohair. Honey. Peanuts, as we shall see anon. And grains
and dairy products and beef and sugar . . . and on and on. If
you can buy it at a supermarket, the chances are it is a politicized product, involved in some government program (do not
forget subsidized water for irrigation) benefiting, and buying
the votes of, America's farmers. Representative Harris Fawell

(R., Illinois) says that in 1990 the federal government paid to *prevent* the production of agricultural goods on 60 million acres, an amount of land about equal to the size of Oregon. Conceivably, this was reasonable. But who, by 1992, believed that such a policy reflected any reasoning unrelated to the reelection desires of farm-state senators and representatives?

Well, then, is agriculture the only sector of the American economy significantly benefiting from government action prompted by the electoral interests of the class of career politicians? Hardly, as a cursory glance at the facts, rather than the rhetoric, of American policy regarding free trade reveals. Protectionism, administered by the Commerce Department but dictated by Congress, is a form of precisely targeted government favoritism for particular firms, industries, unions and communities. It is political crack cocaine, producing quick and fierce addiction. Dealers of the drug of protectionism generate dependent clients whose gratitude is expressed in campaign contributions and votes. So protectionism is an important component of the system for protecting congressional incumbents.

Americans got an unpleasant glimpse of just how protectionist America is when, in late December, 1991, and early January, 1992, President Bush and an equally whiny entourage (consisting primarily of overpaid CEOs of underachieving corporations) toured the Far East. They were a national embarrassment, representing the United States as the crybaby of the Western World.

Their tour got off to a stumbling start in Australia. There Bush, with the representatives of America's industrial anemia in tow, was about to chant the mantra of "fair" rather than free trade when Aussie farmers drowned him out with complaints about huge U.S. subsidies of wheat exports. The Aussies' shouts were not loud enough to be heard all the way to Capitol Hill. And even if those shouts had been heard there, the Aussies' displeasure would not have troubled the senators and representatives who enact the subsidies for the pleasure of grateful wheat-growing voters. (When President Lincoln founded the Department of Agriculture, it had one employee for every 227,000 farms. In 1900 it had one employee for every 1,694 farms.[12] Today it has one employee for every sixteen farms, and the laughter is a little less uproarious when a congressman proposes a law stipulating that there shall never be more Agriculture Department employees than farmers. To be fair to the Department and its personnel needs, it does take many hands to hand out in 1992, $14 billion worth of subsidies.)

Next, the Orient was treated to lectures on "fair trade" from an American government that restricts Jamaica to selling 970 gallons of ice cream a year in America, Mexico to 35,292 bras, Poland to 350 tons of alloy tool steel, Haiti—yes, we are protected from that colossus—to 7,730 tons of sugar. There are import quotas or duties on tampons, typing ribbons, tents, twine, table linens, tapestries and ties, and lots of other things.

Some foreign governments are treating U.S. companies badly, but not as badly as the U.S. government, at the behest of U.S. companies, is treating U.S. citizens. Often the pretext is protection from "dumping." Dumping occurs when a foreign company sells a product in America for "less than fair value." That language leaves Commerce Department bureaucrats empowered by every parochial interest in Congress to do almost anything on behalf of their clients—as the bureaucrats seem to regard them—in U.S. businesses. Bureaucrats "protect" American consumers from paying what the bureaucrats and their congressional masters consider too little for everything from Brazilian frozen orange juice concentrate to Italian pads for woodwind instruments.

Occasionally there actually is real predatory dumping, designed to cripple or extinguish a rival industry in another nation. But most so-called dumping amounts to nothing more than attempts to crack a market or enlarge market share. Does it matter? That depends on what is being dumped, for how long and for what purpose. Some—very few—U.S. industries deserve government protection for reasons of basic national security or economic vitality. Microchips matter more than potato chips. But only private aggrandizement has been served by putting dumping penalties on photo albums, pears, mirrors, ethanol, cement, shock absorbers, roofing shingles, codfish, televisions, paintbrushes, motorcycle batteries, staplers and staples, martial arts uniforms, radios, flowers, bicycles, forklifts, fireplace mesh panels, aspirin and many other goods.

Two kinds of private aggrandizement are linked through the imposition of dumping penalties on such goods. One is the greed of the American producers of such goods. The dumping penalties insulate domestic producers from unrestricted competition and make American consumers a captive market for domestic producers. The other aggrandizement is by the incumbent legislators who authorize the protectionist measures. These legislators reap the reward of political support from those American producers who are dependent on such politicization of markets.

Government subsidies (such as we give agriculture products) usually are foolish, but why not let American consumers benefit from the folly of those foreign governments that use their tax dollars to make American consumption cheaper? Instead, we put countervailing duties on products that foreign governments are foolish enough to subsidize—wool, ham, castor oil, cotton, yarn, scissors, carnations, pistachios, roses, cement, automobile glass, leather apparel, cookware, rice and many other things. Such American protectionism creates artificial scarcities, or artificially high-priced competing goods, as a subsidy for American businesses. If the Commerce Department were abolished, America's standard of living would rise.

James Bovard of the Cato Institute, a Washington think tank, reports that in the last half of 1991 Bush imposed new textile quotas on—consider this list of mighty predators—Nigeria, Indonesia, Egypt, the Philippines, Burma, Costa Rica, Panama and Pakistan.[13] In 1991 a Bush administration official coerced Hong Kong and Korea into cutting their textile exports to the United States. The official called it "a contribution to Operation Desert Storm."[14] America is still a world-class producer of something: cynicism. Such U.S. protectionist measures constitute campaign contributions. They are contributions to the security of the incumbent legislators who mandate the protection for dependent client firms, industries, unions and communities.

Some Commerce Department officials candidly hope that the capriciousness of their decisions will deter foreign exporters. Were everyone candid, they would acknowledge that much of U.S. trade policy, stripped of highfalutin rhetoric about "fair" trade, is just a jobs program. And among the jobs protected by U.S. protectionism are those of many incompetent and overpaid American executives whose companies are weak because they have been protected from bracing competition. Trade policy also is a program to redistribute wealth from unorganized American consumers to well-organized and well-connected commercial interests. Call it Republican socialism. Its result is "lemon socialism," the survival of the feeble. The economic result—the progressive anemia of America's economy—is alarming enough, but it is less alarming than the political process that churns out such decisions by the hundreds, day after day.

There is good news about such decisions. In the early 1990s the country has demonstrated an increased capacity to be scandalized by the everydayness of political practices related to legislative careerism. Thus the drive to limit terms has been fueled by an acid rain of small episodes that were not particularly lurid or even unusual—and that was what made them potent as evidence for the term limiters' arguments. By

1992, advocates of term limits believed that their case was being made for them, constantly and coast to coast, by the behavior of legions of incumbents. Consider just three episodes, one from each side of the U.S. Capitol Building, and one from a state capital. Let us begin in the Senate, where in 1992 a senior member was hatching big plans for a portion of the Central Intelligence Agency.

Having helped win the Cold War, the CIA, or some of it, seemed to be about to reap a reward of a dubious sort. It seemed to be going to Heaven. Or Almost Heaven—West Virginia. Trouble is, many CIA employees did not want to go. They have things (homes, schools, friends, churches) they like in the Washington area where they now work, and they resented the idea of having their jobs packed off to a place a long—up to two hours—commute away. Of course, the bright side of this threat was: It could be worse. Suppose Senator Robert Byrd were from, oh, Idaho. Now, *that's* a commute.

The argument about consolidating 3,000 Washington-area CIA jobs in Byrd's West Virginia may seem like a merely parochial spat. But it exemplifies what is done, day in and day out, in Washington in your name and with your money. And amidst the breaking of crockery and gnashing of teeth about this one of Byrd's many acts of highhandedness, a thought of national importance whispers insistently: Surely we would not be having this argument if we had reasonable limits on the number of terms—say, two—that senators can serve.

Actually, this argument about the CIA would not have raged if the limit were five terms. Byrd, you see, was in his sixth term in 1992. That fact, and his theory of representation-as-rapaciousness, is why he is the much-feared and extremely expensive chairman of the mighty Appropriations Committee.

Byrd, seventy-five on November 20, 1992, has not been in Washington as long as some other legislators. Not as long as Jamie Whitten, the Mississippi Democrat, who was elected thirty-three days before Pearl Harbor. But Byrd has been in the Senate longer than anyone now there who is not Strom Thurmond. Byrd was elected to the Senate in 1958. Before that he was in the House for three terms. Before that he was in West Virginia's Senate, 1951–53, and before that in the state House of Delegates, 1947–51. So he became a professional legislator forty-five years ago, at age twenty-nine, and has had no other career. He is good at what he does. But is what he does good for the nation?

Consider his attempted hijacking of the CIA jobs. The consulting firm hired to advise the CIA did not include the West Virginia site among the top ten sites. Or the top sixty-five. Or even the top two hundred. But suddenly the CIA, tugging its forelock and bowing deeply to Chairman Byrd, asked that the West Virginia site be included in the final four. And, wonder of wonders, it won.

Even if the merits of the site selection case study did not point in one direction—against Byrd—no one could believe that the merits mattered much. Some brave legislators resisted Byrd, a notorious nurser of grudges. In 1992 they stopped the move, at least temporarily. But if the CIA jobs are ever moved (at a cost of at least $1.2 billion), they will join a long parade of pillaged jobs from the IRS, the FBI (2,400 jobs at a $185 million fingerprinting center) and other agencies. For example, West Virginia is taking out of downtown Washington seven hundred jobs from the Treasury Department's—how suitable—Bureau of Public Debt. It is arguable that the federal government should be dispersed, perhaps by dynamite. But it should not be moved in bits, like so much booty, to feed an overbearing senator's unslakable appetite for pork.

When Byrd became Appropriations Chairman in 1989, he vowed to slosh $1 billion into West Virginia in his first six years. He did it in less than three years. More than half a billion dollars in projects and other funds for Almost Heaven were squirreled away in appropriations bills for fiscal 1992. Transportation "demonstration projects" are a notorious form of waste—a slush fund for politicians. (Bike paths for northeast Dade County, Florida, were set to get $2.5 million. The Bicycle Demonstration Transportation Project in Macomb County, Michigan, cost a mere $900,000.) Nearly half—$182 million—of the $387 million for demonstration projects in the 1992 Senate transportation appropriations bill was for West Virginia. That means $182 million was supposed to go to a state of 1.8 million people and $205 million to the other 250 million Americans.

In 1990 Byrd larded more money for Fish and Wildlife Service operations into West Virginia than the President had sought for that agency for the entire nation. No project is too piddling for Byrd to pass up—for example, $80,000 to plan a boat access at Teays Landing, West Virginia. But why are people in Boise and Harlem and Fort Wayne and Watts and everywhere else being forced to ante up $80 million for a new courthouse in Charleston, West Virginia, and $4.5 million to restore a theater in Huntington, West Virginia? Why? Because Byrd boasts that "I want to be West Virginia's billion dollar industry."[15] Because he has been in Congress so long, he can be.

Byrd rose to his current eminence from conditions of severe poverty, and he represents a poor state, so perhaps some of his grasping should be forgiven. Some, but not this egregious sort. His career has become a caricature of a particularly crass and cynical theory of representation. The theory is that election to Congress is tantamount to being dispatched to Washington on a looting raid for the enrichment of your state or district, and no other ethic need inhibit the feeding frenzy.

Senator Daniel Patrick Moynihan tells a story of a Texas congressman, who, in 1916, with what probably passed then, as now, for a troubled conscience, said:

There are a half dozen places in my district where Federal buildings are being erected or have recently been constructed at a
cost to the Government far in excess of the actual needs of the
communities where they are located. This is mighty bad business for Uncle Sam, and I'll admit it; but the other fellows in
Congress have been doing it for a long time and I can't make
them quit. Now we Democrats are in charge of the House and
I'll tell you right now, every time one of these Yankees gets a
ham I'm going to get a hog.[16]

Many participants in the elbow-throwing, shoulder-jostling
scramble for government preferment are uneasy about the difficulty of squaring their participation in the scramble with their
sense of good citizenship. But there comes a point when even
those whose consciences nag them just shrug, throw up their
hands and throw in the towel. They conclude that it is pointless
to hope for a less tawdry process of governance. They decide to
get on with the joyless pursuit of joy, the game of grimly trying
to get their ample portion at the great governmental smorgas-
bord. That point comes when the game becomes so old, so
large, so constant and so inclusive—in a word, so normal—that
any unilateral restraint would not produce any measurable public benefit. It is the point at which groups already receiving,
and campaigning for enlargement of, government benefits are
so numerous that anyone's withdrawal from the competition,
or more moderation in any particular group's pursuit of advantage, would make not a particle of difference. It would not
produce a noticeable subtraction from the clamor. The example
would have no power to begin a contagion of public-spirited
emulation among other groups. So why bother?

Of course "everybody does it." Always have, always will,
to some degree. But surely senators would do it less if they
were limited to, say, two terms. In six of their twelve years
they might think of something—the national interest, perhaps—other than buying votes with the voters' money. The

Framers of the Constitution made provisions—six-year terms; indirect elections—that they hoped would give the Senate a distinctive disposition, one unlike the (they supposed) more parochial and frenetic House. But the Senate today reflects the common culture of Congress, as can be seen by taking a short walk south, to the House side of the Capitol.

In September, 1991, a small legislative episode in the House illustrated the commonness—in several senses—of the congressional culture. The episode was not even reported in Washington. But it was reported in Denver, and that report in Denver papers was the point of the episode. It suggested that an answer to the question, "What ails American government?" is: Representative Patricia Schroeder and the many other career legislators like her.

The congresswoman from Denver is intelligent, witty, well-meaning and warmhearted. Alas, she also is something we simply no longer can afford. She is too costly in money and, more importantly, institutional distortion. It may seem perverse to say that she proves the wisdom of term limits by her legislative embrace of a very admirable idea. But consider what she did with the idea of midnight basketball leagues.

Such leagues in Chicago and other cities take at-risk young inner-city men off the streets and into gyms for basketball and counseling during hours when they might otherwise be getting into trouble. In 1991, at Schroeder's behest, the House Judiciary Committee voted to include almost $3 million (a pittance, but such things grow) in the crime bill to subsidize midnight basketball leagues. The Department of Housing and Urban Development (*et tu*, Jack Kemp?) already had its nose in that tent, with some subsidies. Then Schroeder spoke the four-letter word Washington adores: "More." She favored federal funding for new leagues in suburban and rural areas that are experiencing youth-related problems.

The mentality of Washington's entrenched incumbents is one of the reasons they are entrenched. They believe—really believe—that every good idea out there in America should become a federal program. Let me here reiterate my belief that midnight basketball leagues, in praise of which I have written elsewhere, are a wonderful idea. But in a reasonable society, under a limited government, that judgment is the beginning, not the end of public debate. The debate must take up at least two other questions: Is support for any particular good idea an appropriate federal function? And given the fiscal facts of life nowadays, can the government afford to support even a particular good idea?

While I am at it, let me stipulate that Schroeder is public-spirited. But she also is, strictly speaking, deranged. (Oxford English Dictionary: "thrown into confusion.") She has been reduced, as many career legislators like her have been, to constant confusion about what is and is not temperate, restrained, disciplined, discriminating behavior by government. She has been in Washington so long—elected in 1972, she has spent most of her adult life in Congress—she probably can not fathom how anyone could find anything odd about Washington funding a nice thing like midnight basketball.

She is just doing what people do in Congress and in other legislatures. They get up in the morning, shower, shave or apply their make-up, commute to work, pop open their briefcases, pour a cup of coffee and start spending other people's money. Invariably, they can convince themselves they are not "really" spending anything. "It [the antecedent of the pronoun can be almost any program] will pay for itself." As in: "It is cheaper to buy basketballs than prison cells."

Edward Crane, of the Cato Institute, rightly argues that in a town where the tone of life is set by a ruling class of career legislators, the prevailing mentality makes people weird—strictly speaking, weird. (OED: "out of the ordinary, strange, odd, fantastic.") Most of the people legislators associate with are involved in regulating other people's lives and spending other people's money. Furthermore, microphones are constantly being shoved at them, and soon they believe their preferences are so wise they should be codified.

After prolonged immersion in Washington's culture of ruling, there is not a dime's worth of difference between (as the *Wall Street Journal* puts it) Democrans and Republicrats. That is why there are appropriations bills funding a study of the handling of manure ($37,000); a Stuggart, Arkansas, fish farm ($542,000); a recycling facility in Susquehanna, Pennsylvania ($1 million); the Institute of Peace ($8.3 million); Houston's "Better-Bus" system ($15 million); a study of Afognak Island, in Arkansas ($250,000) and thousands of other projects. Again, let me stipulate, for the sake of advancing the argument, that any—or all—of these projects may be jim-dandy. Each might help make America even more of a land fit for heroes. But, again, there are still those two elemental questions of governance.

Does the federal government have enough money to fund all good ideas? And is the federal government supposed to acknowledge some limits to its reach, some restraints on its activism? We shall see in Chapter 4 that the new ethic of deficit spending serves to erase the first question, and the abandonment of the doctrine of enumerated powers has led to the abandonment of all ideas of limits.

For now, suffice it to note that approximately nine decades before Dr. James Naismith hung peach bushel baskets in the YMCA gym in Springfield, Massachusetts, and invented basketball, President Jefferson saw today's folly coming. When young Senator Clay brought his aching joints into Washington after his long journey from Kentucky over corduroy roads, Jefferson was arguing with Congress about Congress's determination to get into the business of building roads. Jefferson reluctantly agreed to sign the national roads bill, even though there was no mention of roadbuilding in the Constitution's Article I, Section 8, enumeration of Congress's powers. But Jefferson said to Congress: If you guys get into funding even things as basic as roads and canals—if you say the government's "implied powers" (as distinct from those explicitly enumerated by the Constitution) are infinitely elastic—well, sooner or later you will even be subsidizing midnight basketball games in Denver and elsewhere.

Well, O.K., he didn't say that in so many words. But that was his gist, and a glance at the federal budget proves he was right.

We have come a long way, a lot of it downhill, since Jefferson fled the Federal City for the sanity of Monticello, and there is no going back to Jeffersonianism. However, it is reasonable to suppose that term limits compelling the rotation of offices would have two salutary consequences.

If people served in legislatures only briefly, going to them from other careers, to which they would return in a few years, they would have less incentive to shovel out pork. The primary function of pork is to buy gratitude and dependency among clients, qualities that the career legislator can translate into votes, and hence into longevity. And if legislators were not too separated, for too long, from normal citizens and normal life in normal communities, they might retain the ability to discriminate between appropriate and inappropriate functions for the federal government.

Of course derangement by prolonged entrenchment in unchallenged power is not a problem peculiar to Washington or to the public sector. In the early 1990s the roving spotlight of public attention suddenly swung to the issue of private sector extravagance in the compensation of corporate chief executive officers. This subject became, briefly, a national preoccupation in December, 1991, when President Bush took along, on that stumbling, groveling trip to Japan, those extravagantly paid CEOs of failing automobile corporations. Of course abuses in CEO compensation did not begin in the early 1990s, but the recession of those years made the compensation abuses seem all the more egregious. They coincided not only with growing distress in the working and middle classes, but often also with abysmal performances by the corporations that were most lavish toward their CEOs. One reason the issue of CEO compensation has been pulled into prominence in the 1990s is that it is linked to many of the issues raised by the class of entrenched incumbents in Congress. CEOs, too, are insulated from accountability and can pursue their private interests using resources that should not properly be at their disposal for such purposes.

The compensation of CEOs is generally disproportionate and often ludicrous in light of corporate performance. In fact, it often is difficult to determine how much CEOs are paid. Compensation packages can be wondrously—and purposely—difficult to decipher. (The 1990 compensation of International Telephone and Telegraph Corporation's CEO has been estimated at between $7 million and $11.4 million.) But America's CEOs are paid two to three times more than Japan's or Germany's. In Japan, the compensation of major CEOs is 17 times that of the average worker; in France and Germany, 23–25 times; in Britain, 35 times; in America, between 85 and 100-plus times. The American CEO/worker disparity doubled during the 1980s—while the top income tax rate was cut and workers' tax burdens increased because of Social Security taxes. (Japan, Germany and Britain have more progressive tax rates than America.)

In 1990, CEO pay rose 7 percent while corporate profits fell 7 percent. How does something like that happen? CEO compensation is approved by company directors the CEO helps to choose. Sixty percent of all outside directors of the 1,000 largest corporations are themselves CEOs. They are raising the floor beneath themselves.

Economists puzzle about this question: How do you define, measure and appropriately reward individuals' contributions at the pinnacle of complex, sprawling bureaucratized corporations? How do you distinguish between money earned and money merely taken? The slogan "pay for performance" does not take us far. Madonna made $25 million last year? Fine. Her pay is directly a function of performances. If Roger Clemens stops winning for the Red Sox, his $5 million salary will stop. Not so with CEOs.

The CEO of Eagle Picher Industries got a 38 percent pay raise while profits were falling 27 percent and the company was seeking bankruptcy protection. Because times are hard for the auto industry, Ford's CEO took a pay cut last year. But Chrysler's Lee Iacocca took a 25 percent raise—while earnings were falling 17 percent and workers, suppliers and shareholders were being asked to sacrifice.

In 1990 Disney's CEO made more in a day than the average Disney employee made in the year. Is there an economic or moral justification for that, or just a power explanation? Between 1988 and 1991 Reebok's CEO received $40.9 million. But $100 invested in Reebok stock in 1988 was worth only $117 by 1990. In contrast, Nike, which passed Reebok as leader in the sneaker industry as Reebok profits were growing just 1 percent last year, has a CEO who made a three-year total of $1 million in 1988–90 while Nike's return on equity averaged a robust 23 percent a year. Perhaps Reebok's CEO was worth $14.8 million in 1990, but why, precisely? He would have done his job less well for a piddling, say, $7 million? Would he have left the company if paid less? Would the company have done worse with a $7 million—or even $1 million—replacement?

Topping *Business Week*'s annual survey of executive compensation for 1990 was United Airlines' CEO.[17] He received

$18.3 million (1,200 times what a new flight attendant makes) in salary, bonuses and a stock-based incentive plan. United's profits fell 71 percent in 1990.

The word "incentives" is prominent in CEO compensation packages. Think about that. Incentives to do what, exactly? One's job? One's job well? Or better than one would unless lethargy were conquered by lots of cash? Economists worry that many incentive plans encourage a short-term focus on a few numerical goals, such as stock prices. Those can be floated up by a general market rise unrelated to executive performance.

Congress is considering requiring better disclosure of compensation and a strengthening of stockholders' powers to control it. But stockholder democracy is a weak reed to lean on, at least until large institutional investors get angry and involved. Public anger could provoke at least caution in the clubby corporate culture. And antibusiness fever does flare periodically in America.

The fever's causes include resentment of government-conferred wealth (for example, from protective tariffs), fear of monopoly and hugeness (which gave rise to "trust-busting" at the turn of this century), dislike of dependency (such as farmers felt regarding unregulated railroads in the nineteenth century) and disgust with rapaciousness and vulgarity (as in the Gilded Age). This fever of disgust with the business world resembles today's antipathy toward Congress. Both antipathies, toward corporate America and toward Congress, arise from the perception that people wielding authority are not being held to account for their performance, which is frequently inadequate and self-serving.

In 1992 public disgust with the combination of congressional incompetence and congressional pay raises resulted in the absurdity of the 27th amendment. Ratified 203 years after James Madison wrote it, it says a congressional pay raise can not take effect until an election has intervened. This misbegotten amendment, which trivializes the Constitution, is part of the price we are paying for that fever of resentment about prominent people—members of Congress, CEOs—acting in their official capacities, displaying neither skill nor shame, botching their responsibilities but rewarding themselves in ways that mock the idea of accountability.

The climate of impatience, distrust and cynicism fostered by congressional and CEO abuse explained the swift fall of William Aramony in February, 1992. For twenty-two years he had run the United Way of America. From a building on the Potomac waterfront in Alexandria, Virginia, he directed a network of 2,100 local United Way affiliates who together raised $3.1 billion in 1990. But on February 16, 1992, the *Washington Post* published a front-page story headlined "Perks, Privileges and Power in a Nonprofit World."[18] It detailed Aramony's $463,000 annual compensation in salary and benefits, and his hiring decisions benefiting his family and friends. The story also had the kind of small, telling details that impart momentum to this sort of scandal. For example, Aramony traveled to Europe, at United Way's expense, on the Concorde (one-way fare, more than $3,000). Perhaps the most telling tidbit from this private sector, but inside the Beltway, story, was his explanation for his one-year bill of $20,000 for chauffeur services in New York: "I can't afford to be waiting for cabs." Too busy. Too important.

Too bad. On February 27, 1992, he resigned.

∾   ∾

Members of Congress, CEOs, heads of nonprofit institutions—all these have come to be seen as examples of people corrupted by being insulated from competition and accountability, people committed to nothing much other than their own continuation in office, people whose hold on their offices depends on their manipulation of the power of their offices and the resources to which their offices give them access. Regarding members of Congress, term limitation is the surgical remedy.

Because of Congress's recent penchant for pratfalls and scandals, Washington has become the focus of attention pertaining to term limits. But the federal government is not the only government in which protracted incumbency breeds bad behavior. What is called Washington's "Beltway mentality" flourishes far beyond the Washington Beltway, in places like Harrisburg, Pennsylvania. Consider what some exemplars of the mentality did to Cliff Jones.

Jones, a Republican who has served as chairman of the state GOP and in several Pennsylvania cabinet and sub-cabinet jobs, retired in 1991 as president of the Pennsylvania Chamber of Business and Industry. In early autumn of that year he began soliciting support for the GOP nomination for the state Senate nomination in the 31st District. The incumbent senator from that district was a four-term Republican described by one Pennsylvania political reporter (Dennis Barbagello of the *Greensburg Tribune-Review*) as someone "who always votes on issues with the party leadership. And he never addresses the Senate on any issue. State Senate staffers quietly refer to him as a 'lap dog.' "[19]

At 10 A.M. on November 15, 1991, Jones announced he was running. His platform included support for term limits and a pledge to serve no more than two terms. His was a three-hour candidacy.

Around 1 P.M. the Legislative Reapportionment Committee announced a final redistricting plan, including a provision previously unannounced and on which there had been no hearings or public testimony. With this provision, concocted on the eve of Jones's announcement of his candidacy and settled without even the courtesy of a telephone call to him, the committee

had redrawn the lines of the 31st District, splitting communities and school districts, to achieve this result: Jones didn't live
in the 31st District any more. The "nonpartisan" committee
was composed of two Republican and two Democratic legislative members, and a fifth person, currently a Pittsburgh attorney. Under the cover of "nonpartisanship" the two parties
look out for their incumbents' interests. The way they did that
at Jones's expense illustrates a neglected aspect of the term
limits debate. Incumbents opposed to limits argue loftily that
limits are an injury to democracy because voters deserve un-
fettered freedom to choose whomever they want to represent
them. But incumbents often use gerrymandering to choose the
voters, and even the opponents, they want. And that is not all,
or the worst of it, as the outlines shown in figures 1–4 reveal.

These are outlines of basic units of government—congressional districts. They might look like casual doodles, but there
is nothing random about them. Far from it. They were carefully drawn by computers programmed by politicians determined to pick convenient electorates, but doing so in the name
of civil rights. These sketches are the result of the intersection
of idealism and opportunism. Each of these districts is drawn
to make highly probable, if not to guarantee, a particular kind
of winner. They guarantee that the person elected will be from
a particular government-favored ethnic group.

The 1982 amendments to the Voting Rights Act of 1965
mandated, in effect, affirmative action for particular racial and
ethnic groups that Congress deemed insufficiently represented
in Congress. Here is what the amended act actually says:

> 42 USC 1973b "A violation of subsection (a) is established if,
> based on the totality of circumstances, it is shown that the po-
> litical processes leading to nomination or election in the State or
> political subdivision are not equally open to participation by
> members of a class of citizens protected by subsection (a) in that

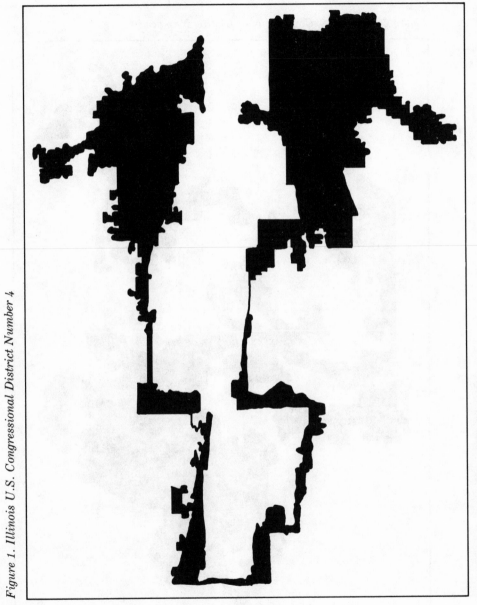

Figure 1. Illinois U.S. Congressional District Number 4

Source: Illinois State Board of Elections

Figure 2. Texas U.S. Congressional District Number 30

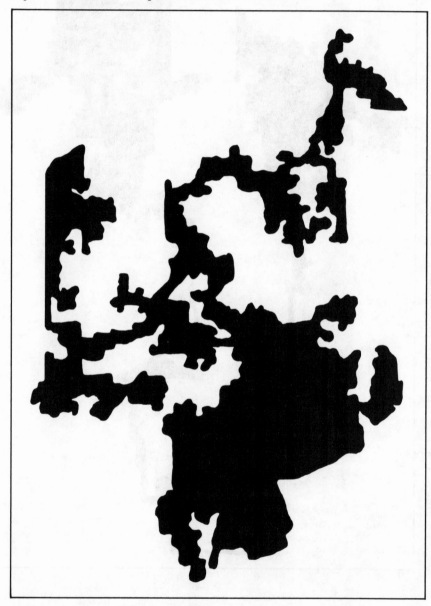

Source: Texas Legislative Council

Figure 3. Florida U.S. Congressional District Number 3

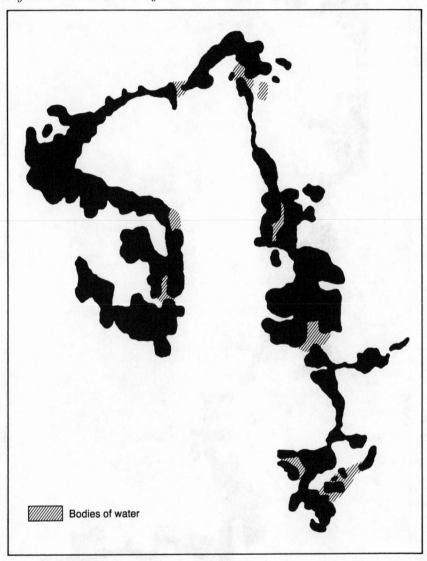

Bodies of water

Source: U.S. Representative Jim Bacchus

Figure 4. North Carolina U.S. Congressional District Number 12

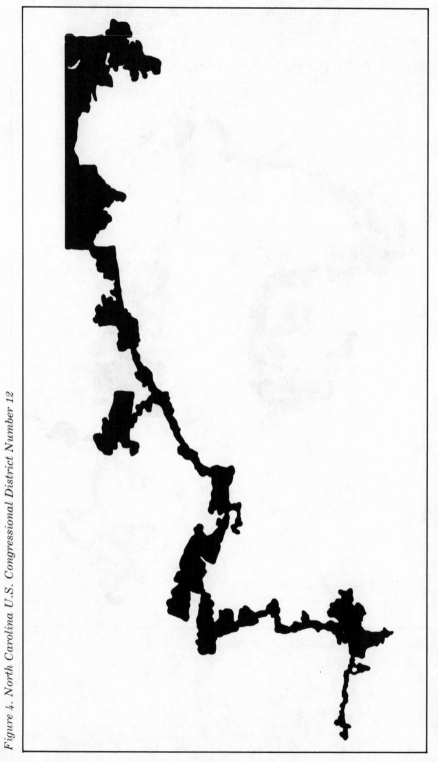

Source: Library of State of North Carolina Assembly

its members have less opportunity than other members of the electorate to participate in the political process and to elect representatives of their choice. THE EXTENT TO WHICH MEMBERS OF A PROTECTED CLASS HAVE BEEN ELECTED TO OFFICE IN THE STATE OR POLITICAL SUBDIVISION IS ONE CIRCUMSTANCE WHICH MAY BE CONSIDERED: Provided, *That nothing in this section establishes a right to have members of a protected class elected in numbers equal to their proportion in the population.*"

This language, especially the murky parts I have emphasized in capital letters and italics, has put the Justice Department and the courts waist-deep in a modern debasement of democracy, a policy of segregating the electorate along racial grounds. That cool, antiseptic language has given rise to the four districts depicted here. These districts represent the unity of bad theory and deplorable practice. The theory is "categorical representation." The practice is gerrymandering. As defined by Samuel P. Huntington, the Harvard political scientist, the doctrine of categorical representation holds that the interests of particular groups can be properly represented only by members of those groups. (People who subscribe to this theory do so selectively. They say that the doctrine applies to blacks, but not to whites. But this need not detain us.) Therefore, categorical representation is a civil right. Therefore, the districts depicted in these remarkable maps represent compliance with a civil rights act.

These four districts are the sort of results that government reaches when it starts to sort out the population for various entitlements on the basis of race or other ethnicity. Consider the fourth district of Illinois, a computer-generated monstrosity invented to sweep together enough Hispanic voters to produce an Hispanic member of Congress. The other three districts were concocted to produce black winners.

North Carolina's handiwork became particularly famous in

1992 when officials of both parties in North Carolina described it as idiotic. It is a district strung along portions of three Interstate Highways, I-85, I-40 and I-77. In some places, one side of Interstate-85 is in one district and the other side of Interstate-85 is in another. The district slithers down these Interstates picking up black voters in three metropolitan areas.

In one sense, such districts are just redundant examples of good intentions producing perverse effects. A civil rights law mandates this ghettoization of representation, and this ghettoization diminishes the incentive of minority and white voters to build inclusive coalitions. But these districts also represent a new dimension of Washington arrogance and bipartisan cynicism in the service of incumbents.

The arrogance, mixed with genuine but misguided idealism, is a fresh form of Washington-knows-best. For many generations—in fact since 1787—it has been understood that the organizing principle of the House is geographic. Hence in the drawing of congressional districts, compactness has traditionally been considered a virtue—not the only virtue, but something desirable, and certainly not a value to be utterly disregarded, as was done in the drawing of the Texas 30th.

Using a Computer Aided Design program (Auto-CAD Release 11), Robert D. Popper, a New York attorney, calculated that the Texas 30th District uses 397.3 miles of perimeter to contain just 222.3 square miles of area. If compactly drawn, the 397.3 miles of perimeter could enclose 12,561 square miles, about as much territory as Connecticut and New Jersey combined. But the Texas 30th encloses an amount of territory slightly less than would be in a box 15 miles square. Popper computes for the Texas 30th a compactness score (the area of a shape divided by the area of a circle with a perimeter of equal length) of just 1.7 on a scale of 100 for maximum compactness. He says a rectangle with the same perimeter length and the same area (and hence the same compactness score) would be

1.1 miles wide and 197.5 miles long—long enough to reach from Boston to New York, or almost from Dallas to Houston.[20]

It is now the law of the land that racial representation shall supplant geographical representation in certain situations. Congressional seats are being included in the spreading racial and ethnic spoils system. A racial entitlement to congressional seats is a disincentive for achieving a truly integrated society. In such a society, not even the cleverest computer program could gather blacks (or Hispanics, or any other group) into a district where they are a majority. Imagine, says the newspaper *Roll Call*, creating a district for twenty-year-olds, and you'll begin to understand the problem.

But many liberal Democrats like extending the racial spoils system to congressional seats. They believe it is healthy for society to heighten racial and ethnic sensibilities and identifications, hence they believe that race and ethnicity are preferable to mere geographic proximity as a basis for political representation. Republicans are all-too-eager to participate in the segregation of black voters—who are heavily Democratic—into a few districts.

What North Carolina has done in the 1990s with its "I-85 District" Mississippi did in the 1870s. More than a century before the 1982 language that was added to the 1965 Voting Rights Act got federal and state governments into the business of selectively segregating the electorate along racial lines, the Redeemers—as opponents of Reconstruction were pleased to be known—in Mississippi were anticipating North Carolina's I-85 district: "Mississippi Redeemers concentrated the bulk of the black population in a 'shoestring' Congressional district running the length of the Mississippi River, leaving five others with white majorities."[21]

What makes North Carolina's "I-85 district" especially interesting is that it is even more preposterous than necessary, even for a racial-entitlement district. A more compact black-

majority district could have been created, a district doing less
violence to the geographic basis of representation. However, it
would have violated the most sacred—the only really sacred—
principle in contemporary politics: Thou shalt not injure an
incumbent. North Carolina could easily have drawn a much
more compact district that still would have made highly probable the election of a black member of Congress, but drawing
it would have taken some reliable Democratic voters from the
district of Representative Charles Rose. Heaven forfend. Di-
lute the almost perfect security of a man who came to Washington in 1972 and thus enjoys the most revered entitlement
America can offer, incumbency? Not a chance.

The incumbency-protection imperative in contemporary
politics has done double duty with the "I-85 district." Rose's
incumbency remains insulated from serious challenge, and a
new district has been created which, it is safe to assume, will
be won by someone who will go on winning it as long as he or
she has breath and the desire to stay in Congress.

However, nowadays more and more incumbents are finding the
business of clawing one's way to Washington and clinging to
office there a game not worth the candle. It has become wea-
risome work demanding the most draining of personal sacrifices. And these sacrifices are not compensated for by the
satisfaction of working in an institution that works well. For
example, in the early autumn of 1991 two congressmen, both
Democrats, both from northern Ohio, but otherwise dissimilar,
announced decisions not to run again. Their decisions gave
outsiders a glimpse into the culture of Congress today and the
texture of lives immersed in it.

When one of the fastest-rising stars in Congress's firma-
ment decides he would rather not try to twinkle any more, his

decision is apt to be an index of that institution's stresses. Dennis Eckart was forty-one in the fall of 1991, when he announced that his sixth term would be his last. In his announcement he expressed a frustration, deeply tinged with guilt, that is felt by many members: "I'm tired of making [family] decisions over the telephone instead of at the kitchen table."[22]

After he said that, about twenty congressional spouses called his wife to ask, "What did you put in his coffee?" And could they borrow a cup of it?[23]

Even when he wasn't traveling to and from his northeast Ohio district—up to forty-five times a year in election years— late sessions in the House often had prevented him from getting home before his son, then eleven, was asleep. Halloween of 1991 had been just the third Halloween he had been entirely free to spend with his son.

Eckart is a liberal. He likes government. He was bred to the business. His father was a Euclid city councilman. When six-year-old Dennis was asked if he wanted to be a councilman he replied, "No. Mayor." In 1960, at age ten, he met candidate Jack Kennedy at a political picnic. He sped through college in three years and law school in two, and after six years in the state legislature he came to Congress in 1980, at age thirty. In 1990 he was one of the few incumbents to improve upon his 1988 majority, winning 68 percent. He was on his way—perhaps just another decade would have done it—to a coveted chairmanship, that of the Energy and Commerce Committee. But last December he left a letter under the Christmas tree promising his wife he would not run again. In September, 1991, he told his constituents:

> For 18 years I have placed my passion for politics and public service above the rest of my family and friends. At a very early age our son, Eddy, used to say that his Dad "shakes hands for a living." One year I was on airplanes more than 90 times. That's

more than the total number of soccer games and swim meets
I've been able to attend."[24]

A few years ago he was asked to give an orientation speech to
freshmen Democratic members. He preached what he had long
practiced: Go home constantly, do as many call-in radio shows
as you can, keep your campaign organization in operation and
a storefront office open. He now says, "I would give a different
speech today."[25]

Like many members, he is dismayed by the increasing
truculence of constituents who no longer ask for things, they
demand them. He is tired of the treadmill of money-raising.
When asked if he would be retiring if there were public financ-
ing of campaigns (a remote possibility, given public hostility to
the idea), he pauses but comes to no conclusion. He does say,
with feeling, "You hate walking around with your hand out."[26]

Most of all, he despairs of ever having elevating, or even
civil, campaigns, given the role of television. The axiom among
his colleagues is, "If you can't explain your vote [on any particular issue] in thirty seconds, it's the wrong vote." He says,
"A thirty-second negative ad can matter more to a candidate's
career than a lifetime voting record." So political discourse
concerns vacuities ("Morning in America," "Competence, not
ideology"). Increasingly, "we debate the picture frame, not the
picture."[27]

Eckart will be saying "enough" at the end of twelve years,
the maximum length of service suggested by many proponents
of term limits. He opposes term limits, but the logic of his
congressional life, and his litany of widely shared dissatisfac-
tions, buttress the case for them. By his own testimony, he led
a doubly distorted life, in his personal affairs—his absence from
his kitchen table—and in his behavior regarding public business. The latter is the business of us all. He does not explicitly
say so, but the purport of his testimony is that he would

have been a better husband and father if he had not been so sunk in careerism. That is a matter between him and his family, but he also strongly suggests that he would have approached public decisions differently if he had not been bent on a lifetime career in Congress, and that is a matter that involves the rest of us. He does not link his experience to term limitations, but he does link the careerist impulse to practical behavior. Remember the speech he says he would no longer give; remember the "If you can't explain it in thirty seconds, don't do it" rule.

In the pell-mell pace of congressional life as he and many other people live it, there is a glaring disproportion, an antic hyperkinesis, an extremism. It arises largely from the professionalization of politics by people who come to Congress, often at an early age, with no earlier career to turn back to, and desperate for lifetime tenure. Members could lead less distorted lives, could spend less time massaging their districts, if they accorded less importance to maximizing their security.

Eckart is a young man with an old soul, the result of a searing experience. No, the experience has not been service in Congress, but rather a lifetime rooting for the Cleveland Indians. He can rattle off the Indians' lineup of 1959, the last time the team was a contender. His retirement will mean he can go to more Indians games. No good deed goes unpunished. His departure from the House, in the interest of his home, is indeed a good deed. There is no disparagement of his congressional career in the observation that nothing in that career has done him more credit than the leaving of it. The same might be said of his colleague Donald Pease.

Pease wants it crystal clear that his decision to leave Congress at the end of 1992, at the completion of his eighth term, does not derive from job dissatisfaction. He likes the work. That's his story and he's sticking to it.

And it's true. Sort of. Up to a point.

This northeast Ohio Democrat speaks with evident sincerity of the pleasures of attending hundreds of pancake breakfasts and rotary lunches and spaghetti suppers and weddings of daughters of people who ring doorbells for him. And if just reading the list makes you weary, you are not cut out for Congress. Your consolation can be that you are normal.

Thirty years ago Pease began the career that led from the Oberlin city council through both houses of Ohio's legislature to Congress. When he became a professional politician, meaning one who regards elective office as a career rather than a leave of absence from one, he made, as a matter of course, a decision normal for that abnormal life, a decision that speaks volumes about, and also conditions, the tone of American politics. He decided on "immersion" in politics, "to go every place, accept any invitation, never to make personal plans."[28] If, he says, friends invite him to dinner two weeks in advance, he thinks: Better wait a week and see if some event—a Farm Bureau meeting, perhaps—might conflict. "It is," he says, "part of the psychology of politicians that you can never do enough."[29]

A coronary by-pass operation and then heart-valve surgery have slowed him this much: He has trimmed his travel to and from and around his district enough to lower the odds on his reelection to, he says, 5-to-1. Those odds are quite comfortable but are way below the 10-to-1 incumbents want to produce—what the vast majority had in 1990: negligible opposition. (Most had no opponent, or an opponent with trivial funds, or an opponent with less than half the incumbent's funds.)

Pease is a slender, sinewy, soft-spoken man with the easy affability common in the House, where, unlike the Senate, collegiality necessarily counts for more than conspicuousness as a satisfaction of the job. Satisfaction? The country's condition that he anticipates ten years hence will be "not good" and "already it's not pleasant being in Congress."[30] There is no consensus in the country about what government should do and, because of deficits (first the Gramm-Rudman restraints, and now the 1990 budget agreement), there are no fiscal tools to work with, anyway.

There are, he says, two ways to curb deficits—spending cuts and tax increases—and voters hate both. Actually, there is a third way, economic growth, but from Pease's district that looks impossible. The district has Cleveland suburbs and a steel mill, two automobile assembly plants and many dairy farms. It has lost upwards of 15,000 high-paying blue-collar jobs in the last decade. A shipyard that employed 1,500 people has closed. It built ships that brought iron ore to many Mid-western steel mills now closed. In the salad days of the 1970s, automotive assembly-line workers were working sixty hours a week, including twenty hours of overtime, pushing their an-nual earnings to as much as $50,000. Today the lines are apt to be closed every other week.

Pease is depressed by the governmental paralysis that prevents creative action. But, again, he wants it clearly un-derstood that he likes the job. Once when Willie Stargell, the Pittsburgh Pirates' Hall of Famer, was dragging himself through an airport to begin a long flight after a night game, he said, "I'm not crying. I asked to be a ballplayer."[31] Pease says, "The demands of a congressional career can tend to crowd out other facets of a person's life," but "I'm not complaining. I recognized the trade-offs, and I accepted them willingly. I would do so again."[32]

But the satisfaction of House service is supposed to come from participation in national success. "Rationalize as we might, the truth is that we are in charge while our nation's future is being mortgaged and its economic strength sapped . . . the bottom line is that we have failed. It's depressing to be part of the corporate 'we'."[33]

Pease may be depressed by the performance of Congress in this era of political careerism. But many opponents of term

limits evidently are not. I say "evidently" because it often is
not clear precisely what they think about Congress today. Consider, for example, the case of Nelson Polsby, the Director of
the Institute for Governmental Studies and a professor of political science at the University of California, Berkeley. Polsby
is a distinguished representative of the scholarly opponents of
term limits. This makes especially fascinating the fact that he
criticizes term limits with this curious argument: Congress is
doing well, and it would do even better if only congressional
careers were not so short.

> It is a delusion to think that good public servants are a dime a
> dozen in each congressional district, and that only the good ones
> would queue up to take their twelve-year fling at congressional
> office. But suppose they did. In case they acquired expertise,
> what would they do next? Make money, I suppose. Just about
> the time their constituents and the American people at large
> could begin to expect a payoff because of the knowledge and
> experience that these able members had acquired at our ex-
> pense, off they would go to some Washington law firm.
>
> And what about their usefulness in the meantime? It would
> be limited, I'm afraid, by the greater expertise and better com-
> mand of the territory by lobbyists, congressional staff, and down-
> town bureaucrats—career people one and all. So this is, once
> again, a proposal merely to weaken the fabric of Congress in the
> political system at large, and thereby to limit the effectiveness of
> one set of actors most accessible to ordinary citizens.[34]

This argument is like a suspension bridge built by an engineer
who did his calculations wrong. The internal tensions do not
support it, they cause it to collapse. Let's look at the pieces.

First, political scientists who oppose term limits would be
well advised not to make their own arguments seem weak by
caricaturing the arguments of supporters of term limits. For
example, supporters do not believe that good public servants

are planted thick on the ground ("a dime a dozen"). But they do believe that potential quality legislators are more plentiful in congressional districts (the average population of a district is approximately 572,000) than critics of term limits seem to think. Surely no one wants to suggest that "good ones" are filling the 535 House and Senate seats today. Neither, surely, is it reasonable to believe that the potential supply of quality legislators is so scanty that if representatives and senators served fewer than twelve years, America would be scraping the bottom of the barrel. There are a quarter of a billion Americans. Surely we have a sufficient supply of talent to allow us to rotate 535 offices.

It is indeed possible that, as Polsby says, people will make money off expertise they have acquired in government. There are some precedents. (We shall come in a moment to James Payne's evidence about this.) But it is peculiar to say that twelve years would be "just about the time" that legislators begin to deliver the "payoff" of the "knowledge and expertise" acquired from incumbency. And it is also odd to say that in "the meantime"—during that long apprenticeship of a dozen years— their "usefulness" is limited by the domination of lobbyists, congressional staffs and bureaucrats, all of whom are "career people."

Well, now.

The vast majority of congressional staffers are not career people. The average length of service is 5.0 years for House staff[35] and 5.7 years for Senate staff.[36] As for lobbyists, they are indeed career people. And they are passionate opponents of term limits because they have valuable investments in long-term relationships of mutual aggrandizement with career legislators. As for bureaucrats, they derive their power largely from being able to serve the long-term needs of career legislators.

But these matters are less important than the suggestion

that a dozen years is the *minimum* time required before sat-
isfactory legislative service can commence. The Constitutional
Convention considered terms of one, two and three years for
representatives. It decided two was long enough to allow legislators to master the duties of the office and short enough to
prevent them from losing what Madison called "an intimate
sympathy with the people."[37] At that time most state legislatures had one-year terms. The argument for three-year terms
(as stated by Madison) was that that length would "bear some
proportion to the extent of practical knowledge, requisite to
the due performance of the service."[38] Now, granted, government has more than quadrupled in size and complexity. But
from that it does not follow that Polsby is right, that twelve
years are required for a legislator to get up to speed.

If legislative service is really that complicated in the modern state, what does that say about the possibility of there
being public comprehension of the public business? What does
it say about the reality of anything even remotely deserving
the appellation "representative government"? If government is
really such an arcane business, how is it that the executive
branch departments and agencies are run, year in and year
out, by Cabinet and sub-Cabinet officers who come into government for stints of eight or (usually) fewer years? Adminis-
tering, say, the Department of Health and Human Services (or
Interior, or Housing and Urban Development, or the Environmental Protection Agency or any of dozens of other departments) is a lot more demanding than representing any
congressional district or running any congressional committee.

Finally, there is the quaint idea that representatives and
senators are "accessible" to ordinary citizens. To be sure, representatives exhaust themselves traveling to and from their
constituencies, attending ceremonial and political functions at
which they are indeed "accessible." But for what? The pertinent question concerns who has access to them where they

work—in Washington. If these legislators—these vessels brimming over, after a dozen years, with expertise—are the few people uniquely qualified to pierce the veil of government's mysteries, then what, exactly, does access to them do for the benighted "ordinary citizens"? If you accept the premise that government is like neurosurgery, only more so, what do the rest of us have to say to these wizards once we are given "access" and are ushered into their presence?

Because this subject has been raised, here is a suitable point at which to say something about the sort of people who in fact have constant access to full-time career legislators. To testify on this subject, we call to the witness stand James L. Payne, an independent scholar who has taught at Wesleyan, Yale, Johns Hopkins and Texas A&M. In one of his projects he asked himself a simple question and came up with a statistically stunning answer. His question was: Why do so many representatives and senators support so many spending programs? The answer he found was that hardly anyone ever testifies against spending.

He studied fourteen different hearings in various House and Senate committees. He tabulated the orientations of 1,060 witnesses concerning the spending under discussion. He found that seven were opponents, thirty-nine were neutral—testifying about something other than the spending—and 1,014 favored spending. Payne knows one reason for such numbers: "In the modern welfare state, we tend to view government as a store, in which we can get the things we need. Going there in order to avoid getting anything seems irrational, and trying to prevent others from getting what they need seems meanspirited."[39]

When Payne discussed his findings, this 145-to-1 tilt in favor of spending, with congressional staff, staffers were surprised the ratio was so low. They already knew what Payne had learned from his analysis of who comes into contact with legislators and their staffs. They knew that "the persuasion process in Washington is highly inbred."[40] The public simply does not know how much so. "The public supposes, because democratic theory says it should be so, that congressional views on spending are mainly affected by opinions and pressures from outside government—from the folks 'back home' or from interest groups 'out there.' This is not the case. *Overwhelmingly, Congress's views on spending programs are shaped by governmental officials themselves.*"[41]

Of the 1,060 witnesses at the fourteen hearings, 47 percent were federal administrators, 10 percent were state and local government officials, and 6 percent were members of Congress testifying to their colleagues. So 63 percent were, in effect, government itself acting as an interest group. Another 33 percent of the witnesses—almost all those who were not government officials—were lobbyists for what purport to be, and are perceived to be, private sector institutions. But, says Payne, these groups are to a large extent extensions of government. Their personnel are often former government officials, thoroughly socialized in government's benign view of its own motives and competence. Furthermore, many of these supposedly private groups are partially funded by government contracts and grants. A list of what Payne calls these "semi-governmental entities"[42] would include the National Council of Churches, the National Education Association, the League of Women Voters, the Sierra Club, People United to Save Humanity (Jesse Jackson's organization), the Gray Panthers and many more familiar petitioners before Congress.

Then there are the consultants who are hired by government, at a cost of about $2 billion a year, to study the government's programs. These people earn their livings evaluating programs. They are not famous for frowning upon the work of the government agencies that hire them. And government agencies are not famous for looking for potentially hostile eval-

uators. Besides, many evaluators are former government officials, steeped in sympathy for what any government agency
wants: more. Often their idea of a useful evaluation of a failing
program is to prescribe "better management"[43] and more
money.

Among members of Congress, the governmental mindset
increases as tenure increases. In both parties there is a correlation between length of service and sympathy for spending
proposals. Analysis of Washington's incestuous, circular form
of government-in-conversation-with-itself suggests a problem
of typology: If rule by king is monarchy, and rule by a single
individual is autocracy, and rule by the people—the demos—is
democracy, then what word do we have for government controlling itself? Payne suggests "autonarchy."[44] That delightful
word suggests both anarchy and self-stimulation (as in auto-
eroticism). How apt.

Payne's research brought him to a conclusion: One way,
perhaps the only feasible way, to counteract the process of
government indoctrinating itself, and to alter the "culture of
spending" in Congress, is to break the closed circle of persuasion by having compulsory rotation of offices—term limits. For
my part, let me be clear that I am not arguing for or against
any particular level of public spending. I am arguing that current levels and patterns of spending are rational only in the
limited sense that they have the political rationale of serving
the job security of incumbent careerists.

Some of the spending that can justly be called pork seems,
at first blush, to be high-minded. Consider "pork barrel science." The fiscal 1992 budget included $684 million in "ear-
mark" payments for about two hundred particular colleges and
universities, an increase of 39 percent over fiscal 1991. These
"earmarked" grants were awarded without competitive review
of their merits by the agencies that Congress was ordering to
finance them. This rapid growth of academic pork coincided

with a much slower growth of more serious science spending—
spending based on merit reviews. For example, money for the
National Science Foundation and National Institutes of Health
increased from fiscal 1991 to fiscal 1992 by only 16 and 8 percent
respectively.[45]

Senator Robert Byrd's West Virginia was, of course, the
biggest recipient of academic pork, as of all other forms. Sixty-
five million dollars, about 10 percent of the national total, went
to West Virginia University and Wheeling Jesuit College. The
university got, for example, $1.5 million for the National Cen-
ter for Alternative Transportation Fuels, and $494,000 for the
Institute for the History of Technology and Industrial Archae-
ology and $247,000 for testing timber-bridge designs, and many
millions more for other programs. Wheeling Jesuit College,
with about 1,400 students and an operating budget of only
about $14 million, received $21 million for, among other things,
construction of the "classroom of the future."[46]

The remaining 90 percent of the academic pork was distributed, with fine evenhandedness, to forty-eight other states.
(Only Delaware was left out.) Perhaps it was in the national
interest for Michigan State University to receive $94,000 for
research on asparagus yield decline and $39,000 for research
on celery, and for Lehigh University to receive $50,000 for
soybean-based ink research, and for Kean College of New
Jersey and twenty-eight other institutions to receive $300,000
to develop educational materials on fishing vessel safety, and
for George Mason University to receive $750,000 for its Cen-
ter for Suburban Mobility and . . .[47] Never mind. The list is
long—very long—and I, like Congress, am not ambitious to
discuss the merits of particular cases. My point is simply that
pork can be served up in the name of knowledge, learning,
science and other good things and still be pork. Whatever one
thinks about this or that program on the list of academic
"earmarks," no one can reasonably think that the resulting

spending, considered in aggregate, represents even an attempt to spend rationally rather than politically. And political spending means, inevitably, spending to serve the spenders' reelection requirements.

Most of the people who read and review books like this may at this point be feeling more than just somewhat virtuous. Few such people participate in the Peanut Program, or raise federally subsidized goats, or keep bees at taxpayer expense, or run subsidized "essential" one-plane airlines. The political diet, so to speak, of the intelligentsia does not include pork, other than the academic variety just examined, right?

Wrong.

Consider a ruckus that erupted in Washington late in the spring of 1992, concerning the federal subsidy for public broadcasting. This is a dispute worth examining at length because it concentrates in one small subject so many aspects of our current discontents. These include disagreement about government's proper purposes; dismay about the deficit and about anything that can be done about it; the advantages the articulate classes enjoy in the competition for the favors of modern government; the power of government-created constituencies to fight for the prosperity of the government agencies that cause the constituencies to exist; the connection between legislative careerism and the refusal of government to recognize limits.

This author helped to bring the row to a rolling boil by wondering, in a column, why, with red ink lapping up to the ship of state's Plimsoll line, taxpayers should be asked to give public broadcasting another $1.1 billion dollars over three years, a 50 percent increase over existing funding levels. This question had already been raised in Congress by some troglodyte Neanderthal Puritan Yahoo philistine reactionary Inquisitorial Victorian barbarian blue-nosed Cromwellian Know-Nothing killjoy spoilsport Savanarolas—that is, conservatives, as the public television lobby portrays them. But people not particularly conservative were asking the same thing.

Needless to say, the Corporation for Public Broadcasting, a filigree put on the Great Society a quarter of a century ago, has ample defenders in Congress. After all, the CPB shovels out subsidies to stations serving virtually every congressional district. The caliber of the arguments of the CPB's defenders can be gauged by this *crie de coeur* from Senator Albert Gore, the Tennessee Democrat: "How many senators here have children who have watched 'Sesame Street' and 'Mr. Rogers' Neighborhood'? . . . This is one thing that works in this country."[48]

How apposite it was, this scene wherein a wealthy legislator, in a chamber planted thick with people like him, called for subsidies for his children's entertainment because the entertainment "works," whatever that means. The Senator, and others who rushed to bow just as deeply before the altars of little children and high culture, surely knows that "Sesame Street" does not need the subsidy it gets. It is produced by the Children's Television Workshop, a multi-media giant grossing more than $100 million a year from programming, publications and licensing fees. But it was easier for the CPB's defenders to take refuge behind the broad feathers of Big Bird than to confront this fact: Public Broadcasting is primarily a middle class subsidy that, like many such subsidies, has now been elevated, in the minds of its recipients and hence in the minds of their representatives, to the status of an entitlement, which puts it just one rung below a civil right in the hierarchy of things the government deals in. However, whatever one thinks of the case made for public broadcasting a generation ago, the case has collapsed in today's utterly transformed technical and fiscal contexts.

The original argument for public television was that over-the-air broadcasting allows only a few competitors, and they are driven to seek a broad, and low, common denominator. That argument has been obviated by technology—by cable and the onset of "narrowcasting." Public television's advocates argued that 90 percent of households can receive it, whereas only 60 percent of households are wired for cable. But leaving aside the rapid spread of cable, the crucial question is: How many of the people in households that are not wired for cable because they can not afford it are watching public television? Not many. Public television's audience always has been economically and intellectually up-scale.

The original rationale for public television was wonderfully sealed against questioning. It was that government had to subsidize particular kinds of programming precisely because so few people wanted them. If the public were more discerning, there would be no need for it. But, then, a discerning public would not object to government providing it. After all, a discerning public is, by definition, discerning about the merits of government provision of services.

The CPB provides 17 percent of the funding for public television stations. But those stations claim 5.2 million voluntary donors.[49] If each would give another $70 a year (less than the average cable subscriber pays for three months of service) they would have raised the $1.1 billion without requiring taxpayers to subsidize their entertainment. And Dr. Laurence Jarvik of the Heritage Foundation has another idea about what to do with the CPB: sell it. Jarvik is confident—and reasonably so—that there now are ample cable, broadcast and home video markets for magnificent work like Ken Burns's Civil War series, so private investors could make and syndicate such quality programming. Because of cable and alternative services, Jarvik says, public television is "a solution in search of a problem."[50]

Walter Goodman of the *New York Times* asks: "Is Dr. Jarvik so satisfied with commercial TV that he can see no room

for future innovation?"[51] To which question the right response
is: Of course not, but does Goodman believe that any possibility
of making improvements in any sector of society is sufficient
justification for a federal subsidy? If not, what makes television
special?

Politically, what is special is public television's audience.
For example, WETA, Washington, D.C.'s public station, says
its contributors have an average household income of $94,583.[52]
That would leave them with $94,513 after sending WETA an
extra $70 to keep themselves and their children (and the sen-
ators' children) wholesomely entertained. WETA's audience
would be an advertiser's dream. Indeed, it is a dream for those
who advertise in WETA's magazine. Thus goverment is entan-
gled in subsidizing competition against private print as well as
broadcasting enterprises.

The public television lobby is, in part, another example of
government-as-an-interest-group. It is government lobbying
itself. It is an effective lobby because it is spread from sea to
shining sea. Furthermore, public television audiences are, like
the members of the American Medical Association, the National Association of Manufacturers and many other muscular
lobbies, largely affluent, educated and articulate. This is why
public television is a paradigm of America's welfare state gone
awry. It is another middle class—actually, upper middle
class—entitlement. If you doubt that the entitlement mentality
is at work here, hear the indignant rhetoric equating any questioning of the subsidy with censorship. Public television provides most of its services disproportionately to people with the
financial and educational means to fend for themselves, but
who have the political competence to bend public power to
their private advantage. Think of it this way: The relationship
of the CPB to affluent America is approximately that of agriculture subsidies to agribusiness.

This line of argument elicited a counter-blast from someone well-versed in Washington's ways—Sharon Percy Rockefeller.[53] She bears the name of a former senator (her father Charles Percy, the Illinois Republican), is married to a senator (Jay Rockefeller, the West Virginia Democrat) and is president of Washington's WETA. With a spirit stronger than the reasoning behind it, she began her rejoinder with some implausible numbers which, if accurate, shatter the rest of her argument. The numbers purported to show that public television's audience is huge (supposedly 80 percent of the population each month) and with demographics that "mirror"—her word—those of the general population. Such numbers make you wonder: Why can no advertisers be found to sponsor the programming that allegedly is so successful at winning huge numbers of viewers who are typical Americans?

Rockefeller said public broadcasting's aim is "good programming, not profit." Of course this lofty disdain for profit-seeking is made possible by successful subsidy-seeking in Congress. She said public television "improves" America, which may well be true but begs the question, which is: In the current (and forseeable) fiscal climate, does public broadcasting—a paradigm of government's ornamental activities, pleasant but inessential—have a strong claim on government's scarce resources? Does it have claims stronger than the homeless, child immunization, the National Institutes of Health and thousands of other competing causes?

Rockefeller said public television is part of government's promotion of "the pursuit of happiness." Actually, it is government in the distorted role of deliverer of happiness. And to whom? To an economically and intellectually advantaged constituency that could and should fend for itself to satisfy its appetite for cultural services. When public television began, before the advent of cable and the VCR, it increased from three to four the choices available to most viewers. Now most households have scores of channels to choose from, including some (e.g., Discovery, and Arts & Entertainment) that offer programming comparable to much of public television's programming.

Rockefeller argued that "more outlets do not necessarily mean more choices; an increase in quantity does not automatically result in more diversity or higher quality."[54] Rockefeller could not deny the explosion of televised diversity. Instead, her argument suggested that any demand the market satisfies must be of dubious quality. And the implication seems to be that no matter how many choices the market offers, government has a duty to add others by offering programs for which the market registers no demand. That argument guarantees that government television can forever, no matter what, be called "necessary." But it achieves this guarantee at a cost. It underscores the perverse rationale for federal subsidies.

The rationale is that no matter how much programming the market provides, government is supposed to provide more. Why? Because its programming is supposed to serve an audience so small or idiosyncratic or devoted to "quality" that market forces, even those now generating a proliferation of programming to a much-segmented market, will not satisfy it. But as noted already, this argument is not available to anyone brandishing the numbers by which Rockefeller purported to prove that public television's audience is just like—because almost identical with—America's entire population.

Rockefeller said, "He [George Will] concludes that government should consign public broadcasting—and by extension other cultural institutions—to the forces of the marketplace."[55] And she likened public television to "public schools, universities, libraries, hospitals, museums, symphonies and national parks."[56] But Rockefeller was making an unreasonable extension. Reasonable distinctions are necessary; let's make some.

Many cultural institutions serving small and primarily affluent audiences should indeed be weaned from dependence on tax dollars, especially federal dollars. And it is not in Rockefeller's interest to put public television on any list with hospitals, which are institutions of life and death, and schools and universities, which are essential for preparing the population for freedom and social competence. Such lists underscore the fact that public television is a social adornment, not a necessity.

Adornments are by definition nice. But can we afford all the adornments it would be nice to have? When one raises the question of cost concerning any domestic program, defenders of that program say (even though the defense budget has declined in real terms for eight years), "The military wastes money!" For example, Bill Moyers, one of public television's adornments, says the military spends $200 million on bands,[57] therefore Congress can vote just five-and-a-half times that sum for public television.

Such crashing non sequiturs (why is the $200 million an argument for more money for people like Moyers, rather than an argument for less money for military bands?) have acquired a kind of crazy plausibility after years of fiscal vandalism. By now the very vastness of the deficit has become an argument for making it vaster. The argument is: Given a deficit of $400 billion, what's another $1.1 billion among friends? What difference does it make?

Columnist Robert J. Samuelson joined the fray about public broadcasting.[58] Taking aim at the argument that a mere $1.1 billion is not enough to do any more damage than the deficit already is doing, Samuelson noted that many other federal spending programs resemble the television subsidies in that they have constituencies, and those similar spending programs add up to serious money. Amtrak, farm subsidies, water subsidies—every constituency for such a program argues, vehemently and sometimes even sincerely, that the program has public benefits that improve America. The costs of such programs mount and soon there is no money for big new government exertions, however meritorious they might be. Samuelson noted that in 1991 Sharon Rockefeller's husband had chaired a national commission on children. It made some expensive proposals. They were effusively praised and promptly dismissed as unrealistic because there is a shortage of money. "If Senator Rockefeller wonders why," wrote Samuelson, "he should look across the breakfast table."[59]

Samuelson knows that the CPB's $1.1 billion is not standing between children and adequate government provision of services. Rather, his point is that the public will not countenance serious tax increases until spending is controlled, which suits the political class just fine because that class wants neither tax increases nor spending cuts. So the minuet of the incumbents continues. The public says: No new taxes until spending is disciplined. The political class says: No particular discipline will make any difference. Samuelson sums up his philippic as follows:

> But both parties are pleased, because neither truly wants to raise taxes or cut spending. The paralysis is sustained by special pleaders like Rockefeller who have a vested interest in the status quo: that is, massive deficits without political pressures to cut the least-justified programs. . . . The attitude is live and let live: I'll keep my favorite program, you keep yours. We can no longer tolerate this casual cynicism. People like Sharon Rockefeller enjoy unwarranted public sympathy because they defend programs deemed "worthy." In fact, she and her ilk are prime defenders of the deficits. Irresponsibility has become respectable, even chic.[60]

Here the argument about public broadcasting subsidies ended, with the side I was on urging Congress to ask two simple questions about cutting the CPB's funding: If not here, where? If not now, when?

Who won the argument? Your answer will depend on your

point of view. Who won the political fight? No question. No contest. Sharon Rockefeller's side won. The CPB's subsidy was voted in full, in a Senate landslide, 84 yeas, just 11 nays.[61]

If something as marginal as public television can successfully defend its subsidy, clearly future spending cuts—if any—will come only at the expense of Americans less affluent, less educated and less skillful in Washington than public television's aggressively moralistic constituency. Public television is a paradigm of government's role as servant of the comfortable and defender of the strong at the expense of the future. The battle in Congress over the CPB subsidy was contemporary government writ small, in two senses. It involved a relatively small amount of money. And it turned on the small calculations of incumbents eager to spend money out of empty pockets in order to please small but intense and attentive groups of voters.

Many informed and public-spirited people argue that government is spending a portion of the GNP too large for the long-term vigor of the economy, and in the process is distorting the operations of democracy. Other reflective and honorable people argue with equal vehemence that government is spending too little on public investment (in infrastructure, education, research, medicine, culture) to maintain society's civility and vitality. And it is even conceivable that someone, somewhere, sincerely believes the current level of public spending is just right. In fact, the current level is about what the level has been for a decade. However, no thoughtful person can be pleased with the current pattern of public spending. This is not just because every faction has had to compromise. No, the source of dissatisfaction is more serious than that. It is the widespread and unquestionably correct sense that the allocation of scarce public resources is determined to a large and growing extent not by calm deliberation about public needs but by the runaway dynamism of a scramble by incumbents attending to their career needs by dispensing favors as different as wool subsidies and Masterpiece Theater.

The problem of government itself becoming an interest group is as old as politics. Aristotle defined a corrupt regime as one that rules for its private good rather than the public good.[62] Jefferson similarly defined "corruption" as "a legislature legislating for its own interests."[63] Jefferson was twenty-one centuries distant from Aristotle and is less than two centuries distant from us. However, his world more closely resembled Aristotle's than ours in this particular: Eighteenth-century American government had a relatively limited capacity for such "legislative corruption." Jefferson could not have imagined the myriad ways in which a modern state enables a legislature to acquire interests of its own and to advance them.

One dramatic difference between America's public mind today and that mind in the eighteenth century, and to a large extent even in the nineteenth and part of the twentieth, is this: Back then, there were many areas of life that government, especially the federal government, was at least hesitant about regulating, subsidizing, taxing or otherwise bringing under its sway. Today there are few such areas. Now there are few limits to the areas in which legislators can operate to confer the favors that are the currency for purchasing perpetual incumbency. That currency has considerable purchasing power.

The accompanying graph and table shown in Figure 5[64] tell the same story. The declining line on the graph charts the rise of legislative careerism.

Figure 5. Turnover Rates in the House

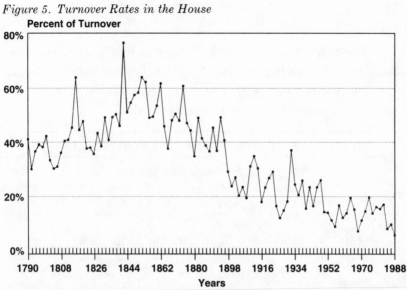

Source: Calculated from information contained in Congressional Research Service Report. Reproduced from Trudy Pearce, *Term Limitation: The Return to a Citizen Legislature*, p. 18. Copyright © 1991. Used with permission of the U.S. Term Limits Foundation.

TURNOVER RATES IN THE HOUSE OF REPRESENTATIVES

Year	%Turnover	Year	%Turnover	Year	%Turnover
1790	41.5%	1858	49.6	1924	17.9
1792	30.8	1860	53.5	1926	13.6
1794	37.1	1862	61.5	1928	16.3
1796	39.6	1864	46.2	1930	19.5
1798	38.7	1866	38.2	1932	37.7
1800	46.2	1868	48.3	1934	25.6
1802	34	1870	50.6	1936	21.8
1804	31	1872	48.2	1938	26.9
1806	31.7	1874	60.6	1940	17
1808	36.6	1876	47.3	1942	24.6
1810	40.9	1878	44.7	1944	17.9
1812	41.3	1880	35.5	1946	24.6
1814	45.6	1882	49.2	1948	27.1
1816	63.7	1884	41.9	1950	15.8
1818	44.8	1886	39.4	1952	15.6
1820	47.9	1888	37.2	1954	12.9
1822	38.2	1890	45.9	1956	10.6
1824	38.5	1892	37.4	1958	18.2
1826	36.2	1894	49.4	1960	13.8
1828	43.7	1896	41.2	1962	15.4
1830	39	1898	30	1964	20.9
1832	49.3	1900	24.9	1966	16.8
1834	41.2	1902	28	1968	9
1836	49.4	1904	21.5	1970	12.9
1838	50.4	1906	24.6	1972	16.1
1840	46.3	1908	20.7	1974	21.1
1842	76	1910	32	1976	15.4
1844	51.1	1912	35.6	1978	17.7
1846	54.7	1914	31.3	1980	17
1848	57.4	1916	19.3	1982	18.6
1850	58.2	1918	24.4	1984	9.9
1852	63.8	1920	27.8	1986	11.5
1854	62	1922	30.1	1988	7.6
1856	49.2				

The modern postwar era of American politics can be usefully said to have begun in 1952, when Truman retired, breaking the organic link with the New Deal. Table 1 shows the
pattern of seniority in the House since 1952.[65]

TABLE 1.   SENIORITY OF REPRESENTATIVES, 1953–1991

	Percentage of representatives serving								*Mean*	*Median*
Congress	1 term	2 terms	3 terms	1–3 terms	4–6 terms	7–9 terms	10+ terms	*Total*	*term*	*term*
83d (1953)										
Percent	18	14	12	44	29	16	10	100	4.9	4
Seats	78	61	53	193	127	70	42	432		
84th (1955)										
Percent	11	17	13	42	26	19	12	100	5.2	4
Seats	50	74	58	182	115	84	54	435		
85th (1957)										
Percent	9	11	16	36	31	17	16	100	5.5	5
Seats	40	46	69	155	133	74	71	433		
86th (1959)										
Percent	18	10	10	38	30	17	15	100	5.6	4
Seats	79	43	43	165	131	74	66	436		
87th (1961)										
Percent	13	15	8	36	29	18	17	100	5.8	5
Seats	55	65	35	155	126	77	74	432		
88th (1963)										
Percent	15	13	13	41	24	19	17	100	5.7	5
Seats	66	55	55	176	104	81	74	435		
89th (1965)										
Percent	19	14	11	44	22	18	17	100	5.5	4
Seats	83	60	47	190	94	78	72	434		
90th (1967)										
Percent	14	15	12	41	25	16	17	100	5.6	4
Seats	60	65	54	179	110	70	75	434		
91st (1969)										
Percent	8	15	14	37	31	15	18	100	5.7	5
Seats	36	65	58	159	132	64	76	431		

92d (1971)										
Percent	11	10	13	34	29	16	20	100	6.0	5
Seats	48	45	57	150	127	69	87	433		
93d (1973)										
Percent	16	11	10	37	30	16	18	100	5.7	5
Seats	67	49	41	157	131	67	78	433		
94th (1975)										
Percent	20	14	10	44	24	19	14	100	5.4	4
Seats	86	61	42	189	102	81	61	433		
95th (1977)										
Percent	15	21	12	48	21	17	14	100	4.6	4
Seats	64	92	54	210	90	73	60	433		
96th (1979)										
Percent	18	14	17	49	22	16	13	100	5.0	4
Seats	77	61	76	214	96	70	55	435		
97th (1981)										
Percent	17	17	13	47	28	14	11	100	4.9	4
Seats	73	75	57	205	120	60	50	435		
98th (1983)										
Percent	18	14	16	49	28	11	13	100	4.6	4
Seats	80	63	68	211	121	48	55	435		
99th (1985)										
Percent	9	19	14	41	32	13	14	100	4.7	4
Seats	39	81	60	180	141	55	59	435		
100th (1987)										
Percent	11	8	17	37	33	14	16	100	5.6	5
Seats	48	37	74	159	144	63	69	435		
101st (1989)										
Percent	8	12	8	28	38	20	14	100	5.8	5
Seats	33	54	33	120	167	86	60	433		
102d (1991)										
Percent	10	9	11	30	31	21	17	100	6.2	5
Seats	42	41	47	131	137	92	76	435		

Note: Percentages may not add to totals because of rounding.

Sources: Congressional Directory, 1953 through 1985; *Congressional Quarterly Weekly Report*, October 11, 1986; November 8, 1986; January 7, 1989; November 10, 1990; *The Almanac of American Politics 1990* (Washington, D.C.: National Journal, 1989).

Reprinted by permission from Norman J. Ornstein, Thomas E. Mann and Michael J. Malbin, *Vital Statistics on Congress 1991–1992* (Washington, D.C.: Congressional Quarterly, Inc., 1992), pp. 19–20.

Table 2 follows the pattern of recent Senate seniority.[66]
The mean and median years of service are now approximately
the same in both Houses, and are approximately equal to the

TABLE 2.   SENIORITY OF SENATORS, 1953–1991

| Congress | Number of senators serving | | | | Total | Mean years service | Median years service |
	6 years or less	7–12 years	13–18 years	19 years or more			
83d (1953)	46 (16)	29	14	7	96	8.5	7
84th (1955)	42 (14)	37	8	9	96	8.4	7
85th (1957)	37 (10)	36	13	10	96	9.6	9
86th (1959)	42 (20)	30	14	12	98	9.4	8
87th (1961)	42 (7)	25	22	11	100	9.7	9
88th (1963)	42 (12)	26	18	14	100	9.9	7
89th (1965)	29 (8)	36	16	19	100	11.1	9
90th (1967)	28 (7)	34	19	19	100	11.6	9
91st (1969)	32 (14)	32	17	19	100	11.2	11
92d (1971)	25 (10)	24	29	22	100	11.5	11
93d (1973)	40 (13)	20	20	20	100	11.2	9
94th (1975)	35 (11)	22	23	19	99	11.5	9
95th (1977)	42 (17)	25	13	20	100	10.6	9
96th (1979)	48 (20)	24	10	18	100	9.6	7
97th (1981)	55 (18)	20	10	15	100	8.5	5
98th (1983)	43 (5)	28	16	13	100	9.6	7
99th (1985)	32 (7)	38	18	12	100	10.1	9
100th (1987)	26 (13)	44	16	14	100	9.6	8
101st (1989)	31 (10)	26	29	14	100	9.8	10
102d (1991)	30 (5)	23	28	19	100	11.1	11

Note: Figures in parentheses are the number of freshmen senators. Senators who are
currently in their first term are listed under the "6 years or less" column.

Sources: Congressional Directory, 1953 through 1985; Congressional Quarterly Al-
manac (Washington, D.C.: Congressional Quarterly, various years); Congressional
Quarterly Weekly Report, October 11, 1986; November 8, 1986; November 12, 1988;
November 19, 1988; November 10, 1990.

Reprinted by permission from Norman J. Ornstein, Thomas E. Mann and Michael J.
Malbin, Vital Statistics on Congress 1991–1992 (Washington, D.C.: Congressional
Quarterly, Inc., 1992), p. 21.

length of service—twelve years—envisioned as the maximum permissible in many term limitation proposals. But behind the mean and median years of tenure numbers are the facts shown in tables 3 and 4.

In the entire history of the House of Representatives the success rate for incumbents seeking reelection has rarely fallen below 70 percent. Indeed, it has been lower in only seven of the 102 elections: 1842, 1854, 1862, 1874, 1890, 1894 and 1932. That last date is emblematic.[67]

It is no mere coincidence that in the six decades since 1932, when the New Deal—and, in some senses, modern government—began, there has been no election in which fewer than 79 percent of House incumbents seeking reelection were successful. This has occurred because the modern state, with all its spending, subsidizing, regulating and patronage powers, is a fecund source of support for incumbents seeking to satisfy constituencies. In fact, there have only been two elections when the incumbents' reelection rate was below 80 percent. One was in 1938, the year of the reaction against President Roosevelt's Supreme Court–packing plan. The other was in 1948, when President Truman successfully ran against the "do-nothing" 80th Congress. And in both of those elections the rate was barely below—79.1 and 79.3 percent respectively.

In every election from 1790 through 1810, reelection rates for House incumbents exceeded 90 percent. But that was when the party system was just taking shape, and before mass participation in elections. In only four elections between 1810 and 1950—in 1818, 1822, 1926 and 1928—did the incumbents' reelection rate exceed 90 percent. But in the twenty-one elections from 1950 through 1990 the rate has exceeded 90 percent seventeen times and has never fallen below the 86.6 rate of 1964.[68] Those four elections in which the rate fell below 90

TABLE 3.　MEMBERS OF THE UNITED STATES HOUSE OF
REPRESENTATIVES, 1ST THROUGH 102ND CONGRESS: 12 OR
MORE YEARS OF SERVICE AT END OF CONGRESS OF
RECORD[69]

Congress	Consecutive Service
1st (1789–1791)	0
2nd (1791–1793)	0
3rd (1793–1795)	0
4th (1795–1797)	0
5th (1797–1799)	0
6th (1799–1801)	2
7th (1801–1803)	3
8th (1803–1805)	5
9th (1805–1807)	5
10th (1807–1809)	9
11th (1809–1811)	11
12th (1811–1813)	15
13th (1813–1815)	13
14th (1815–1817)	12
15th (1817–1819)	7
16th (1819–1821)	3
17th (1821–1823)	3
18th (1823–1825)	3
19th (1825–1827)	4
20th (1827–1829)	8
21st (1829–1831)	7
22nd (1831–1833)	14
23rd (1833–1835)	13
24th (1835–1837)	9
25th (1837–1839)	8
26th (1839–1841)	7
27th (1841–1843)	6
28th (1843–1845)	3
29th (1845–1847)	4
30th (1847–1849)	4
31st (1849–1851)	3
32nd (1851–1853)	2
33rd (1853–1855)	2
34th (1855–1857)	5
35th (1857–1859)	6
36th (1859–1861)	6

Congress	Consecutive Service
37th (1861–1863)	2
38th (1863–1865)	1
39th (1865–1867)	3
40th (1867–1869)	3
41st (1869–1871)	2
42nd (1871–1873)	2
43rd (1873–1875)	9
44th (1875–1877)	4
45th (1877–1879)	3
46th (1879–1881)	4
47th (1881–1883)	5
48th (1883–1885)	9
49th (1885–1887)	13
50th (1887–1889)	18
51st (1889–1891)	23
52nd (1891–1893)	19
53rd (1893–1895)	22
54th (1895–1897)	19
55th (1897–1899)	18
56th (1899–1901)	18
57th (1901–1903)	19
58th (1903–1905)	35
59th (1905–1907)	51
60th (1907–1909)	66
61st (1909–1911)	77
62nd (1911–1913)	74
63rd (1913–1915)	68
64th (1915–1917)	62
65th (1917–1919)	71
66th (1919–1921)	65
67th (1921–1923)	58
68th (1923–1925)	67
69th (1925–1927)	91
70th (1927–1929)	107
71st (1929–1931)	125
72nd (1931–1933)	121
73rd (1933–1935)	102
74th (1935–1937)	86
75th (1937–1939)	77
76th (1939–1941)	75
77th (1941–1943)	86
78th (1943–1945)	97

Congress	Consecutive Service
79th (1945–1947)	102
80th (1947–1949)	100
81st (1949–1951)	114
82nd (1951–1953)	119
83rd (1953–1955)	130
84th (1955–1957)	139
85th (1957–1959)	152
86th (1959–1961)	142
87th (1961–1963)	153
88th (1963–1965)	169
89th (1965–1967)	155
90th (1967–1969)	150
91st (1969–1971)	168
92nd (1971–1973)	171
93rd (1973–1975)	167
94th (1975–1977)	168
95th (1977–1979)	146
96th (1979–1981)	132
97th (1981–1983)	115
98th (1983–1985)	117
99th (1985–1987)	142
100th (1987–1989)	158
101st (1989–1991)	178
102nd (1991–1993)	198

percent were in 1958, a recession year in the middle of Eisenhower's lame-duck term; 1964, the year of the anti-Goldwater landslide; 1966, the correction of the unnatural swing in the previous election, and 1974, the year of the post-Watergate disgust. Even in those four years the incumbents' success rates were 89.9, 86.6, 88.1 and 87.7 percent. In 1980, when Ronald Reagan's highly ideological campaign partially succeeded in "nationalizing" Senate elections, twelve incumbent senators, all Democrats, were defeated. That year the Senate incumbents' reelection rate was just 55.2 percent. But the rate for House incumbents was 90.7 percent.

The success rate of Senate incumbents seeking reelection has been remarkably similar in the eras before and after 1914,

TABLE 4.   MEMBERS OF THE UNITED STATES SENATE 1ST
THROUGH 102ND CONGRESS
12 OR MORE YEARS OF SERVICE AS OF THE BEGINNING OF
EACH CONGRESS[70]

Congress	Consecutive Service
1st (1789–1791)	0
2nd (1791–1793)	0
3rd (1793–1795)	0
4th (1795–1797)	0
5th (1797–1799)	0
6th (1799–1801)	0
7th (1801–1803)	1
8th (1803–1805)	0
9th (1805–1807)	0
10th (1807–1809)	0
11th (1809–1811)	1
12th (1811–1813)	1
13th (1813–1815)	1
14th (1815–1817)	0
15th (1817–1819)	1
16th (1819–1821)	1
17th (1821–1823)	1
18th (1823–1825)	1
19th (1825–1827)	1
20th (1827–1829)	1
21st (1829–1831)	3
22nd (1831–1833)	1
23rd (1833–1835)	2
24th (1835–1837)	3
25th (1837–1839)	3
26th (1839–1841)	5
27th (1841–1843)	2
28th (1843–1845)	2
29th (1845–1847)	1
30th (1847–1849)	1
31st (1849–1851)	1
32nd (1851–1853)	1
33rd (1853–1855)	1
34th (1855–1857)	1
35th (1857–1859)	2
36th (1859–1861)	5
37th (1861–1863)	6

Congress	Consecutive Service
38th (1863–1865)	3
39th (1865–1867)	4
40th (1867–1869)	5
41st (1869–1871)	5
42nd (1871–1873)	6
43rd (1873–1875)	5
44th (1875–1877)	4
45th (1877–1879)	4
46th (1879–1881)	3
47th (1881–1883)	5
48th (1883–1885)	5
49th (1885–1887)	8
50th (1887–1889)	9
51st (1889–1891)	17
52nd (1891–1893)	20
53rd (1893–1895)	23
54th (1895–1897)	20
55th (1897–1899)	19
56th (1899–1901)	18
57th (1901–1903)	18
58th (1903–1905)	16
59th (1905–1907)	15
60th (1907–1909)	20
61st (1909–1911)	19
62nd (1911–1913)	15
63rd (1913–1915)	14
64th (1915–1917)	17
65th (1917–1919)	14
66th (1919–1921)	13
67th (1921–1923)	18
68th (1923–1925)	18
69th (1925–1927)	19
70th (1927–1929)	17
71st (1929–1931)	22
72nd (1931–1933)	25
73rd (1933–1935)	23
74th (1935–1937)	22
75th (1937–1939)	21
76th (1939–1941)	21
77th (1941–1943)	21
78th (1943–1945)	20
79th (1945–1947)	21

Congress	Consecutive Service
80th (1947–1949)	20
81st (1949–1951)	21
82nd (1951–1953)	19
83rd (1953–1955)	20
84th (1955–1957)	18
85th (1957–1959)	23
86th (1959–1961)	27
87th (1961–1963)	34
88th (1963–1965)	33
89th (1965–1967)	36
90th (1967–1969)	38
91st (1969–1971)	34
92nd (1971–1973)	43
93rd (1973–1975)	39
94th (1975–1977)	43
95th (1977–1979)	32
96th (1979–1981)	29
97th (1981–1983)	25
98th (1983–1985)	26
99th (1985–1987)	28
100th (1987–1989)	30
101st (1989–1991)	37
102nd (1991–1993)	49

when the nation changed from electing senators by state legislatures to direct election. Before 1914, 75 percent of the 805 incumbents who sought reelection were reelected. Since 1914, 72 percent of the 1,124 incumbents seeking reelection have been successful. Over all, since 1790, 73 percent of incumbents seeking reelection have succeeded. In only twelve of 100 election years have the incumbents' success rates fallen below 60 percent (in 1846, 1866, 1870, 1880, 1910, 1912, 1916, 1922, 1930, 1932, 1946 and 1980). The success rates have exceeded 70 percent in 60 of the 100 election cycles.[71] But the most interesting fact about the Senate incumbents' success rates is that they are lower than those of House incumbents. In the House, which is supposed to be more tied to the vicissitudes and turbulence of public sentiment, the overall success rate for incumbents seeking reelection since 1790 is 85 percent. It was 81 percent before 1914 and has been 89 percent since then.[72]

The results of gerrymandering to enhance the security of incumbents can be seen in table 5.[73] It reveals the fluctuating disparities between party strengths as measured in the popular vote and as measured in House seats won since World War II.

Two of the most salient statistics in the term limits debate are those about the number of incumbents seeking reelection in each election cycle, and the number being reelected. Tables 6 and 7[74] reveal the similar tendencies in the House and the Senate.

During the Jeffersonian era congressmen came and went with what today seems remarkable rapidity. Politicians passed through Congress and then often passed on to, or back to, what we now consider, anachronistically, "lower" offices. "A typical career sequence early in the nineteenth century would be local office, state office, U.S. House, and back to the state House."[75] But as the national government grew in importance, ambition turned, like the needle of a compass, toward Congress. "No longer was every politician eligible for and equally likely to seek every other office. The musical chairs of the early nineteenth century were replaced by a tacit consensus among politicians about appropriate career development."[76] The era of the career congressman was at hand.

The development of that era was speeded by the nature of the government's revenue base at the time. In the second half of the nineteenth century, the federal government's heavy reliance on tariff revenues gave Congress a double-barreled weapon in its struggle for institutional aggrandizement. Every imposition of a tariff was a valuable favor for some interest. And the revenue raised by tariffs was used for conferring fa-

TABLE 5. POPULAR VOTE AND HOUSE SEATS WON, BY PARTY, 1946-1990

| Year | Democratic candidates | | Republican candidates | | Change from last election[a] | | Difference between Democratic percentage of seats and votes won |
	Percentage of all votes[b]	Percentage of seats won	Percentage of all votes	Percentage of seats won	Percentage of major party votes	Percentage of seats won	
1946	44.3	43.3	53.5	56.7	6.4R	12.8R	-1.0
1948	51.6	60.6	45.4	39.4	7.9D	17.3D	9.0
1950	48.9	54.0	48.9	46.0	3.2R	6.6R	5.1
1952	49.2	49.1	49.3	50.9	0.1R	4.9R	-0.1
1954	52.1	53.3	47.0	46.7	2.6D	4.2D	1.2
1956	50.7	53.8	48.7	46.2	1.5R	0.5D	3.1
1958	55.5	64.9	43.6	35.1	5.0D	11.1D	9.4
1960	54.4	60.0	44.8	40.0	1.2R	4.9R	5.6
1962	52.1	59.4	47.1	40.6	2.3R	0.6R	7.3
1964	56.9	67.8	42.4	32.2	4.8D	8.4D	10.9
1966	50.5	57.0	48.0	43.0	6.0R	10.8R	6.5
1968	50.0	55.9	48.2	44.1	0.3R	1.1R	5.9
1970	53.0	58.6	44.5	41.4	3.4D	2.7D	5.6
1972	51.7	55.8	46.4	44.2	1.7R	2.8R	4.1
1974	57.1	66.9	40.5	33.1	5.8D	11.1D	9.8
1976	56.2	67.1	42.1	32.9	1.3R	0.2D	10.9
1978	53.4	63.7	44.7	36.3	2.8R	3.4R	10.3
1980	50.4	55.9	48.0	44.1	3.2R	7.8R	5.5

TABLE 5, *continued*

1982	55.2	61.8	43.3	38.2	5.2D	5.9D	6.6
1984	52.1	58.2	47.0	41.8	4.1R	3.6R	6.1
1986	54.5	59.3	44.6	40.7	2.4D	1.2D	4.8
1988	53.9	59.8	45.5	40.2	1.1R	0.5D	6.5
1990	54.0	61.4	45.0	38.4[c]	0.1D	1.6D	8.5

[a] Data show percentage-point increase over previous election in votes or seats won by Republicans (R) or Democrats (D).

[b] Republican and Democratic percentages of all votes excludes districts in which candidates ran unopposed and no vote was recorded: for 1978, 8 districts from Arkansas, Florida, and Oklahoma; for 1980, 12 districts from Arkansas, Florida, Louisiana, and Oklahoma; for 1982, 11 districts from Florida and Louisiana; for 1984, 16 districts from Arkansas, Florida, and Louisiana; for 1986, 14 districts from Florida, Louisiana, and Oklahoma; for 1988, 16 districts from Florida and Louisiana; for 1990, 12 districts from Florida and Louisiana.

[c] For 1990, total percentage of seats won—Democratic and Republican—does not equal one hundred due to the election of Bernard Sanders, an independent candidate from Vermont.

Sources: Congressional Quarterly Weekly Report, June 11, 1977, 1141; March 31, 1979, 571; April 25, 1981, 713; November 11, 1982, 2817–2825; February 19, 1983, 387; April 15, 1985, 687; March 14, 1987, 484; May 6, 1989, 1063; February 23, 1991, 487; Thomas E. Mann and Norman J. Ornstein, eds., *The American Elections of 1982* (Washington, D.C.: American Enterprise Institute, 1983).

Reprinted by permission from Norman J. Ornstein, Thomas E. Mann and Michael J. Malbin, *Vital Statistics on Congress 1991–1992* (Washington, D. C.: Congressional Quarterly, Inc., 1992), p. 50.

TABLE 6. HOUSE INCUMBENTS RETIRED, DEFEATED, OR REELECTED, 1946–1990

Year	Retired[a]	Total seeking reelection	Defeated in primaries	Defeated in general election	Total reelected	Percentage of those seeking reelection	Reelected as percentage of House membership
1946	32	398	18	52	328	82.4	75.4
1948	29	400	15	68	317	79.3	72.9
1950	29	400	6	32	362	90.5	83.2
1952	42	389	9	26	354	91.0	81.4
1954	24	407	6	22	379	93.1	87.1
1956	21	411	6	16	389	94.6	89.4
1958	33	396	3	37	356	89.9	81.8
1960	26	405	5	25	375	92.6	86.2
1962	24	402	12	22	368	91.5	84.6
1964	33	397	8	45	344	86.6	79.1
1966	22	411	8	41	362	88.1	83.2
1968	23	409	4	9	396	96.8	91.0
1970	29	401	10	12	379	94.5	87.1
1972	40	390	12	13	365	93.6	83.9
1974	43	391	8	40	343	87.7	78.9
1976	47	384	3	13	368	95.8	84.6
1978	49	382	5	19	358	93.7	82.3
1980	34	398	6	31	361	90.7	83.0
1982	40	393	10	29	354	90.1	81.4
1984	22	409	3	16	390	95.4	90.1

TABLE 6, *continued*

1986	38	393	2	6	385	98.0	88.5
1988	23	408	1	6	401	98.3	92.4
1990	27	406	1	15	390	96.0	89.7

[a] Does not include persons who died or resigned before the election.

Sources: Congressional Quarterly Weekly Report, January 12, 1980, 81; April 5, 1980, 908; November 8, 1980, 3320–3321; November 10, 1984, 2900; October 11, 1986, 2398; November 8, 1986, 2844; November 12, 1988; *National Journal*, November 6, 1982, 1881; November 10, 1984, 2147; November 10, 1990, 2719.

Reprinted by permission from Norman J. Ornstein, Thomas E. Mann and Michael J. Malbin, *Vital Statistics on Congress 1991–1992* (Washington, D.C.: Congressional Quarterly, Inc., 1992), p. 58.

TABLE 7. SENATE INCUMBENTS RETIRED, DEFEATED, OR
REELECTED, 1946–1990

Year	Retired[a]	Total seeking reelection	Defeated in primaries	Defeated in general election	Total reelected	Reelected as percentage of those seeking reelection
1946	9	30	6	7	17	56.7
1948	8	25	2	8	15	60.0
1950	4	32	5	5	22	68.8
1952	4	31	2	9	20	64.5
1954	6	32	2	6	24	75.0
1956	6	29	0	4	25	86.2
1958	6	28	0	10	18	64.3
1960	5	29	0	1	28	96.6
1962	4	35	1	5	29	82.9
1964	2	33	1	4	28	84.8
1966	3	32	3	1	28	87.5
1968	6	28	4	4	20	71.4
1970	4	31	1	6	24	77.4
1972	6	27	2	5	20	74.1
1974	7	27	2	2	23	85.2
1976	8	25	0	9	16	64.0
1978	10	25	3	7	15	60.0
1980	5	29	4	9	16	55.2
1982	3	30	0	2	28	93.3
1984	4	29	0	3	26	89.6
1986	6	28	0	7	21	75.0
1988	6	27	0	4	23	85.2
1990	3	32	0	1	32	96.9

[a] Does not include persons who died or resigned before the election.

Sources: Congressional Quarterly Weekly Report, January 12, 1980, 81; April 5, 1980, 908; November 8, 1980, 3302; November 6, 1982, 2791; November 10, 1984, 2905; October 11, 1986, 2398; November 8, 1986, 2813; November 12, 1988; November 10, 1990.

Reprinted by permission from Norman J. Ornstein, Thomas E. Mann and Michael J. Malbin, Vital Statistics on Congress 1991–1992 (Washington, D.C.: Congressional Quarterly, Inc., 1992), p. 59.

vors on other groups. "The adoption of tariff barriers to protect domestic industries for every product from 'agate to zinc,' for example, meant that the economic welfare of communities throughout the country became tied to national policies. Moreover, the tariff produced substantial treasury surpluses, and congressmen found themselves in the happy dilemma of how to spend the revenues as a growing number of solicitous groups offered suggestions."[77] The steady and dramatic increase of the importance of Congress as a maker of federal policy, and of federal policy as an allocator of wealth and opportunity, made congressional service more attractive to some people and less attractive to others. For the professional politician, the increased power and prestige of Congress made the hardships involved more endurable. "For the amateur, however, the hardships became *less* endurable. Heavier workloads and longer sessions meant longer absences from home and business. Slowly, the amateurs were replaced by the professionals."[78]

In William Dean Howells' novel *Indian Summer*, published in 1886, there is an oblique reference to a member of that vanishing species, the amateur. A female character is introduced with this information: "She had married a leading lawyer of her Western city, who in due time had gone to Congress, and after his term was out, had 'taken up his residence' in Washington, as the newspapers said. . . ."[79] That is a suggestive, perhaps illuminating phrase, "after his term was out." The congressman served a while—perhaps a single term; it is not clear—then retired. That was the old way. (Then he took up residence in Washington. That was a taste of the new.)

Between 1860 and 1920 the average length of House service doubled from two to four terms. "As more incumbents returned and as the sessions grew longer, the House moved from a temporary way-station where anonymous amateurs and professional politicians alike stopped over on their way to other

careers, to a stable social system with all its trappings."[80] Propelled by the regional and class dimensions of the contest between William Jennings Bryan and William McKinley, the
great realigning election of 1896 shoved the nation toward a
political sorting-out. Because of the polarizing effect of this
campaign, after 1896 both parties had a larger number of safe
congressional seats. Hence there were more members who
could contemplate long legislative careers.

As many such careers matured, there came the "revolt of
1910." Confident members eager for long careers rose against
the power of a few House leaders—the Speaker and a few
committee chairmen—to shape all members' career chances by
dispensing or withholding the keys to power, such as choice
committee assignments. The principal reform resulting from
the revolt was the seniority system. It made careers more
attractive both to careerists and to their constituents.

Careerism suited the temper of the turn of the century.
Careerism came to be identified with modernity—professionalization and specialization, and policy and political "sciences"—in
a nation always receptive to the appeal of the modern. It is symbolic that when the first Congress elected in this century convened in 1901, it was the first in American history in which
fewer than 30 percent of the members were freshmen.

The twentieth century has seen the steady ripening of
careerism. This development probably would not have surprised the nineteenth-century political scientist who noted one
of the stimulants to careerism—the severe individualism of
politics in a party system like America's.

More than a century ago, at Johns Hopkins University, a
young professor with a bright (if then unimagined) political
future wrote that American parties "are like armies without
officers, engaged upon a campaign which has no great cause at
its back. Their names and traditions, not their hopes and policy, keep them together."[81] Today, even more than in 1885

when Woodrow Wilson wrote that, parties are, particularly in
congressional races, mere money-raising and money-
distributing operations, and not even the most important rais-
ers and disbursers. The parties' names mean little because
their traditions mean next to nothing to today's electorate,
which has a mean age of 41.7. No traditions can have much
purchase on the affections of a public that knows little history.
President Franklin Roosevelt, denounced as "Vallandighams"
those who advocated negotiations with Hitler. Roosevelt, who
had an amazingly acute sense of how to communicate with the
American masses, clearly assumed that his reference would
have wide resonance with the general public. How many Americans today would recognize a reference to Ohio's Copperhead,
Clement Vallandigham, the most prominent of the Northern-
ers sympathetic to the Confederacy—or a reference to Cop-
perheads, for that matter?

Running for Congress is today an activity akin to pure
entrepreneurship on the part of candidates who put themselves
forward. They find a market (a district) and a market niche (a
potential majority to be cobbled together from various factions); they merchandise themselves with advertising paid for
by venture capitalists (contributors) who invest in candidates.
The return on this investment is access to decision-makers and
influence on legislation and other government actions. The vast
majority of contributions are, in effect, investments in incumbents. Those investments involve low risks in House races. As
Everett Carll Ladd of the University of Connecticut and the
American Enterprise Institute notes, contests for House seats
occupy an awkward middle ground in American politics, where
voters are apt to have an information deficit that works to the
advantage of the incumbents.

In highly visible races such as those for president, senator, and
governor, voters often do acquire enough information to make

up for the decline of the guidance that party ties long provided. At the other end of the spectrum, in elections for school-board members, aldermen, and other local officials, voters often have enough close-up, personal knowledge to reach reasonably informed judgments. House races and some other "intermediate" contests are where we now have our problem. Here, party voting is no longer decisive, but substantive knowledge of the candidates' records is insufficient to furnish a substitute base. Enjoying huge advantages in resources for self-promotion, incumbents can't readily be challenged so long as they avoid public scandal.[82]

Consider just one of the resources for self-promotion, free mail. In the second half of 1991, according to the National Taxpayers Union, House members more than doubled their already exuberant use of the franking, or free mailing, privilege. In the first half they spent $14.3 million. In the second half they pumped up the volume to $30.4 million. In the last three weeks of 1991 they spent $10.5 million, enough to spew out more than 85 million pieces of mail. This spurt was partly a function of the decennial redistricting. As a result of a loophole carefully stitched into a 1990 "reform" of the law regulating franking, mailings can be sent by members to addresses outside their districts, to households within the redrawn lines of a district in which the member plans to run in the next election. The original and only proper rationale for the franking privilege is to facilitate, between members and constituents, the communication necessary for the latter to judge how the former is fulfilling the office conferred upon him at the last election. The loophole expanded the use of franking for purely campaign purposes.

Franking is not a negligible campaign advantage. In 1991, 185 House members spent more on mailings than the average challenger to a House incumbent spent ($108,506) in 1990. The $10.5 million spent by members just in the last three weeks of

1991 equaled *all* the money raised in 1991 by *all* nonincumbent candidates for House seats. Furthermore, even though every American is represented by two senators and just one representative, the House spent $6.5 million more in just the last quarter of 1991 than the Senate spent in all of 1991. In the frenetic final three weeks of 1991 the House spent as much as the Senate did in the first nine months. In 1991 senators spent on average 6.3 cents per address on franked mailings. House members spent 42.3 cents. Members reelected in 1990 with 55 percent of the vote or less spent 50.6 cents per address, 20 percent more than the House average.

A former member of the staff of Jim Mattox, who was a Democratic Representative from Texas, remembers applying for a job with Mattox:

> "Let me tell you what this job is all about," he said as he brandished an envelope during my job interview. "I'm in a district full of Republicans and the newspapers hate my guts. The TV stations are out to get me. I'm always barely a step ahead of the political undertakers and I win by a couple of percentage points if I'm lucky. The only chance I have is mail." He paused for a moment and waved the envelope bearing his personal signature, or frank, which means that it can be mailed at taxpayer expense. "We are going to mail, mail, mail and then mail some more. You're going to mail until you run out of ideas. Then you're going to talk to the rest of the staff until they run out of ideas. After that you're going to come to me and mail until *I* run out of ideas. And when that happens, we're going to staple my picture to pages of the goddamn Yellow Book and mail them out, too, and lemme tell you, you cain't *ever* run out of them sons of bitches."
>
> We laughed, and the job was mine.[83]

Members' mailing allowances are, to put it mildly, generous, and the relevant law, written by incumbents with incumbents' advantages in mind, permits members to spend up to $25,000 more than their mailing allowance by transferring funds from their office expense or staff salary accounts. Eleven members did so. Thirty-two members spent more than $100,000 just in the last quarter of 1991. Only twenty-nine senators spent more than $100,000 on mass mailings during all of 1991.

House members did not exhaust all their energies on mailings in 1991. In one two-day period in the spring of 1992, members of the House churned out 58 million pieces of franked mail. By the summer of 1992 Congress's franking excesses had cost Congress the support of a normally sympathetic voice, that of the newspaper *Roll Call*. That paper's patience snapped when the editors examined reports of franking in the first quarter of 1992. These reports, said a *Roll Call* editorial,[84] "reveal that we have been naive" and that "scores of Members are using the franking privilege mainly to win votes" rather than for more public-spirited communications. One awaits the great awakening when *Roll Call* recognizes that most members are using the whole government mainly to win votes. But let us stay with what has shocked *Roll Call*. In the first quarter of 1991 House members spent $5.9 million on franking. In the first quarter of 1992 they spent $10.7 million, an increase of 83 percent that *Roll Call* called "astounding." The difference between 1991 and 1992? The former was not an election year. *Roll Call*, slow to anger but splendid when aroused, thundered: "Members cannot be trusted with the frank under current terms." *Roll Call* does not like to entertain the thought that a different kind of member—members serving under term limits—might be much more trustworthy. Instead, *Roll Call* proposed allowing members just one mass mailing a year, at the end of each year, to report on the year past and on plans for the year ahead. If that mailing were abused, then *Roll Call* would favor eliminating the frank for mass mailings, allowing it to be used only for replies to constituent mail. Then *Roll Call* said: "Or, better yet, allow challengers to mail three free letters for every one

free letter that a member sends out. Now, *that* would kill
franking in very short order."

The franking privilege is but one, and hardly the most
important, of the incumbents' many advantages. The modern
state is a treasure trove of such advantages. In fact, the modern state is one big advantage. That was even more obvious
than usual as the dust from the House bank brouhaha began to
settle in the spring of 1992 and incumbents went home to try to
mollify their constituents. That process of mollification demonstrated what is really wrong with modern government. Consider the case of two congressmen from Georgia, Charles
Hatcher, a six-term Democrat from a mostly rural district in
the southwestern corner of the state, and Newt Gingrich, the
second-ranking Republican in the House (the Republican
Whip), seeking an eighth term in a suburban Atlanta district.

Hatcher bounced 819 checks while failing to balance his
checkbook in 35 of the 39 months under investigation. So he was
included on the list of twenty-two members who were deemed
by the House Ethics Committee to have abused their banking
privileges. Was he in trouble back home? Some, partly because
redistricting left him with a black majority district. As this book
goes to press in July, 1992, he has been forced into a run-off for
the Democratic nomination. But in spite of bounced checks and
redistricting he was still formidable because two things that
matter a lot in his district are peanuts and tobacco. Guess who
is chairman of the House Agriculture Subcommittee on Peanuts
and Tobacco. Hatcher is, and in that capacity he was the prime
mover behind the 1990 reauthorization of the Peanut Program.

Under it the government sets price supports for peanuts
and attempts to regulate production. This raises the price of
American-grown peanuts above the cost of imports, which
therefore must, of course, be penalized by import quotas. (The
quota is 1.2 million pounds of peanuts per year, which would
amount to approximately two imported peanuts per year per
American, if the quota were filled. This quota achieves the

result that would be achieved by a 90 percent tariff.) This means that American consumers pay more than necessary—more than the price that a free, as opposed to a politicized, market would set—for peanuts. In addition, under the Peanut Program, the government must occasionally intervene to buy up a glut of peanuts that can not be sold at the subsidized price. The government did that in 1991 at a cost of about $100 million.

Most Americans have better things to do (do their jobs, raise children, wash the storm windows, watch ESPN) than read the fine print in agriculture appropriations bills, so most Americans do not have even the foggiest idea that any of this is happening. However, the peanut farmers and their suppliers and truckers and workers pay close attention. And they are duly grateful to and protective of the congressman whose seniority enables him to turn the federal government into a powerful siphon, sucking money out of the wallets of consumers and into the pockets of his constituents. Says Danny Fillingame, the owner of a farm supply business in Hatcher's district, "I don't think the peanut farmer can afford to lose Charlie Hatcher."[85] It is a reasonable assumption, considering where Fillingame is from and what he does, that he fancies himself a conservative and is fed up with Washington and its profligate ways, particularly with welfare payments that produce a dependent welfare class in cities. A dependent class of peanut farmers in southwest Georgia is another matter. Eunice Mixon, a farmer and a Democratic county chairman in Hatcher's district, understands: "Everybody thinks the government needs to be reined in and everybody thinks their own cause is holy. People aren't dumb; they just think they're special."[86]

The people up in Cobb County, on the north side of Atlanta, know they are special, because Newt Gingrich says so. He bounced a couple of checks, including one for $9,463 sent to—could this have been an ideological statement?—the Internal Revenue Service. By the spring of 1992 he was beginning to be perceived as one of those unsavory creatures he had long

been excoriating for fun and profit. He was beginning to seem
like a supple, nimble Washington insider, soggy with the perverse values of "the system" and out of touch with ordinary
folks. So he took radical remedial action.

He decided that, come to think about it, he did not need,
did not want and would not any longer tolerate the chauffeur-
driven Lincoln Town Car that has been a traditional perk for
House Whips of both parties. His $60,540-a-year driver was a
detective who packed a gun and doubled as Gingrich's security.
A bodyguard is modern Washington's most coveted, because
most status-conferring, perk. The driver-detective's name was
exquisitely right: George Awkward. Gingrich's decision to embrace asceticism by jettisoning his limousine was perhaps
prompted by the fact that when Representative David Bonior
(D., Michigan) was elected Democratic Whip in 1991 he refused
to accept a car and a driver.

But getting rid of the embarrassing opulence of the car
and driver was just a final filigree on Gingrich's appeal to Cobb
County's restive and surly voters. He was facing a serious
threat to his incumbency in the Republican primary. Hence he
was in danger of losing his career as a critic of career legislators and their use of Congress as an incumbency-protection
device. So, although he is a rhetorical supporter of term limits,
he resorted to precisely the sort of rhetoric that produces the
revulsion that fuels the drive for term limits. He said: "If you
had the choice between the No. 2 ranking Republican in the
House or you can have a freshman who doesn't have any idea
who the Cabinet members are, has never met any of them and
has never worked with the President, which one do you think
can do more for Cobb County?"[87]

With an almost—only almost—admirable forthrightness,
he was asking: Which one of us is more of a well-wired, pork-
producing, inside-the-Beltway operator? He was promising:
Keep sending me back to Washington and I will keep bringing

home the bacon. With that argument, made while this is being written, Gingrich may have saved his career as a professional legislator, but he ended his career as the scourge of the "corruption" of the welfare state in the hands of career legislators. And he unwittingly made himself a textbook example of why term limits are now necessary. In the past Gingrich has made powerful arguments for term limits. Now he has become a powerful argument for limits. He has become a case study of the primacy of careerism in the life of the modern congressman. His entreaty to Cobb County—*please* pick me; I can "do more" for you—is a crystalline expression of the degradation of the idea of representation.

That idea got a much better exegesis 218 years before Gingrich made such a hash of it.

On November 3, 1774, Edmund Burke delivered a thank-you speech[88] to some people who, upon hearing it, may have wished they had not done what he was thanking them for. They had just elected him to Parliament. His speech was to the voters of the bustling commercial city of Bristol. After felicitously expressing his gratitude, he proceeded to, as it were, step back and put some distance between himself and those who had embraced him. He said, "I am sorry I cannot conclude without saying a word on a topic" then on many minds. And he proceeded to speak his excellent mind on the theory of representation. By the time he finished the Bristol voters may have been murmuring: *"Now* he tells us . . ."

He told them that he rejected the popular theory that a representative should feel bound by "instructions" issued by his constitutents concerning how he should vote in Parliament. This doctrine, he said, is incompatible with the duty of a representative, rightly understood. Certainly, he said amicably, a representative should "live in the strictest union, the closest correspondence, and the most unreserved communication with his constituents." But all he was saying was that a representative should hear, understand and empathize with his constituents. "Their wishes ought to have great weight with him; their opinions high respect; their business unremitted attention." But, he said, a representative does not owe obedience. He owes something more than his "industry." He owes his "judgment."

And not just his judgment about how best to achieve what his constituents say they want. No, a representative is duty-bound to exercise his judgment about ends as well as means. His job is not just to help constituents get what they want; he also is supposed to help them want what they ought to want. He should try to reconcile them to his understanding of their duties as citizens. And if he can not do that, he is nevertheless obligated to disregard their desires and follow his judgment. This is an obligation to them. Again, he owes them his judgment.

Burke was taking issue with something that had been said to Bristol voters by another man they had just elected, a man more pliable—and probably at that moment more pleasing—to them. Burke noted: "My worthy colleague says his will ought to be subservient to yours." Burke tried to soften the blow of his disagreement by saying that if government were a mere matter of willfulness, an endless clash of wills, then "yours, without question, ought to be superior." But. With Burke, such a bow to popular sentiment often presaged a "but." "But government and legislation are matters of reason and judgment, and not of inclination; and what sort of reason is that in which the determination precedes the discussion, in which one set of men deliberate and another decide, and where those who form the conclusion are perhaps three hundred miles distant from those who hear the arguments?"

They were, he said, sending him to a capital, but not a foreign capital. He was going to Parliament, not to "a *congress* of ambassadors from different and hostile interests, which interests each must maintain, as an agent and advocate, against other agents and advocates." He should not be guided by merely "local purposes" or "local prejudices." "Parliament," he said, "is a *deliberative* assembly."

So should the U.S. Congress be, although that evidently is news to Newt Gingrich. He promised unsleeping toil in Washington to satisfy the interests and slake the appetites of Cobb County. Thus he promised to participate, calculate and negotiate. He promised to participate energetically in the Washington bazaar. He promised to calculate Cobb County's wishes and the most efficient ways of meeting them. He promised to negotiate with other—what? "ambassadors from different and hostile interests"?—well, other members so that he could maximize Cobb County's "clout." A telling word, "clout," so common in Washington conversation. It conjures up a scene of physical strife, of forces colliding with other forces in a maelstrom of sheer willfulness, a process devoid of—to cite three of Burke's telling categories—reason, discussion and deliberation.

What Gingrich did not promise to do was to deliberate.

The 1770s are a long time distant from the 1990s. Bristol, England, is a long way from Cobb County, Georgia. But those distances of time and space are as nothing compared to the philosophic—the moral—distance between the austere declaration of independence that Burke delivered to the electors of Bristol and the pledge of servility that Gingrich laid at the feet of the voters of Cobb County. We have come a long way in two centuries, much of it downhill, in our understanding of representation. That is a core category in the political philosophy and civic morality of a republic. It is time resolutely to turn round and reascend to the high ground mapped long ago by reflective Americans who explored this terrain.

CHAPTER 2

The Recovery of Deliberative Democracy

W hat's new? Not much. Not in American political
argument, at any rate. Almost all of the basic subjects of American controversy were present by
1776, or shortly thereafter. Think about it. What current controversy was not alive and kicking, or at least clearly foreshad-
owed, in the last three decades of the eighteenth century?

Today's controversy about the proper role of Congress is
not just an echo of an earlier argument, it is a continuation of
America's oldest argument. This argument is a scarlet thread
of continuity running through American history. The controversies about the Stamp Act (1765) and the Townsend Acts
(1767) prompted an American consciousness and hence helped

to ignite American history. Remember the rallying cry: "No taxation without *representation*." And as the Framers understood, discussion of the meaning of representation and the proper role of Congress is incomplete without consideration of the appropriate composition of Congress. So today's quickened interest in term limitations is, strictly speaking, quite traditional.

The name of Samuel Osgood, a Massachusetts man, is an answer to a trivia question: Name one of America's first politicians retired by term limits. In 1784 the Committee on Qualifications of the Continental Congress undertook "to make an inventory of [the] present stock of members to determine . . . whether any members were tarrying beyond their appointed terms."[1] The Committee declared Osgood "incapable of being a Delegate in Congress after the first day of March, 1784, he having been a Delegate three years since the ratification of the Articles of Confederation."[2] Osgood was (in the limpid language of his time) restored to his private station. The Republic got along without him. It also got on with its fruitful reflections about how to design a government that did not need to presuppose or provide for any indispensable political individual or class.

Many political philosophers have argued that the health of a republic is served by periodic recurrences to first principles. A republic is, by definition, a form of government that presupposes some broadly dispersed thoughtfulness: The people are supposed to make choices, having first taken time to think. Today the health of the American republic requires reestablishment of contact with first principles, particularly with those pertaining to the idea of representation.

At the beginning, or very near the beginning, of all political philosophy there is this stark question: Who shall rule? There are three basic answers to it: One, a few, or many. The American Founders' answer was that the many shall rule but they shall do so through a few. They shall do so under arrangements that are *constitutional*; they shall do so under arrangements designed to condition the way power is used, including the ends for which it is used. The U.S. Constitution has a history. But does it also have an "essence"?[3] It has a trajectory over two centuries, in which its open-textured language has been construed to accommodate exigencies. But does the Constitution, properly construed, serve certain core values? Unquestionably it does.

The Framers' audacious aspiration was to establish a system that would have the "aptitude and tendency"[4]* to produce representation characterized by the virtues of calmness, reasonableness, civility, detachment and long-headedness—a due concern for the long term. The Framers, not being romantics or sentimentalists, knew that whatever else virtues are, they are not "natural." They are the results of nurture and artifice. The Framers intended the institutions they designed, and hence the Constitution itself, to be nurturing artifices.

In the greatest single essay on American politics, Federalist Paper No. 10, Madison says that representation—the delegation of decision-making "to a small number of citizens elected by the rest"—is supposed "to refine and enlarge the public views."[5] As Harvey Mansfield, professor of government at Harvard, says, the Founders believed that the function of representation is to add reason to the popular will.[6] Their delicate task was to devise a system of representation sustained by the people's support but insulated from the people's merely momentary inclinations. The Framers of the Constitution strove to constitute deliberative democracy. At the core of it would be a Congress whose members would have both opportunity and incentive to transcend the maelstrom of

---

* All quotations from *The Federalist*, edited with Introduction and Notes by Jacob E. Cooke, copyright 1961 by Wesleyan University Press by permission of University Press of New England.

private interests and to engage in deliberation about the public good.

The Constitution is not a preachy, overbearing document. It is fundamental law, but it does not lay down the law about the goals of American life. At least it does not other than in quite general language. The Preamble enumerates the six objectives that the Framers and the rest of the ratifying generation did "ordain and establish" the Constitution "in order to" achieve. You remember: "to form a more perfect union, establish justice, insure domestic tranquility, provide for the common defense, promote the general welfare, and secure the blessings of liberty to ourselves and our posterity." The Constitution has been compared to a loose-fitting suit of clothes. The most apposite comparison would be to work clothes—or play clothes. The Constitution does not bind during strenuous exertions. Or, to change the metaphor, it has, like a limber body or some well-designed machines, "play in the joints." (The words are those of Oliver Wendell Holmes.)

But all this does not mean that the document embodies indifference about the way we live or the purposes for which we, collectively, live. Rather, it means that the working of the institutions constituted by the Constitution is supposed to shape, slowly and imperceptibly but surely, both the political manners and the political objectives of the American people. And anyone who thinks political manners and objectives are not related in complex, subtle and consequential ways has not been paying sufficient attention to the lessons of modern history.

A constitution should shape political behavior, and such shaped behavior should shape national character. Thus in a constitutional system such as ours, statecraft is soulcraft, always and inevitably. Constitutional choices are, at bottom, choices about the behavior we wish to encourage. Hence constitutional choices are about the kind of people we want to be, and the kind we want to honor with elevation to office.

Furthermore, the proper function of the U.S. Constitution, as its Framers understood it, is to constitute a government that is controlled by the people but that also controls them. In fact, it controls them through the very process of being controlled by them. It establishes popular sovereignty in that it is supposed "to elicit reason from the people rather than to impose it on them."[7] However, the eliciting is done by the creation of constitutional distance between the people and those who are chosen by the people—chosen to make decisions in the people's name and on their behalf.

To say that popular sentiments and passions should be "controlled" by the government is not to say anything that, properly understood, should offend libertarian spirits. It is not to say that the controlling should be done by coercive or other authoritarian measures. Rather, popular sentiments and passions should be controlled by the very functioning of the government. That is, in the normal course of things, the proper operation of the political process through the government should deepen, mellow, mature and leaven sentiments and passions. This is what Madison meant when, in Federalist No. 51, he wrote, "You must first enable the government to control the governed; and in the next place, oblige it to control itself."[8] First things first.

Rereading Madison, Mansfield marvels: "Control the people! What statesman today could speak so frankly of the first necessity of popular government?"[9] The answer to that question is: Any statesman could who would take the trouble to clarify for the people what it actually is that so troubles them about their government. What is troubling them is, I believe, their sense that they are the problem, or at least a large part of it. Americans criticize their government with increasing virulence, but they know they are deeply implicated in the conduct of popular sovereignty. They are ashamed—vaguely but acutely—of their government, and hence, inescapably, of themselves. They do not know it, and would not take comfort from knowing it, but they are resenting a development that was anticipated.

Alexis de Tocqueville worried about the capacity of democracy to "degrade men without tormenting them."[10] The sensible worry about democracy in America today is that the public is being degraded by the government's constant concern for the public's happiness. What is galling to the public, and what makes the public grumpy in a way that suggests embarrassment and an uneasy conscience, is that the government has been doing what the public has demanded and what the government has promised. Government has been being "responsive."

In any election season, if you listen carefully you will hear the telltale language of current politics. Usually there are a few recurring words or phrases that are indices of current hopes, angers or confusions. In the 1790s there was much argument about "factions" and "parties," which many people thought were inimical to national unity and public virtue. In the Jacksonian era political rhetoric reverberated with the language of economic aspirations and anxieties, with warnings that the Bank of the United States, that "monster," would produce a proliferation of "speculation" and other unworthy ways of acquiring wealth. In the 1850s the temper of the darkening time was encoded in arguments about "sectionalism" and "popular sovereignty."

In any era, popular passions can be unpacked from the vocabulary that is the common currency of political discourse. Today the telltale word is "responsive." And the tale it tells is both deeply felt and profoundly mistaken. Listen carefully. You will hear the word "responsive" in demands issued by voters to politicians and in promises made by politicians to voters. Voters demand a more responsive government; politicians promise to be responsive. What is odd is that never has government—never has any government anywhere—tried as hard as the American government does, with the help of so many devices, to know and conform to popular opinion. Politicians are aided by sophisticated means of measuring the breadth, intensity and nuances of public opinion, and of many demographic components of the public. As a result, government has become a sensitive instrument, trembling at even the slightest tremor of opinion or appetite. And any compact, intense and organized interest group can cause a tremor.

This is not government by deliberation, it is government by "clout." The test of a faction's clout is its ability to get its appetites translated into government action with maximum speed and minimum alteration. The test is the faction's ability to reduce government, on as many issues as possible, to no more than a recording, ratifying and brokering agency. It is understandable, if not admirable, that factions have this aspiration. What is dismaying is the fact that today's servile government aspires to no higher purposes than those of recording, ratifying and brokering.

People who actually like this style of government—who like the theory, if not the actual practice—call it direct democracy, the immediate and emphatic response of government to the public's will, or at least to the public's willfulness. This notion of democracy possesses the virtue of clarity and the vice of simplicity and has never lacked adherents. In this century its adherents have been simultaneously mistaken and correct. They have been mistaken about what the nation needs but correct (and mistakenly disapproving) about what the Framers thought the nation would always need.

Several political movements—the Progressives at the turn of the century, and then the New Dealers—have criticized the Constitution on the grounds that the Framers' purposes are no longer appropriate to the nation's situation. The Progressive movement's intellectuals seemed to suppose that any impediment to the direct and prompt fulfillment by government of popular desires is antidemocratic, and therefore the Constitution is antidemocratic in many parts, and in spirit. Such critics argued that the Constitution prevented, or at least intolerably inhibited, necessary actions by the federal government. The critics were correct about one thing: inhibitions were among the Framers' intentions. But the inhibitions were supposed to prevent action. Rather, they were supposed to facilitate deliberation prior to action.

Woodrow Wilson, "the first American president to criticize the Constitution,"[11] began doing so long before he became President, in his writings as a professor of political science. He and other twentieth-century reformers have argued that the Constitution's flaws are inherent in the Framers' political purposes. With the checks and balances made possible by the separation of powers, and with federalism, the Constitution purposely places other political goals above the goal of efficiency. It gives particularly short shrift to efficiency as it is defined in the populist manner, as the ability to act swiftly and boldly in response to public sentiment. The rival goals to which the Framers gave support include the prevention of tyranny and the ability of representative institutions to be deliberative bodies.

The soundest argument for term limits involves no such Wilsonian criticism of the Framers' intentions, no implication that those intentions are not suited to today's situation. Rather, the argument is that term limits are necessary for the fulfillment of the Framers' intentions in the nation's present situation, one the Framers did not anticipate, and could not have.

Mansfield correctly says that the Constitution has an "explanatory power."[12] The Constitution does not merely enable, or empower, or tell us to do certain things in certain ways. It also tells us why we do, or should do, certain things. It tells us this if we inquire into it in the right way. Serious reflection about the logic and structure of the document, including the Framers' philosophy and the intellectual milieu of their era, can tell us why we do some of the things we do. And such reflection can even tell us why we should amend the document.

Today such reflection tells us that an amendment limiting congressional terms would conform to its spirit and improve its aptitude and tendency to serve the core goal of republicanism. That goal is deliberative democracy through representatives who function at a constitutional distance from the people.

In the era of America's founding, the most frequent arguments for term limits were that limits would be prophylactic measures against tyranny. Thus the Massachusetts delegation to the Constitutional Convention was specifically instructed "not to depart from the rotation established in the Articles of Confederation."[13] Delegate John Adams believed rotation would "teach" representatives "the great political virtues of humility, patience, and moderation without which every man in power becomes a ravenous beast of prey."[14] Adams's colleague, Elbridge Gerry, said, "Rotation keeps the mind of man in equilibria [sic] and teaches him the feelings of the governed" and counters "the overbearing insolence of office."[15] Adams and Gerry were echoing the thinking that had produced Article VIII of the Declaration of Rights in the Massachusetts Constitution of 1780, which declared that citizens have a right to expect "public officers to return to private life" "in order to prevent those, who are vested with authority, from becoming oppressors."[16]

Today the sensible reason for enacting term limits is not to forestall oppression but to nurture deliberation, meaning a disposition to reason about policies on their merits rather than their utility in serving the careerism of legislators. A deliberative institution is one in which members reason together about the problems confronting the community and strive to promote policies in the general interest of the community. The deliberative process involves identification and investigation of social needs, the evaluation of programs currently attempting to meet those needs, and the formulation of new legislative remedies for recalcitrant problems. On the surface, Congress seems to be in the business of informing and persuading—the essence of a deliberative process. However, "reasoning on the merits of public policy is not the same thing as registering constituent opinion at each stage of the legislative process."[17] The increase of Congress's spending on its own staff and travel, the openness of Congress to television, and the proliferation of subcommittees (in 1992 there were 146 House and 87 Senate subcommittees, plus the 8 subcommittees of the 4 joint committees) have had the effect of increasing "the opportunities, incentives, and rewards for non-deliberative behavior, specifically for the kind of public self-promotion that serves a legislator's electoral ambitions but does not contribute to serious reasoning about public policy."[18]

A distinction must be drawn between public pedagogy and mere posturing in the service of careerism. The pedagogy—Congress's teaching and informing function—is public in two senses. It involves Congress teaching itself in public, and it involves Congress teaching the public. "In a deliberative legislative body the members meet together in committees and the full body in order to educate and learn from one another. It is more and more the case in the U.S. Congress that these forums have become platforms for members to reach outside audiences, in order to impress their constituents or develop statewide or national reputations."[19] The processes that James L. Payne examined in his study of the "culture of spending" (see Chapter 1) are processes of brokering, not deliberating. They are attempts by representatives of client groups to negotiate the satisfaction of as many demands as possible. They are not attempts to persuade anyone of anything.

You might think that senators weighing the confirmation of presidential nominees, particularly nominees to the judicial branch, would be deliberative, if they are ever going to be. However, remember the two confirmation processes the public has seen most closely, the hearings on the nominations to the Supreme Court of Judge Robert Bork and Judge Clarence Thomas. Those hearings were spectacles that involved precious little that deserved to be dignified as "deliberation." Regardless of what one thought of either nominee, surely no one believes that the senators on the Judiciary Committee were as much concerned about the merits of the thoughts they were hearing from the nominees as they were about what they were hearing from interest groups that were feverishly mobilizing mass pressure on the committee. Does anyone doubt that the behavior of the Judiciary Committee would have been markedly different—never mind better; just different—if its members had been serving under a regime of term limitations? Would not the hearings have been different, in tone and substance, if the senators had not been calculating the impact on their careers of the questions they asked, decisions they made and poses they struck in front of the national audience?

Former Representative Charles A. Vanik, a man of dry wit and withering judgments, says that members of Congress can be "deliberate and thoughtful" but only "in the time that remains after what I am going to list now."[20] He then lists nine "essential functions" that have priority over deliberating. Significantly, he lists them in this order: political action; general service to the constituent communities ("cut the budget but get your hometown every darn dollar you can squeeze out of Washington");[21] service to individual constituents (helping them get passports and visas, helping to find Aunt Min's lost Social Security check, helping Uncle Ralph win his dispute with his health care provider); committee work; meetings with the media; meetings in Washington with constituents, visitors and contributors ("Now, who do you spend more time with?");[22] travel time; time in the district office; time for family and personal life.

> Now after all of the aforesaid, there may be time for deliberation on the national issues which confront the Congress. Now it could be readily seen that a congressman has little time left for this very, very important function. In many situations, he follows the leader on voting issues. You know, you vote with others whom you trust and whom you feel have had time for deliberation, and whose views are generally in line with yours. Sometimes you stagger into the room, you don't even know what they're voting on. How did George vote? Okay. It used to be a lot more difficult when they didn't have the votes put on the monitors. Now you can just look up there and decide how to vote. The deliberative time is such time as is required to see how someone else voted.[23]

Vanik says that "about two-thirds of the average member's votes are follow-the-leader votes."[24] However, he does not despair. He says that "knowing which leader to follow constitutes deliberation. . . . Deliberation does not always demand independent judgment."[25] He is putting a comforting construction on the behavior of an institution that is doing too much, and doing much of it poorly. It is an institution with a frenetic pace and a high level of stress and dissatisfaction, in part because its members no longer draw distinctions between what government should and should not do. They are too busy to draw distinctions, busy exploiting the full panoply of uses to which the modern state can be put to serve legislative careerism.

In politics, as in human affairs generally, there is always a gap between theory and practice. But the gap between the practice of representative government, as Vanik and many others describe it, and the theory propounded by the Founders, has become alarmingly wide. The Founders' theory, as explained by Madison in Federalist No. 57, is that the House

... is so constituted as to support in the members an habitual recollection of their dependence on the people. Before the sentiments impressed on their minds by the mode of their elevation, can be effaced by the exercise of power, they will be compelled to anticipate the moment when their power is to cease, when their exercise of it is to be reviewed, and when they must descend to the level from which they were raised; there for ever to remain, unless a faithful discharge of their trust shall have established their title to a renewal of it.[26]

Notice that the danger against which the precaution of frequent elections was taken was the danger of having representatives who were not sufficiently solicitous about the immediate "sentiments" of the people. The requirement of frequent elections would, the Founders believed, prevent the representatives' minds from losing the fresh, deep stamp of public opinion. This loss is hardly a worry today.

Today's representatives will be forgiven for feeling like puppies on very short leashes that are held by very short-tempered masters. Representatives are, to put it mildly, not apt to feel prevented by time and distance from being acquainted with public opinion, not in this age of talk-radio call-in shows, fax machines, carpet-bombing of Congress by telegrams, and all the other technologies for what the Constitution calls petitioning for redress of grievances—grievances often sharpened by the news media's instant communication of the representatives' actions. Small wonder that we suffer from too many representatives who are hyperresponsive and oversolicitous. They are armed with many modern techniques for measuring and controlling opinion, so they can stay in perfect conformity with the sentiments of the disparate publics in their districts.

But does such carefully calculated and slavishly maintained congruence between the representatives' behavior and the public's sentiments constitute, on the part of representatives, a "faithful discharge of their trust"? Surely not. Because if it does, then there is no place in democratic theory—no room in the idea of representative government—for the concept of leadership.

Now, bookshelves groan beneath the weight of volumes about this or that facet of leadership—leadership in politics, business, athletics, religion or elsewhere. These volumes exhort individuals to exercise it and/or exhort the people to submit to it. These volumes define it as a function of charisma, or rhetoric, or this, or that. But perhaps the very idea of leadership is dispensable, or at least of secondary importance, in the working of representative government. We can say most of what needs to be said about good government without recourse to the word "leadership," with its intimations of an indispensable role for a charismatic visionary. The idea of judgment—back to Bristol!—should suffice.

Remember, a republic is a society presumed to have a broad diffusion of thoughtfulness. In a republic, persuasion rather than inspiration—reason rather than emotion—is supposed to move the citizenry. Judgment—what Burke said he owed Bristol, whether or not Bristol wanted it—is the outcome of thought, of reasoning. A deliberative legislature, composed of people exercising judgment, can do what leaders are supposed to do. It can inspirit people by the dignity of its deliberations. It can persuade by the gravity of its procedures as well as the plausibility of its conclusions. This is the noble power possessed by ordinary people who take up the republican task of deliberating for the community, in public. Let us call these deliberating people "leaders." Let us call what they do "leadership." But let us not lose sight of the fact that what they are doing is deliberating. What they are exercising is judgment.

Someone once defined political leadership as the ability to inflict pain and get away with it—ideally, short-term pain for long-term gain, but pain nonetheless. That is too stark a definition, but it is useful because it makes an elemental distinction: People do not need to be "led" to do what they want to do, any more than it takes "leadership" to get the kids to go to McDonald's. However, in politics, leadership usually does not involve clear choices between pains and pleasures, or wants and antipathies. The primary task of political leadership is to help people decide what it is that they really want. It is a commonplace of everyday life that when you face a difficult choice between competing alternatives, often the least helpful advice is, "Do what you want." For polities as well as individuals, the problem is to know what they want. And because polities as well as individuals are ethical entities, the question always must be complicated by this consideration: What *ought* we to want?

Among the commonplaces of American experience are polls showing strong public support for increased government spending on health, education, welfare, the environment, transportation, worker safety, fighting crime—on everything, in fact, except foreign aid—and equally strong support for lower taxes and for reducing the deficit. This is where leadership comes in. Leadership does not amount merely to being "responsive" to such contradictory polling data. Rather, leadership involves clarifying and persuading. It involves explaining the incompatibility of many aspirations, the conflict between many rights, and many goods, the tensions between short- and medium- and long-term goals, the need to balance private and collective preferences, and the current generation's obligation to coming generations. Thus in republican government, leadership, properly understood, is not substantially distinguishable from a process—the public process of making judgments in deliberative assemblies.

In Federalist No. 63, James Madison (probably; perhaps the author was Hamilton) adumbrated the necessity that the Senate be somewhat insulated from public passions. He argued

that "such an institution may be sometimes necessary, as a defense to the people against their own temporary errors and delusions." There will, he said, be occasions when people will be "stimulated by some irregular passion, or some illicit advantage, or misled by artful misrepresentations of interested men." Then the people may demand measures they will later regret. Therefore there must be institutional arrangements to encourage a "cool and deliberate sense of the community."[27] Cool and deliberate, as opposed to hot and unreflective. A sense of the community, rather than a mere aggregation of individual clamors.

In the context of today's concerns, special attention should be paid to Madison's felicitous phrase "illicit advantage."[28] One problem, and arguably the central problem, afflicting governance today is just this: There no longer is an ethic, or a political philosophy, or a constitutional doctrine that encourages people to distinguish between licit and illicit advantages from government. Certainly the problem of governance today is rarely that of turbulent passions. Quite the contrary, the problem is the everydayness of, the routinization of, the banality of the process by which private interests methodically seek to bend public power to private purposes.

And the problem today is not the "misleading" of the public by artful and unscrupulous leaders. Rather, the depth, sweep and seriousness of the problem is apparent from this fact: The public does not need to be led, or misled, into the maelstrom of competition for government preferment. The public plunges in exuberantly, with an energy that betokens a clear (or perhaps deadened) conscience. Indeed, you may well wonder: What is there to be ashamed of, now that the distinction between licit and illicit advantages seems quaint and even unintelligible?

In simpler times and simpler societies, as in this country at the beginning of the American Revolution, the problem of pol-

itics—note the definite article: *the* problem—was understood to
be the conflict of interests between the rulers and the ruled.
Soon—very soon: by the time the Constitutional Convention
convened in 1787—a sadder but wiser America knew better.
By then Americans had lived through revolutionary upheaval
and untidiness, and through what historians have come to call
the "critical period" of American history, the period of institutional flux and weakness under the Articles of Confederation.
By 1787 a new realism had dawned like thunder. It involved
recognition that in a republic the ruled as well as the rulers—
the sovereign people as well as their government—could be a
threat to the nation's happiness, prosperity and liberty. The
American people saw that popular sovereignty did not solve all
political problems, it posed new ones.

This fact, so obvious to us, seemed novel and perverse to
many generations that were preoccupied with the simple, clean
dichotomy between rulers and ruled. The crux of the problem
in the 1780s and 1790s was that "the people" were not a single
organic unity. The American people had not been of one mind
even when pounded together on history's anvil by the hammer
blows of Britain's aroused imperial power. The American people had not been fused into a single harmonious whole by the
heat of shared revolutionary ideology.

The first ten words of the Constitution are "We the People
of the United States, in order to . . ." Those words are the
beginning of the Preamble, which is a statement of intention-
ality by a unity, the American people. But when are we "a
people"? Are we always one? Always to the same extent? It is
a premise of our pluralism, and a glory of our open society, that
we are not always, and for all purposes, united, or even aspir-
ing to unity. Indeed, we are rarely in serried ranks about
anything short of war, and, come to think about it, rarely even
about war.

However, it is not just nice, it is often necessary for even a pluralistic, open society to think and act as a community. Now, the word "community" implies unity, but a unity short of unanimity. It is unity compatible with an easy, friendly, neighborly acceptance of differences within a framework of consensus on essentials. But a community needs institutions that reconnect its actual diversity with its need for some unity. One of those institutions is government.

Government is, or at any rate should be, the instrumentality through which the community attains self-consciousness and speaks its mind. But the very hyperkinesis of modern government makes it more difficult for the community to feel common bonds. A society riven by rivalries that arise from competition for government preferment is a society unable to think of itself as a single community, and hence unable to act as one.

To understand how much times have changed, and how our worries have changed with them, remember some of the language of *The Federalist* that was quoted earlier. Remember what Madison called "the cool and deliberate sense of the community"[29] and Hamilton called "cool and sedate reflection":[30]

> The republican principle demands, that the deliberate sense of the community should govern the conduct of those to whom they entrust the management of their affairs; but it does not require an unqualified complaisance to every sudden breeze of passion, or to every transient impulse which the people may receive from the arts of men, who flatter their prejudices to betray their interests. . . . When occasions present themselves in which the interests of the people are at variance with their inclinations, it is the duty of the persons whom they have appointed to be the guardians of those interests, to withstand the temporary delusion, in order to give them time and opportunity for more cool and sedate reflection.[31]

Hamilton was worried about volatility, both the turbulence of mobs (Daniel Shays would soon be on many minds) and the

whims of intense factions or flighty majorities. But under today's lumbering Leviathan of a government, the problem is not
forces that are "sudden" or "transient." Rather, the problem is
a deadening permanence of implacable and entrenched interests that are prospering off their mutually aggrandizing relationships with career legislators. What these relationships give
rise to is not instability but governmental gridlock. That is the
result of strong interests defending, and expanding, their prerogatives.

You may say that Hamilton's colleague, Madison, is partly
to blame for this. You may argue that we have what Madison
wanted, or at least that the sorry condition of contemporary
government is what Madison's principles must produce in modern society. It is true that Madison wanted a multiplicity of assertive, self-interested factions. That multiplicity was supposed
to prevent the coalescing of a stable, and hence potentially oppressive, majority. However, the Founders—and Madison was
the subtlest of them—had more complicated aims than the mere
avoidance of oppression. They also wanted a government with
an "aptitude and tendency" to behave responsibly.

It is not true that the Framers sought simply to set in
motion a maelstrom of factional scrambling. They did not assume that whatever outcome resulted from such scrambling
could be called—indeed, by definition would be—the public
good. The Framers were realists about the inevitably large
role of interestedness in human affairs, but they also were
committed to popular sovereignty. And precisely because they
were realists, they saw that majority rule, meaning governance in accordance with the wishes of the majority, requires
"framing." This is so because the existence of majority opinion,
of public opinion properly understood, can not be assumed. The
will of the community does not announce itself spontaneously;
it does not well up naturally like a mountain spring; it does not
exist until helped into existence.

The Framers believed that a wholesome commitment to popular sovereignty is more than just compatible with, it *requires* inhibitions on the speed and directness with which popular sentiments can be transmuted into public policy. Thus the Constitution contains various provisions designed to shape popular inclinations by the very process of recording, sifting and measuring them. These provisions are intended to increase the probability that public sentiments will be leavened by thoughtfulness as they pass along the way to becoming law. These provisions include a bicameral legislature, which slows and simmers legislation by passing it through different bodies differently constituted; and an independent executive branch headed by a president with the power to wield a qualified veto against legislation; and a Supreme Court, composed of members who can be removed only by impeachment, and are empowered to exercise judicial review.

And add to that list of leavening provisions another item: the Bill of Rights.

It was instructive, and at times amusing, that the quickening of interest in term limits coincided in 1991 with the Bicentennial of the Bill of Rights. The air was thick with praise of the Bill of Rights as a—even as *the*—bulwark of American liberty. However, many of the people loudest in their praise were just as loud in denouncing term limits. Term limits, they said, violate the morality of democracy because they limit choice and thus abridge the people's sovereignty.

But notice this. The first word of the First Amendment is "Congress." Congress is a repository of popular sovereignty. And what comes after that word in the First Amendment? A stern denial of the people's right to make, through Congress, certain choices: "Congress shall make no law . . ." The people's freely elected representatives, in Congress assembled, are not allowed to make any law respecting an establishment of religion, or prohibiting the free exercise thereof, or abridging the freedom of speech or of the press, or the right to peaceably assemble or to petition the government for a redress of grievances. If term limits are un-American because they limit popular sovereignty, then so, too, is the First Amendment un-American. In fact, of course, the First Amendment proscribes certain kinds of choices in order to guarantee the democratic values of an open society. So do term limits.

The First Amendment comes first in the Bill of Rights because the freedoms and rights it concerns are fundamental. Freedom of speech and press and the right to petition for redress of grievances are fundamental to the functioning of republican government. Such government presupposes society's capacity for deliberation. Again, remember: Man is a political animal because he is a language-using animal. Note well that it is the use of language—not something as vague as "expression"—that the Framers explicitly protected. Language is intrinsically connected with reasoning, and hence with two indispensable facets of popular government, persuasion and deliberation.

The protected freedoms of speech, press and petition are necessary to the functioning of republican government, but they are not sufficient for the flourishing of such government. The deliberative life of a polity can not be realized unless there are institutions through which the eddies of mere public opinions are translated into a public's judgments.

The point of representative government is that people do not decide issues, they decide who shall decide. The hope is that this shall mitigate the tendency of popular sovereignty to degenerate into the mere registering of the willfulness or "feelings" of the many rather than the judiciousness of a few. The few, the representatives, are selected by the many to perform the task of expressing the public will at one remove from the public. The object is to create constitutional space in which reasoning, rather than mere responsiveness, can occur.

In the measured words of Alexander Hamilton from Federalist No. 68, the "aptitude and tendency" of the Constitution is to encourage a particular kind of politics, and a particular kind of people. What kind? It shall suffice to say, in both cases, the aim is reasonableness. The Constitution's aptitude and tendency is, as Mansfield says, "to elevate the will of the people to their intention."[32] And here we come to the heart of the matter, the distinction between mere willfulness and more refined, serious and admirable manifestations of the public mind.

God is in the details, and in political philosophy the details often are adjectives. We speak of the difference between mere will and well-considered intentions. Or the distinction between passing whims and settled desires. Or between momentary desires and reflective aspirations. In each case the crucial difference denoted by the adjectives concerns the degree of reasoning involved. And that, in turn, is a result of deliberation.

The Latin origin of the verb "deliberate" is in the word "deliberare," the root of which is "librare," meaning "to weigh," from "libra," meaning "scales." The Oxford English Dictionary's definition of "deliberate" is "to weigh in the mind; to consider carefully with a view to decision." So a deliberative body has a collective mind, which it makes up without haste—in a deliberate manner.

The opposite of a deliberative body is a merely ratifying body, one that exists only to affirm decisions made elsewhere. The presidential nominating conventions of both parties have become ratifying bodies, formalizing the results of state primaries and caucuses. And there are many people who seem to think that the modern media of mass communication have rendered representative institutions much less important than they used to be. The media supposedly have done this by making the deliberative functions of representative institutions redundant. Some people say that because of the rich array of modern media, representative institutions are, if not quite superfluous, certainly drained of the dignity that attaches to the necessities of democracy.

The new theory is that the myriad forms of mass communication, including those used for measuring and shaping opinion, have acquired a quasi-governmental role. Journalism in particular has (so the theory says) really become the fourth branch of government, and in doing so it has usurped much of the function of, and has demoted, the First Branch. The old theory was that Congress's deliberative function takes inchoate public sentiments and other impulses and causes real public opinion to take shape and acquire weight. The new theory holds that this function of Congress is no longer very important. It is not important because real public opinion is formed, honed and given fully adequate expression "prior to" any workings of representative institutions, through the mass media. Therefore government is, and ought to be, primarily a ratifying instrument, or a recording device, like a seismograph—a seismograph that, when jiggled by tremors of opinion, produces laws.

American society is indeed amply, even abundantly, served by news media, both print and broadcast. Virtually every subject is covered, and virtually every viewpoint is represented, in some accessible newspaper, magazine or broadcast. Therefore every American individual, perusing a newspaper or watching television can find the information necessary for forming an opinion about the large issues of public affairs. Because of these modern media, public opinion, as we normally discuss and measure it, is a pervasive fact. It has been such a fact since mass literacy and cheap newsprint democratized the habit of reading newspapers.

But here is a puzzle. Does this public opinion mean that *the public* has an opinion? Every individual has a right to know, and the ability to know, many things, including what he or she thinks about this and that. But does the aggregation of all these individuals—these individuals reading and hearing things through the media—amount to opinion held by "a public"? By "public opinion" we should mean something other than, something richer and more political than, the mere tabulation of private judgments arrived at in private.

For public opinion to be truly of a public, and to be political, it must be more than a one-way flow of sentiment from individuals to . . . whom? Or what? Not, surely, just to poll-takers standing on the nation's stoops. And not just to a government that receives and records the sentiments passively, like a telephone answering machine. For an agglomeration of individuals' opinions to become the opinion of a public, properly understood, the flow of communication should be circular. The sentiments of individuals, and of individual factions, should indeed flow to a representative government. But there, in bodies that are both representative and judicious, these sentiments should become the stuff of deliberation. And by the action of such a political body on the raw material of public sentiment, those sentiments can acquire the shape and weight of truly political principles and arguments and judgments.

This process should be observed by attentive constituents of the deliberating politicians. The observation is assisted by journalism and by such political communications as party publications and legislators' newsletters. Such communications complete the circle. And the members of the public, being attentive to and hence participants in this process, become a *public*.

Here we are tiptoeing to the edge of intellectual waters that are deep and murky. The fundamental question is this: Can the philosophy of individualism convincingly explain how we actually come to know things, and how we reason? Do we really think and reason as individuals, or are our language and categories of thought community property? Do our language and categories evolve, with an autonomous life of their own?

At the core of modern philosophy is the problem of epistemology and the principle of private judgment—each person deciding on his or her own what he or she thinks about the world. Modern philosophy, with its focus on the individual's private judgments about the information served up by the senses, has a strongly individualist bent. But it may not accurately depict how individuals, who are also social creatures, learn and think. It certainly does not adequately explain how man, the political animal, fulfills his political dimension.

For a sum of private sentiments to become a public's opinion, those sentiments need institutional shaping and expression. The passage of many sentiments through political institutions should, like the passage of metal through a furnace, refine and temper the sentiments. Public opinion, as it percolates up from millions of individual encounters with information and opinions, is unformed and incomplete until it has been passed through a deliberative body.

It has been argued that the media are among the forces that have eroded the forms of representation that were constructed to encourage deliberation. The media, says Mansfield, "confirm and culminate the trend toward formless nonelective representation."[33] But that is not representation at all. The media may fancy themselves mere checks on state power, but they have become both more and less. They have become instruments for bypassing representative institutions. However, they remain less than agencies of representation.

The media furnish people with news, broadly—very broadly—defined. (Sometimes the news is information; sometimes it is just snippets of rhetoric; sometimes it is mere pictures.) As the media do this, and especially as they do it with the immediacy of broadcasting, and particularly the immediacy of broadcast pictures, there develops an expectation of, and almost a vague duty of, reciprocal immediacy from the audience. The audience—the "people" as passive spectators—is expected to have instant "reactions."

It is indicative that the common question posed by journalists to the person-on-the-street after an event (a notable presidential speech or action, or an important congressional vote) is not, "What do you think about it?" but rather "How do you feel about it?" The latter question—"How do you feel?"—is one of the telltale locutions of the age. Feelings can be quick and easy. Feelings are not necessarily produced by reflection, any more than is a skin rash. Feelings can be produced as easily as a head of foam is produced on a stein of beer. And feelings can be just as insubstantial as foam. So feelings are more "democratic" than thoughts. Thoughts are not as universally distributed. Our society considers feelings to be morally complete and self-legitimizing. Therefore it seems natural to say that the principal criterion of good government is "responsiveness." Responsiveness means quick action to assuage feelings. And, as has been noted, the highest encomium for a politician today is that he or she is "responsive."

If there is no appeal to any standard higher than how people "feel," it is impertinent to advocate institutions and forms that will improve upon feelings. If feelings are all we aspire to, there is no point in trying to transmute them into anything higher, such as considered judgments. As Tocqueville observed, "Men living in democratic ages do not readily comprehend the utility of forms: they feel an instinctive contempt for them."[34] But of course. Forms, such as institutions and their procedural requirements, are not just for recording things, they are for attaining things. Governmental forms are not mere "matters of form," they are practical means of achieving things more complex, more nuanced, more durable and deliberated than "feelings."

Impatience with inhibiting forms and indifference to shaping institutions has contributed to the decline of Congress. And that decline has not just coincided with, it has contributed to the making of the modern presidency. Congress has lost the status and esteem—including the self-esteem—that went with its deliberative function. And the presidency has acquired a plebiscitary cast as the instrument of a rolling, year-round, year-in-year-out, nonstop referendum on the nation's destiny. In the new way of thinking about things, the president—any president—is supposed to be a tribune of the people, hearing or, even better, sensing their yearnings and calling them to exertions and greatness. (Tribune McKinley? Tribune Coolidge? The mind boggles.) There seems to be a consensus, fuzzy but insistent, that the presidency should be an institution of national intimacy. Presidents are expected to cultivate a direct, unmediated relation with the nation, both summoning and shaping its feelings.

One of the costs of Congress's decline is that the presidency has taken on, and is buckling under, new responsibilities, including responsibility for the nation's emotional well-being. Presidents are expected to perform a confused and constitutionally problematic kind of representation. Evidence of this transformation of the presidency is everywhere. Consider, for example, the fog of rhetoric that replaced the smoke of fires after the Los Angeles riots of April, 1992.

President Bush tried to blame the riots on the domestic programs put in place by Lyndon Johnson. A number of Democrats and editorialists criticized the president and his Republican echoes for disregarding the fact that Republicans "had been in power for 20 of the last 24 years." What Bush said was silly. What his critics said was symptomatic of a distortion of American government brought on by a fixation with the presidency. By "in power" Bush's critics meant "in the White House." Republicans had not been in power sixteen blocks to the east on Pennsylvania Avenue, or in most governorships, or in most state legislatures, or in many mayor's offices. The idea that to possess the presidency is to be "in power" suggests that in America political power is unitary and possessed entirely by the head of the executive branch of the federal government.

Why do so many people talk like that? Why does anyone speak in that way, thereby suggesting something that everyone familiar with the separation of powers and with federalism knows to be untrue? The reason is an unhealthy obsession with the presidency. The phrase "in power" reeks of it. Let us call it, in the modern academic manner (academics, including Professor Woodrow Wilson, helped to create it) president-centrism. This obsession has been a long time coming and is by now so familiar as to seem "natural" or, in political language, constitutional. It seems to be the normal order of things. But there was a time when things were quite different. That time was all the time prior to this century.

The evolution of the presidency into its current prominence—its current condition of swollen size and pretensions—began with this century, with the eruption into the middle of the nation's consciousness of a protean force named Theodore Roosevelt. He was the first president who was regularly filmed by that harbinger of the graphic revolution in communications, the movie camera. He was himself a harbinger of the president as a permanent presence in American life. With TR began the practice of "the rhetorical presidency." Woodrow Wilson, the man who soon would be TR's detested rival, supplied the theory for the transformed presidency.

The phrase "rhetorical presidency" is from Jeffrey K. Tulis's book of that title.[35] Tulis, of the Department of Government at the University of Texas at Austin, says that since the presidencies of Theodore Roosevelt and, even more importantly, Woodrow Wilson, popular rhetoric—rhetoric designed to produce mass effects—has become one of the principal tools of presidential governance. To today's Americans, this seems altogether proper: Should not a president be a leader of public opinion, constantly inspiriting the polity? Perhaps not. Tulis's historical research reminds us that this unquestioned premise of our contemporary political culture is quite questionable.

Not only is the rhetorical presidency, with its routine direct appeals to the public, a twentieth-century invention, it is built upon behavior strongly discouraged by the Founders' eighteenth-century theory of constitutional propriety. And that theory controlled nineteenth-century practices. Until Theodore Roosevelt, all presidents—with one exception (Andrew Johnson) that confirms the rule—communicated primarily with the legislative branch rather than with the people. This meant that most presidential communications were written rather than oral, a form more readily suited to deliberative reasoning. The deliberative communications between presidents and Congress were public, meaning accessible to all, but not popular, meaning designed to sway the populace. Before Theodore Roosevelt, presidents gave few public speeches, and the few were mostly patriotic orations on ceremonial occasions. Very few dealt with particular policies or attempted to move the nation in any direction by moral suasion.

Tulis calculates that the average number of speeches given annually by the first three presidents were: Washington, three; John Adams, one; Jefferson, five. The fourth president, Madison, who led the nation in a war that resulted in his house being burned, and who might have been expected to feel a need to appeal to the people, gave no speeches for popular audiences. Monroe averaged just five such speeches a year. John Quincy Adams averaged one a year. So did Andrew Jackson, supposedly our first populist "leader of the people."[36] And so it went in the nineteenth century. Remember, at the dedication of the military cemetery at Gettysburg, Lincoln was very much the secondary speaker on the program. The one nineteenth-century president who did go out campaigning to raise public support for particular policies—his Reconstruction program—wound up on trial in the Senate, charged with, among other things, using improper rhetoric. One of the articles of impeachment brought against Andrew Johnson charged that he,

> . . . unmindful of the high duties of his office and the dignity and propriety thereof . . . did . . . make and deliver with a loud voice certain intemperate, inflammatory, and scandalous harangues. . . . Which said utterances, declarations, threats, and harangues, highly censurable in any, are particularly indecent and unbecoming in the Chief Magistrate of the United States, by means whereof . . . Andrew Johnson has brought the high office of the President of the United States into contempt, ridicule and disgrace.[37]

Tulis says that approximately one thousand "unofficial" popular speeches were delivered by the twenty-four presidents from Washington through McKinley.[38] More than half of those were delivered by three presidents in the second half of the nineteenth century: Rutherford B. Hayes (126), Benjamin Harrison (296) and William McKinley (130). Almost all the speeches by these three were given on "tours" designed for presidents to "see and be seen."[39]

Benjamin Harrison's speeches "on tour" were filled with passages like this: "I . . . will not enter into any lengthy discussion here. Indeed, I am so careful not to trespass upon any forbidden topic, that I may not in the smallest degree offend those who have forgotten party politics in extending this greeting to us, that I do not know how far I should talk upon these public questions." And: "But, my countrymen, I had not intended to speak so long. I hope I have not intruded upon any ground of division." And: "You ask for a speech. It is not very easy to know what one can talk about on such an occasion as this. Those topics that are most familiar to me, because I am brought in daily contact with them, namely, public affairs, are in some measure prohibited to me."[40] McKinley, the immediate predecessor of the prolix Theodore Roosevelt, gave no speech that even alluded in passing to the sinking of the *Maine*, or the Spanish–American War, or the passage of "Jim Crow" laws or U.S. policy toward the Philippines.[41]

McKinley can usefully be called the last premodern president. The birth of the modern presidency can, for convenience, be dated from Theodore Roosevelt's campaign for the Hepburn Act of 1906, which regulated railroads. Here in TR was Hamilton's "energy in the executive," but it was put to a use the Founders had not anticipated. Here was a statesman not acting as a brake on public opinion. Rather, the Rough Rider was putting a saddle and a bridle on public opinion, the better to control that stallion as he spurred it. Theodore Roosevelt justified his bold attempt to shape opinion by presidential action as a prophylactic measure against volatile, uncontrollable opinion. Roosevelt thought that what he was doing was justified by the gravity of the legislation at issue. Railroad regulation did indeed involve what Tulis calls "regime-level" issues.[42] Those issues included the meaning of the "public interest" and the principles upon which the pursuit of economic gain shall be conducted in a nation that encourages such gain. While Roosevelt was pioneering a political practice for what he considered extraordinary circumstances, the president of Princeton University was watching, and thinking.

When Woodrow Wilson became President of the United States he wanted to do what Roosevelt had done, only more constantly. Wilson, the most nimble theorist to serve as president since Madison, devised a theory that would present as a virtue what Roosevelt had regarded as a necessity. Wilson's theory made the rhetorical presidency routine.

He knew he was reforming—almost refounding—American politics. He was doing so boldly, on the basis of a critique of the Founders' principles. Sixteen years before he became President—four years before Theodore Roosevelt became

President—Wilson wrote: "Policy—where there is no absolute and arbitrary ruler to do the choosing for a whole people—means massed opinion, and the forming of the mass is the whole art and mastery of politics."[43] The Founders had seen direct appeals to the people as inherently incompatible with the indirectness that facilitates deliberative government. Wilson saw such leadership as the indispensable catalyst of deliberation. But he justified it by semantic sleight-of-hand, by changing—you might say by hollowing out—the concept of deliberation.

He said that strong rhetorical leaders must advance deliberation by acts of "interpretation."[44] He meant that leaders must discover what is in the hearts of the masses. However, what is in those hearts can be a function of the leader's power of persuasion, "and persuasion is accomplished by creeping into the confidence of those you would lead."[45] The Founders saw tension between the requirement of government by popular consent and the need to insulate government's deliberative processes from unmediated public opinion. Wilson dissolved the tension, by terminological fiat. He linked, somewhat murkily, the idea of deliberation with the process of managing, or creating, or discovering public opinion.

Most of the rhetorical activities by which Americans today define presidential leadership were, in the nineteenth century, stigmatized as inimical to constitutional values. But as Tulis says, for many of the Founders "demagogue" and "popular leader" were synonyms. Nearly all references to popular leaders in the Founders' writings are pejorative.[46] "Indeed, the term 'leader,' which appears a dozen times in *The Federalist*, is used disparagingly in all but one instance, and that one is a reference to leaders of the Revolution."[47]

The Founders prescribed what strikes modern Americans as extreme modesty in the presidential role. But the Founders' prescription fits the Founders' fundamental purposes. Those

purposes were to "give effect to the distinction between public and private life."[48] This the Founders tried to do by limiting government's purposes to the provision of security, the
promotion of prosperity and the protection of rights. It
should not be surprising that the development of the rhetorical presidency coincided with the weakening of the nation's
commitment to the Founders' notion of politics circumscribed
in a narrow public sphere. The president began to be everywhere, moving about by railroad and then by airplane. Soon
he was "in the air" in another sense, first his voice on the
radio and then his image on television. It is no mere coincidence that as the president began to be everywhere, so did
the federal government.

The rhetorical presidency blurs—no, erases—the distinction between campaigning and governing. Governance tends to
become "a continuation and reduplication of campaigning."[49] It
is of course arguable that the rhetorical presidency is an example of Darwinian adaption in politics. Perhaps it is a necessary antidote to paralysis in our pluralistic constitutional
system, given the nature of the modern welfare state and the
multiplicity of aggressive factions constantly petitioning the
government for preference. And it is arguable that the rhetorical presidency often has been, and now generally is, indispensable for energizing the government during crises, such as
World War II or the racial conflict that followed the war. But
what makes Tulis anxious, and should make the rest of us
anxious, is the fact that the rhetorical presidency has become
routinized. It is now ordinary, not a rare response to extraordinary circumstances.

The Founders' ethic of political speech, which Tulis calls "a
'common law' of rhetoric,"[50] held that any presidency that appeals to, and attempts to manipulate, public opinion would
constitute an anticonstitutional preemption of the deliberative
process that was the Constitution's crowning achievement. The

skeletal idea of American constitutionalism, the frame on which the flesh of institutions is arranged, is the idea of indirect governance. The rhetorical presidency, with its plebiscitary overtones, subverts the structure of indirectness. Presidential appeals made directly to the people are made over the heads of, and often against, Congress. Thus, they are made against the institution of representation through which the Founders expected public opinion to be filtered, shaped and matured.

Since Woodrow Wilson, two factors, one ideological and one technological, have produced in America an attitude toward the presidency that amounts to a watery caesarism. Americans persist in trying to see in whomever is president an embodiment of the nation's will and a distillation of its moral sense. The ideological reason for this is the belief, derived from a crude understanding of democracy, that because a president is chosen by a process involving more voters than any other process, he must be invested with special moral dignity. The technological reason is the apparatus of modern communications—television, particularly. This apparatus has made the presidency the constant, because the convenient, focus of journalism. Television journalism is slave to inherently superficial news gathering instruments—cameras. They have to be pointed at something, and a president is an easy, often mindless choice. Furthermore, many modern technologies of communication enable presidents to speak directly to the public. Before the advent of broadcasting, presidents were required, by the paucity of alternatives and by the doctrine of appropriate behavior, to deal with the American people by deliberating with the people's representatives. No more.

Clearly the working of the U.S. Constitution in our complex, continental nation depends on factors nowhere mentioned in the document—a document written when the American population was 4 million people, 80 percent of whom lived within 20

miles of Atlantic tidewater. These factors include political parties and modern technologies of communication and transportation. However, to acknowledge this does not amount to
subscribing to the theory that the government created by the
Constitutional Convention now requires continuous presidential shaping of public opinion. That theory means that the vitality, even the viability, of the constitutional order today
requires extraconstitutional factors—particularly the means of
mass communication—that did not exist and were not dreamed
of in the Founders' era.

If the modern theory of presidential government is true,
America's political energy and coherence are permanently held
hostage to the attributes of particular presidents. The expectations resting heavily on the rhetorical presidency make it
generally improbable that the winner of a presidential election
will possess the unusual traits and skills that fit the post-Wilson
notion of the presidency. This expectation makes Americans
perpetually susceptible to disappointment, and hence to political dyspepsia.

What happens when the nation is conditioned to demand
presidents suited to the "rhetorical presidency" and the nation
gets instead a president with negligible rhetorical skills and
political purposes smaller than those skills? What happens is
something like the Bush presidency.

Poor George Bush. He has been genuinely perplexed by
the public's desire for him to supply what he calls "the vision
thing." And, worst of all, he has had a difficult act to follow.
How appropriate it was that his predecessor, so suited to the
rhetorical presidency, had a resonant middle name: Ronald
Wilson Reagan. Reagan was a conscious emulator of Franklin
Roosevelt, whose first experience in national government was
in the administration of Woodrow Wilson. Wilson wrote the
rules of the new game. Years before he became president, he
had a vision of having "the vision thing":

> A nation is led by a man who . . . speaks, not the rumors of the street, but a new principle for a new age; a man in whose ears the voices of the nation do not sound like the accidental and discordant notes that come from the voice of a mob, but concurrent and concordant like the united voices of a chorus, whose many meanings, spoken by melodious tongues, unite in his understanding in a single meaning and reveal to him a single vision, so that he can speak what no man else knows, the common meaning of the common voice.[51]

And when at last he was inaugurated, Wilson affirmed the new burdensomeness of the presidency—the duty of being a visionary:

> At last a vision has been vouchsafed us of our life as a whole. We see the bad with the good, the debased and decadent with the sound and vital. With this vision we approach new affairs. . . . This is the high enterprise of the new day; To lift everything that concerns our life as a nation to the light that shines from the hearthfire of every man's conscience and vision of the right. . . . We know our task to be no mere task of politics but a task which shall search us through and through, whether we be able to understand our time and the need of our people, whether we be indeed their spokesmen and interpreters, whether we have the pure heart to comprehend and the rectified will to choose our high course of action.[52]

The urgent need to restore Congress to vigor, self-respect, respectability and its rightful place in American governance has been underscored by the Bush presidency. The fact that Bush became president when he did was serendipitous for people who advocate term limits in a spirit friendly to Congress. Bush has dramatized the danger of excessive reliance on the presidency as the locus of energy and purposefulness for the national government. Bush has at least been useful by demonstrating what happens to that reliance when the president is a stammering cipher.

Bush is the most narrow-gauge president in living memory, and even his narrow interest and supposed competence is ill-suited to his moment on center stage. He prepared throughout most of his adult life to play the role of conductor of the West's side of the Cold War. Then he found that conception of the presidency suddenly anachronistic. On November 9, 1989, the Berlin Wall was breached, just 293 days after his inauguration. After that, Bush seemed perplexed by his surroundings, the executive branch of government. He seemed to wonder: What can all this be for? He was purposeful only when Iraq's invasion of Kuwait gave him a brief opportunity to pluck up the Commander-in-Chief's baton. When not dealing with foreign policy—when trying to look interested in the domestic questions that are of most interest to most Americans—Bush was a blank. But, to repeat, he has been a useful blank. By his very vacuousness he has called attention to the cost to the country of the Congress's eclipse, an eclipse caused in part by the careerism of professional legislators.

Bush may be a less substantial figure than most of his forty predecessors in the presidency, but he is not much less substantial than many of them. And just at the moment when Congress's misadventures and the term limit idea are focusing attention on the issue of congressional reform, Bush's performance in the presidency has forced Americans to face this question: Is the quality of American governance now dependent on the skills, intellectual energy and moral seriousness of a single person? Must the quality fluctuate with the attributes of the presidents—people whose most conspicuous attributes are apt to be an obsessive mastery of the politics of their party's presidential nomination process and the mechanics of assembling at least 270 electoral votes?

We like to fancy that the twentieth century has been an age of reason, empiricism, science and, therefore, sturdy immunity to superstition. However, in this century's tenth decade, Americans still have not shaken the superstition that sustains the constitutionally unseemly preoccupation with the presidency. The superstition amounts to a belief in political alchemy. In the Middle Ages, alchemists hoped to develop a chemistry that would turn lead into gold. In our age, many Americans believe in an equally implausible alchemy-by-elections. They believe that an election can turn the base metal of an ordinary politician into the gold of a moral visionary. How else, other than by such a belief, can one explain the incessant invocation of "presidential leadership," the insistent turning toward the president, even toward one such as George Bush, to provide the nation with moral guidance?

In the aftermath of the Los Angeles riots of 1992, even before the embers of burned buildings had cooled, there was a call—reflexive and nearly universal—for President Bush to speak about the meaning of it all and to indicate what we should do about it. What explains this strange turning toward a man who, in sixty-seven previous years of life, had never shown noticeable interest in, or the slightest aptitude for, saying helpful things about the great questions of justice that should drive discussion of domestic policy? The explanation is one, or both, of two superstitions. One is the idea, facially implausible and refuted by ample evidence, that proficiency at the skills of presidential politics is evidence of an elevated nature. The other is the belief that the presidential office works an ennobling transformation on its occupant.

The public's excessive expectations of presidents involve the public in putting all its eggs—all its hopes for good government—in one basket. That is not smart. Or necessary. Congress can contribute. And it would contribute much more than it recently has done if it were constituted differently, under a regime of term limits.

The Founders were institutional theorists who understood the limits of cleverness in crafting institutions. There are severe limits to what the inventiveness of institution-makers can achieve. Any representative institution's capacity for deliberation will always be to some extent contingent on the kinds of people elected to it. So the wisdom of term limits depends, in part, on the consequences term limits will have on the sociology of a legislature. What kinds of people, at what points in their lives, will run for legislative offices, and for what reasons? We can not know in advance the answers to those questions. However, it is a reasonable surmise that term limits would improve the composition, and hence the "aptitude and tendency," of Congress.

We have today a professional Congress. A leading scholarly proponent of term limits, Professor Mark P. Petracca, of the University of California at Irvine, argues that "the professionalization of politics" contradicts the core values of representative government. This is so, he says, because "a profession entails a set of role relationships between 'experts' and 'clients' in which the 'professional' is an expert who offers knowledge and judgment to clients." By making a career of politics, the professional "disconnects and distances"[53] himself from those he or she ostensibly represents. This leads to attenuation of the "communion of interests and sympathy of sentiments" (Madison's words, in Federalist No. 57) that should characterize republican government. Such government, says Petracca, should be characterized by a "close connection" between the rulers and the people.

This argument contains a measure of truth, but it is, I believe, on balance unhelpful to the best case for term limits. It is certainly true that service in Congress, particularly now that year-round sessions are normal, often causes the career politician to develop a mentality unlike that of the constituents he or she represents. The legislative life—a full-time vocation of spending other people's money and regulating other people's lives—is peculiar. Someone who lives it for years on end may have difficulty maintaining an empathetic relationship with the workaday world "out there," beyond the Potomac.

However, advocates of term limits should bear in mind that it is imprudent to couch any argument to Americans in language that disparages professionalism. Americans believe, as Napoleon did, in "careers open to talents," and Americans are mightily, and properly, respectful of people who can make a profession out of a talent. There are few forms of praise more purely American than the phrase, "He's a real pro." To most Americans, the term "professional" does not merely mean the opposite of amateur. A professional is not just someone who is paid for doing something. Professionalism also implies proficiency, a mastery of theory and practice that elevates a trade to the dignity of a profession. So the adjective "professional" modifying the noun "politician" does not necessarily add to whatever stigma the noun may carry.

At least it does not unless and until it is demonstrated that the skills, expertise and attitudes characteristic of professional politicians are irrelevant to, or inimical to, the good functioning of government. That can, I believe, be demonstrated. It is illustrated by thousands of things like Representative Schroeder's desire to federalize Midnight Basketball. To those who dismiss such examples as "merely anecdotal," a proper response is that a sufficiency of anecdotes makes a pattern that confirms a theory. The pattern, in this case, is the federal budget, a thick volume that speaks volumes about the way the government makes choices.

A particularly weak argument for term limits is that professionalism in politics is deplorable because it "distances" the politician from the public. In fact, when professionalism is invested in the service of careerism, and when it means the skillful prolongation of tenure in elective office, then the worst feature of professionalism in politics is that it obliterates the proper distance between the representatives and the represented.

The political "distance" that Harvey Mansfield praises is, he says, necessary for two purposes.[54] One is to enable deliberative processes to proceed. The other, and related, purpose is to preserve the government's authority. A government incapable of deliberation is incapable of the dignity that deserves, and earns, respect. Without respect, government's authority seeps away. Term limits would strengthen the authority of representatives who deliberate at a constitutional "distance" from those they represent. But that authority does not entitle representatives to make a claim offensive to democratic sensibilities—the claim that they constitute a class possessing exceptional virtue and insights not accessible to ordinary citizens.

When Burke told the electors of Bristol that he rejected the practice of "instruction," he did so in the name of deliberation. Perhaps his notion of deliberative representation was more suited to the aristocratic society in which Burke lived than to the young American republic, whose Framers had a different idea. Granted, any election is inherently an exercise in elitism, because elections assume that some people are more eligible than others—better than others—for the purpose of exercising public authority. Otherwise it would be reasonable, because easier, to allocate offices by lot.[55] And perhaps Burke in his address to the Bristol electors meant to imply that representatives should be different from, because wiser and more virtuous than, the people they represent. And therefore, representatives should feel free, and even morally obligated, to act on their personal views rather than the views of the voters. That may be a defensible elitism. However, it is not the doctrine the American Framers subscribed to when they established popular sovereignty expressed through majority rule among deliberative representatives.

What the Framers tried to frame was a set of institutions, and hence a process, that would "actualize the deliberative sense of the community" by having the citizenry "do its reasoning through its representatives." These representatives are supposed to "share the basic values and goals of their constituents." And the process is a success if "the results of their deliberations would broadly approximate what the people themselves would have decided had they engaged in a similar reasoning process."[56]

But what is this we are referring to as "reasoning"? Aristotle said that man is not merely a social animal, he is a political creature because of his capacity for reasoned speech.[57] But reasoning—as distinct from brokering—has precious little to do with life as lived by members of a professional political class determined to be career legislators. Just listen to the language of good people on the verge of despair—that is not too strong a description—about Congress's failure to be a deliberative body.

By June, 1992, six Michigan congressmen with a total of 110 years of seniority—of fifty-five terms—had announced their retirements. One was Bob Traxler, age sixty. He said eighteen years were all he could stand. He had run up 201 overdrafts at the House bank, but he insisted, in strong language, that this had nothing to do with his decision to quit. Proclaiming himself "frustrated and angry," he said: "I am so deeply grieved by what I have seen happen to our country that I have, on several occasions, privately been driven to tears. It is as if I am hemorrhaging inside. I can no longer endure the pain."[58] A few weeks earlier, when Representative William S. Broomfield of Michigan, age seventy, announced his retirement, he sounded a similar lament. Describing service in Congress as "intolerable," he said, "I can't tell you how upset I've been. The frustration, the gridlock . . . and, of course, the scandals, the anti-incumbency, the term-limitation movement."[59]

It was peculiar that Broomfield included the term limitation movement on his list of factors that have made congressional careers unpleasant. The term limitation movement is a response to the totality of complaints that Broomfield, Traxler and others made as they said goodbye to careerism and the kind of Congress it has produced. For example, when Senator Warren Rudman, the New Hampshire Republican, announced his decision not to seek the third term he almost certainly could easily have won, he delivered a withering blast at Congress's practices: "Here we are, getting zero done, staying up to midnight debating amendments that everyone knows won't become law, because somebody wants to get a press release out." The purpose of the press release is self-promotion. The reason for the self-promotion is reelection. A few days after Rudman spoke, Senator Jack Danforth, the Missouri Republican, said, "I have never seen more Senators express discontent with their jobs. . . . I think the major cause is that deep down in our hearts we believe that we have been accomplices to doing something terrible and unforgivable to this wonderful country. Deep down in our hearts we know that we have bankrupted America and that we have given our children a legacy of bankruptcy. . . . We have defrauded the country to get ourselves elected."[60]

The most direct way to combat such defrauding is to inhibit the dynamic of careerism. Term limits will do that. At first blush, term limits might seem like an exercise in what conservatives consider dreamy liberalism of an especially quaint, anachronistic and discredited sort. Term limits might seem to be an attempt to tame deep and turbulent cultural forces by putting fresh words on old parchment, and to do so in the hope of reforming human nature. However, that is not at all the spirit of the term limits movement.

On the contrary, term limits are a paradigm of Madisonian accommodation to the hard facts of human nature. Sensible advocates of term limits do not believe that anything straight can ever be made from the crooked timber of humanity; least of all do they believe that constitutional provisions have the power to effect such transformations. Rather, term limitation is a simple, spare reform to alter the incentives that are relevant to entry into, and behavior while in, public life.

As the Founders understood, incentives are levers by which the behavior of human beings—creatures characterized by "interestedness"—can be influenced. The absence of term limits is a temptation to legislative careerism. Enactment of limits will perform a winnowing function, discouraging certain kinds of people from seeking legislative offices. Limits also will discourage occupants of those offices from entertaining the kind of aspirations that result in behavior that subordinates the public interest to the tactics useful for prolonging legislative careers.

Term limitation is not a "silver bullet" that can slay political sin. Term limits can not cage, securely and forever, the unruly passions of aggrandizement that sleep lightly, when they sleep, in modern Americans, passions that contemporary politics purposely arouses. There are no such "silver bullets" in politics or in any other human enterprise. Besides, no one wants to purge from politics the traditional arts and crafts and skills of negotiating, conciliating, logrolling and the rest. However, term limitation is an attempt to enlarge the domain of deliberation, to improve government's "aptitude and tendency" to behave reasonably.

Granted, the goal of reasonableness is rarely reached by radical measures. And it must be acknowledged that term limits are a radical measure, at least in the etymologically strict sense that they strike at the roots of a problem. The problem is legislative careerism. However, it is hyperbolic to refer to term limits as a revolutionary idea. In political contexts, "revolutionary" connotes hostility toward the fundamental principles of a polity. Neither the proper motives nor any conceivable consequences of term limits are revolutionary. Quite the contrary. The rationale for term limits is recovery of some of this Republic's animating principles, such as deliberative democracy, and representation, properly understood. Term limits are a reform—albeit a radical one—as the Oxford English Dictionary defines "reform": "the amendment of some faulty state of things." The OED's first two definitions of the verb "to reform" are "to renew, restore, re-establish" and "to convert, bring back, or restore (a thing or person) to the original form or state, or to a previous condition."

Strictly speaking, reform understood that way is impossible. It is unlikely in human affairs generally, and it is impossible in the political life of a great nation that has whirled and swirled two centuries away from its Founders' era. Change is constant; nothing lasts; the past is not coming back. That is why Heraclitus, who said that all is flux and that one can never set foot in the same river twice, should be required reading for all politicians, and for all political commentators.

No sensible advocate of term limits regards limits as a panacea for all the ills of American governance, still less as a way of curing those ills by restoring a long-lost Golden Age when republican virtue was pristine. Such an age never was nor ever will be. Besides, supporters of term limits must confront the fact that the Framers of the Constitution did not include term limits in their handiwork, even though the Articles of Confederation provided a precedent for them.

What makes the argument about term limits so interesting, as well as important, is precisely this: It highlights some ways in which the nature of American governance, and hence the nature of American citizenship, has changed in two centuries. Also, it teaches this useful lesson: Measures that were not deemed necessary for the nurturing of important values in one era can become necessary for nurturing those values in a very different era. The crux of the case for term limits is that we want to preserve or resuscitate some of the core political values of the Founders' generation in an utterly changed political and social setting.

Just how changed things are can be gauged by imagining what was in the mind of the most important Founder 209 Decembers ago.

CHAPTER 3

The Revival of Classical Republicanism

O n December 23, 1783, George Washington went before Congress in Annapolis to tender his resignation as commanding general of what remained of
the army that had made a nation and thereby moved mankind
onto a new and ascending path. Earlier that year he had rendered perhaps the most crucial of his many vital services to the
nation. He had restrained the rebelliousness and reinforced the
loyalty of the understandably restive soldiers. In what arguably still stands as the most critical moment in more than two
centuries of American history, Washington had held back the
rebellious despair of an army whose justifiable grievances could
have caused it to overthrow civilian authority, such as it then

was. That would have presaged the disintegration of the nation into a clutter of weak and probably warring little entities. The army's bloody footprints in the snows of the wartime winters had testified to the poor provision made for it by the Continental Congress. That Congress was too institutionally weak to compel assistance from the states, which were jealously guarding their sovereignty. The soldiers had often lived off the land "like beetles off a leaf,"[1] and when many of them left the army they were as destitute as they were triumphant.

So in December, 1783, Congress, in its civilian plainness and political impotence, would have been an object of Washington's disdain, had he blamed it, as many of his soldiers did, for the destitution they had endured while many Americans prospered. But that was not how Washington probably saw the legislature as he was ushered into the Hall of Congress. In the words of Washington's finest biographer, James Flexner, "His physical eye saw a tiny, powerless body of some twenty men, hardly worth, Napoleon would have thought, the whiff of grapeshot that would so easily have sent them flying; but in his mind's eye, Washington saw gathered before him the power that was to grow down the centuries, the dignity of a great nation."[2]

General Washington, like the American officers at the surrender of Charleston three years earlier, thought of Congress not as what it was but as what it could and should be. He thought of it not as a frail vessel of flawed men and their rivalries but as the incarnation of a free nation.

Dignity is in the eye of the beholder, and few who behold Congress today consider it dignified. To some extent Americans are judging Congress severely to avoid judging themselves at all. It may be that the nation today is faithfully portrayed in Congress the way Dorian Gray was portrayed in his portrait. Be that as it may, the brute fact is that most Americans regard Congress with contempt. But a republic can not long despise its legislature and respect itself.

If the flinty realists who framed this Republic saw the condition of Congress today, they probably would be saddened but not shocked. They knew that what they accomplished—a judicious founding—could do no more than increase the probability of political happiness. Nothing is guaranteed in politics. That is why political philosophers are great worriers. They often gaze upon the social order and conclude:

> Take but degree away, untune that string,
> And, hark! what discord follows . . .[3]

The philosophic politicians among America's Founders were like that. They were anxious lest they make small mistakes at the nation's beginning that would have large consequences later. In this anxiety they were men of their age. The eighteenth century is known to us as the Age of Reason, but its most reasonable statesmen knew the limited role of reason in human affairs. A sense of permanent impermanence was in the eighteenth-century air.

The most famous work of history written in the English language was published during the American founding and dealt with a recurring fascination of Western political thinkers, the decline and fall of the Roman empire. Gibbon's six-volume work, published between 1776 and 1788, was avidly read by people apprehensive about something that had made Plato, and has made many philosophers since him, apprehensive. It was the possibility that societies—all sorts of societies—can easily slip into the grip of decay. This worry linked Machiavelli with the ancients. Machiavelli, so unlike the ancients in so many ways, shared with them an intense interest in the problem of preventing decay, and the possibility of regenerating a society when decay has not been kept at bay. These are the themes—degeneration and regeneration—that connect today's two controversies about the condition of Congress and the meaning of representation with the largest and most enduring arguments of the Western political tradition.

If the term limitation movement can not convincingly connect itself with a political philosophy—with perennial themes and values of the Western tradition and American political experience rather than with merely epiphenomenal discontents of a season—then it will not succeed, and should not. Fortunately, it can connect. In fact, term limitation is an idea nourished by two intellectual streams. One is the Founders' understanding of the institutional prerequisites for deliberative democracy, as adumbrated in the preceding chapter. Another intellectual stream is the idea of classical republicanism. That idea had a larger role in the American founding, and hence has a larger relevance to contemporary American governance, than most Americans realize.

In a justly famous aphorism, John Maynard Keynes said that "practical men, who believe themselves to be quite exempt from any intellectual influences, are usually the slaves of some defunct economist."[4] Keynes was an economist, so forgive his belief in the primacy of economists. His larger point, put with his customary verve, is valid: "I am sure that the power of vested interests is vastly exaggerated compared with the gradual encroachment of ideas." Those whom Keynes rather unkindly called "academic scribblers"[5] sometimes are, in fact, if not on purpose, people of considerable practical consequence. There are today, for example, some American historians whose arguments might, and should, shape the thinking of people who have never heard of them. It would be particularly desirable for those historians' arguments to percolate among the people now participating in arguments about the depressing trajectory of America's representative institutions. Fortunately, the slow seepage of scholarly disputation into the broader culture may already be quietly exerting a gravitational pull on people who do not consciously feel it. Cultural osmosis is at work. The vocabulary of public discourse is being leavened by the revival, in academic settings, of some sturdy old concepts and categories, such as those of classical republicanism.

A timely survey of current thinking about the role of classical republicanism in the founding era is *The Political Philosophy of Thomas Jefferson.*[6] The author, Garrett Ward Sheldon, is a professor of political science at the Clinch Valley College of the University of Virginia. While describing some intellectual currents in the late eighteenth and early nineteenth centuries, he illuminates how those arguments echo in the late twentieth century. He is doing intellectual archeology, tracing the several threads of thought that Jefferson wove into the fabric of his philosophy. However, one result of his research is a deepened understanding of today's dissatisfaction with the functioning of contemporary American democracy. To read his essay is to understand that the term limits movement has a richer intellectual pedigree than it knows.

The American Revolution arose not only, or even primarily, from grievances about such material matters as taxation and regulation of trade. To be sure, sparks struck by the Stamp Act, the Townsend Acts and other provocations from Westminster set the colonies ablaze. But why were the colonies such combustible tinder? What is the explanation for such a swift coalescing of the new American consciousness, and the consequent rapid unraveling of the British position in the American colonies? Between 1760 and 1776 something that had seemed unthinkable and indeed had barely been thought of—a desperate revolutionary wager for independence—came to seem (in the title of the most important nongovernmental publication in American history, published in 1776) a matter of "common sense." What happened to cause this abrupt change?

What happened is that some ideas got spread around. Ideas account for the astonishing acceleration of events in the decade and a half that midwived the modern world. Ideas explain what seems to be the disproportion between the colonists' grievances and their worldshaking and history-making response. Perhaps never before or since has philosophy been such an intensely practical subject. The era of the founding of the United States is especially powerful evidence for the school of historians that says not only that ideas have consequences, but that only ideas have large and lasting consequences.

Sheldon's book is part of an argument currently enlivening the writing of early American history. From the mother lode of Jefferson's philosophy, Sheldon mines a gleaming nugget of an insight. It is that we have too often slighted one of the two strands of philosophy that deserve equal dignity as intellectual progenitors of this Republic. The strand that has not been neglected is the liberalism derived from the writings of John Locke, especially from his *Two Treatises on Government*. The insufficiently appreciated strand is that of classical republicanism. The ways in which these two philosophies complement each other, and the tension between them, is relevant to America today.

For several decades now, historians have debated the sources and qualities of the American Revolution. The debate has turned on the supposed primacy of John Locke's ideas of individualism, natural rights and limited government. Individualism: Locke portrayed mankind as a loose—very loose—aggregation of autonomous and almost asocial individuals. Natural rights: These individuals possess, prior to political association with others, certain rights by virtue of their nature. Limited government: These rights-endowed individuals ("endowed by their Creator," says the Declaration of Independence) associate politically only to make more commodious each individual's enjoyment of these rights.

Recently, however, there has been increased appreciation of the saliency of other notions, those of classical republicanism. These include the ideas of social man, the central impor-

tance of public participation in civic life and the struggle of the
virtuous people out in the country to contain the corruption
associated with those who cluster around the central power,
like a court around a king.

Until recent decades—until, we may say, the late 1960s—
there was a broad and, it seemed, durable consensus among
historians. It held that an understanding of Lockean liberalism
was not merely necessary but was virtually sufficient for understanding this Republic's origins, its founding and its early
course. An influential and characteristic formulation of the consensus was that "Locke dominates American political thought
as no thinker anywhere dominates the political thought of a
nation."[7] That was written in 1955, when, from the center of
Europe to the South China Sea, Marxism was an established
civil religion enforced by state terror. Nevertheless, Louis
Hartz, who wrote that, had a point. Marxism was only an
imposed and alien orthodoxy; we now know how utterly it
failed to sink roots into the social soil. In contrast, Locke's
liberalism permeates America's political vocabulary and institutions.

Locke portrayed man as a mild and essentially congenial
creature, semisocial but basically isolated while in a "state of
nature." In that state he is a materialist. He possesses a "natural right" to life, liberty and property. In Locke's understanding of government, men make a rational, if unenthusiastic,
choice to leave the state of nature. They enter into a social
contract with kindred spirits who seek from government a severely limited service. They seek only relief from the generally
mild inconveniences and insecurities of the state of nature.
These inconveniences and insecurities are primarily the results
of disputes between people exercising their natural rights. The
government they create is essentially an arbitrator—a referee.
Thus the government that arises from Lockean liberalism is
inherently limited in its purposes and scope by the impulse that

gives rise to it. That impulse is the desire for the protection of the private rights and acquired interests that predate government.

For many years the practice of locating the intellectual origins of the American polity entirely in Lockean liberalism had, for historians and other intellectuals, the attraction of tidiness. It also had, in this century, the advantage of political utility. As Sheldon says, "Locke's emphasis on private property and conflicting material interests led quite easily into the progressive (and later Marxist) school of historical interpretation that focused upon economic, social and institutional factors in explaining political ideas and actions in America."[8]

Then the consensus began to fray.

In the 1960s classical republicanism became a rival of Lockean liberalism as an explanatory concept in the writing of early American history. The crucial difference with Lockean liberalism is the emphasis classical republicanism gives to man's natural sociability. That sociability entails both a need and a disposition to participate in civic life and to develop and display public virtue. In 1969, J. G. A. Pocock, backed by rich and persuasive scholarship, said, in effect: Mr. Locke, move over and make room for credit to be given to another philosophic contribution to the making of the first modern nation. Pocock extracted from the writings of Aristotle, Cicero, Machiavelli and others a coherent political philosophy that first appeared in Ancient Greece and Rome, later resurfaced in Renaissance Italy, then resonated in eighteenth-century England and became a fighting faith in revolutionary and postrevolutionary America.[9] But in America it was alloyed with Lockean liberalism and was often lost sight of.

Classical republicanism is rooted in Aristotle's notion that man is a political animal. Man, to Aristotle, is not political in the tentative, limited and diffident manner of the Lockean man who enters into political society only negatively, as a necessary concession to inconveniences. Rather, said classical republicans, man is political in the sense that his nature can not be realized, and his natural inclinations can not be fulfilled, without active involvement in a political order—a particular kind of political order. It is a kind that makes possible political participation, which Aristotle considered a defining attribute of citizenship. Such a political order is right for man's nature. Which is to say, it is a natural right.

Classical republicanism stressed the economic independence of the individual as a prerequisite for satisfying the individual's social nature through political participation in a virtuous republic. Virtue, Sheldon notes, is a decidedly non-Lockean concept, because it involves the individual in sacrificing some self-interest for the common good.

The reappearance of classical republicanism in eighteenth-century England reflected a quickened concern about civic virtue and the decay of political life. Classical republicanism was the rallying doctrine of the country gentry. That gentry saw itself as the force of countervailing virtue against the wealthy, corrupt and dependent "court" faction that inevitably flourishes when great power is concentrated in a central government in a vast metropolis. In England in the sixteenth and seventeenth centuries considerable political tension existed between the sovereign and the class of landowners who had to bear most of the financial burden of the sovereign's government. The tension was not just about money. It also concerned the apportionment of power and respect, and different visions of how English society and government should evolve. This struggle for supremacy was often spoken of as a contest between "court and country." The "country" party—if it is not too anachronistic to use the word "party" about this faction—thought of the court not just as the sovereign but as the gaggle of interests that fastened like leeches on the seat of government in a corrupt and corrupting political city.

It would be crashingly incongruous to call the "country" faction democrats. They did not seek substantial extension of political participation to those below them. Neither were they republicans. They wanted to tame and trim the crown's prerogatives, but they did not seek to abolish it. On the other hand, they were making more than a narrow argument on behalf of the material and political interests of their class. They also were formulating a moral stance. It was, in a sense, an echo of earlier political philosophers and would soon reverberate in America. It was an echo of the tradition of those ancients in Greece and Rome, and subsequent thinkers such as Machiavelli, who worried about political arrangements that work against the very virtues that the political arrangements presuppose. And the English "country" faction was an anticipation of the revival, across the ocean, of an intense, and intensely practical, debate about the problems of defining and nurturing republican virtue.

In the last decade of the eighteenth century in America, as the two-party system began to coalesce from the cooling dust of the revolutionary explosion, the "court versus country" distinction was a useful analogy that Jeffersonians put to partisan use. They invoked it in their rivalry with Hamiltonians. Jeffersonians were grounded in, and spokesmen for, the rural yeomanry who, Jeffersonian theory held, were disciplined by agrarian life to the virtues requisite for freedom: individualism, hardihood, self-reliance. It suited Jeffersonian political purposes to portray Hamiltonians as sunk in metropolitan corruption. Hamiltonians, said Jeffersonians, were seeking private gain from proximity to an overreaching and overbearing central government.

This was a caricature, but like all caricatures it was a distortion developed from a kernel of truth. Jeffersonians did, indeed, believe in a sociology of virtue. Their sociology entailed agrarianism, localism and decentralism. And Hamiltonians did in fact favor considerable (for that day) concentrations of power in the federal government. Hamiltonians wanted that government to possess power sufficient to promote credit, commerce and industry. That would necessarily mean urbanization, which would sever many people, and hence popular government, from what Jeffersonians considered indispensable—the ennobling influences of life on the land.

To be fair (as Jeffersonians and Hamiltonians rarely were to one another), Hamilton himself had a clear and noble moral vision. It involved a social revolution as important, Hamilton thought, as the political revolution that had just been effected. And Hamilton thought that without the second—the social—revolution, the political revolution would prove to have been a barren achievement. He cast his cool gaze on history and on his contemporary situation and came to a conclusion many others have come to before and since. He concluded that social progress is always propelled by the exertions of an industrious minority. For this minority, in the modern age, money must be the means as well as the measure of achievement. A society plastic to the power of money may be susceptible to crassness, vulgarity and corruption, but it also is apt to be an open society, with a large cohort of the industrious. Thus, Hamilton thought, it would be decidedly superior to a Jeffersonian society.

Hamilton's best modern biographer, Forrest McDonald, rightly insists that Hamilton saw the free working of sound money as a solvent to wash away the rigidities of a Jeffersonian society, a form of society that Hamilton thought would suffocate social energies. Hamilton considered Jeffersonianism partly a sentimental celebration of rural existence and partly (sometimes simultaneously) the self-interested ideology of a retrograde class. Against this, and on behalf of a more fluid and vital America, Hamilton proposed to unleash the creative force of money. "For money," McDonald writes, "is oblivious to class, status, color, and inherited social position; money is the ultimate, neutral, impersonal arbiter. Infused into an oligarchical, agrarian social order, money would be the leaven, the fermenting yeast, that would stimulate growth, change, prosperity, and national strength."[10]

Jefferson said: Keep the factories, financiers and cities in Europe. Democracy depends on yeomen dispersed over vast spaces (hence the Louisiana Purchase). Hamilton saw cities in America's future. Although in 1790 America's largest city, Philadelphia, had a population of 54,391 (about the size of Rapid City, South Dakota, today), Hamilton was the first political thinker for urban America. He saw in Jefferson's vision not the romance of bucolic life but an indolent, oligarchic caste society suffocating America's promise.

Hamilton's rival vision was contained in one of the most important public documents in American history. His "Report on Manufactures" made the case for tariffs, a central bank, public works and other government assistance to commercial development, but was not just a statement of economic policy. The "Report" was an exercise in statecraft as soulcraft. He aimed at nothing less than a change in the American character. Like Jefferson, Hamilton took seriously the social ecology of virtue. He wanted a different society because he had a different idea of virtue for individuals and the nation.

America never really had a choice between Hamiltonian and Jeffersonian futures. The forces—scientific, industrial, financial, organizational—that made the modern world were going to erupt. Nothing Jeffersonians could have done would have made the Atlantic a barrier to them. Furthermore, it is, on balance, good that they erupted. Modernity has meant a vast improvement in conditions for the mass of mankind. And when Hitler and Stalin got factories, it was good that we had some, too.

Still, there is a tragic dimension to Hamiltonianism, and to

American history. Hamilton had a healthy distrust of human nature but was not wary enough. He underestimated the difficulty—the impossibility, it seems—of keeping government limited and reasonable once it becomes a big player in the game of creating and allocating wealth. Hamilton had an austere, even noble, vision of a people energized by the spirit of perpetual improvement. He did not foresee the degradation of political and economic life that would result when government became an arena for entrepreneurship, engulfed in a feeding frenzy of people bending public power to private purposes.

Prescient Jeffersonians saw that the kind of government Hamilton favored would lend itself to exploitation by individuals and interests animated by lust for private gain. However, in extenuation of Hamilton's responsibility for our current discontents, let us stress that we have today a central government that has grown mighty beyond Hamilton's dreams of federal supremacy. Still, he planted the intellectual and institutional seeds from which today's regulatory and therapeutic welfare state grew into the huge engine it is. Therefore the systemic problems of this government, particularly the deep dissatisfaction with the style and substance of the politics such a state generates, are, in a sense, part of Hamilton's mixed legacy. Hence it is reasonable to consult the Jeffersonian tradition for guidance concerning possible corrective measures.

Jefferson's life of public involvement was so long, and his intellectual life had so many facets, that one comes upon portions of the Jeffersonian tradition wherever one turns when examining the American political tradition. This is certainly true when considering the tradition—one might better say the ethic—of term limitation. George Washington's voluntary retirement after two terms in the presidency established the ethic by example. But it might not have done so if Jefferson had not chosen to make the ethic explicit.

Halfway through President Jefferson's second term the

nation found itself sailing in increasingly choppy waters. It was embroiled in disputes with France and Britain over the rights of neutral nations' shipping during the war between those two nations. In June, 1807, the issue of impressment of members of U.S. ships' crews by British Navy ships reached a crisis point. The U.S. frigate *Chesapeake* was fired upon by the British frigate *Leopard*. The *Chesapeake* struck its colors, four Americans were taken away on the *Leopard*, and the new nation's sense of dignity was lacerated. Jefferson's proclamation ordering British warships out of American territorial waters was followed by a British proclamation ordering still more aggressive searches for British subjects serving on the crews of American ships. Congress then passed the Embargo Act, which divided the nation in the most dangerous way, along its regional fault line, North against South. New England merchants were especially injured and angry.

Meanwhile, the American public was increasingly alarmed by evidence of Aaron Burr's conspiracy to separate Western states from the Union. So it was not surprising that, beginning in November, 1806, and with increasing urgency, local meetings of Jefferson's party, the Republican Party, began petitioning him to seek a third term. Soon nine of the seventeen state legislatures and one territorial government joined the call for him not to retire.

Jefferson did not respond until December, 1807, and then he replied only to the addresses from state legislatures. He was emphatic. He said he felt as obligated to put down the burdens of the presidency as he had felt duty-bound to take them up. Because the Constitution had not limited presidential terms, custom must do so. Otherwise the office might become, *de facto*, one held for life. "I should unwillingly be the person who, disregarding the sound precedent set by an illustrious predecessor, should furnish the first example of prolongation beyond the second term of office."[11] Jefferson's position was praised by the editor of the *Richmond Enquirer*. He said that if Jefferson had allowed himself to be persuaded by the nation's emergency to serve another term, a "less virtuous and more ambitious" successor might "seize upon any lowering speck in the distant horizon, perhaps to conjure up an imaginary danger, that he might shield his ambition under a similar excuse. Mr. Jefferson's retirement wrests this plausible pretext from the hands of his successors. They will see from his example, that no crisis, however fruitful in danger or in war *can* justify the prolongation of their term of office."[12]

Jefferson surely knew that the question of improper "prolongation" of tenure in office involves values that were first, and arguably best, discussed by the ancients. Historian Bernard Bailyn maintains that although other American thinkers of the founding era used classical allusions "ornamentally," Jefferson was a "careful reader"[13] of the ancients. However, he was not an acolyte in awe of them. Aristotle and other Greeks, said Jefferson, never mastered the task that confronted the American Founders. It was the task of preparing a middle ground "between a democracy (the only pure republic, but impractical beyond the limits of a town) and an abandonment of themselves to an aristocracy, or a tyranny independent of the people."[14]

The American solution was a government of what Jefferson called "the second grade of purity." We should not be distracted by the resonance his language has today. The added ingredient of representation was—is—not an impurity. Representation is a necessity "where the citizens can not meet to transact their business."[15] And the idea of representation contains its own standard of purity. That standard can be expressed negatively, as the avoidance of what Jefferson called the "detestable game" and "base scramble"[16] for public funds and other private advantages from public power. That game rages today on a scale far beyond Jefferson's worst nightmares.

This twentieth-century scramble may be in part a consequence of seventeenth- and eighteenth-century theories of human nature. Are human beings only mildly social creatures, moved primarily by the desire for self-preservation and avoidance of the "inconveniences" that the state of nature has for property holders? Do they, therefore, enter into only chilly political associations with other materialistic individuals who are similarly motivated by private interests? If people are described this way—and therefore taught to be this way—by the public philosophy, we should not be surprised or aghast when the politics that results from such narrow utilitarian calculations turns out to be the sort of scramble that Jefferson detested.

Such scrambling, which legislative careerism intensifies and term limitation would abate, is incompatible with good citizenship. Civic virtue means a steady predisposition to prefer the public good to private advantages when they conflict. Term limitation would also help to reinvigorate our understanding of citizenship by reemphasizing the value of civic participation. Aristotle taught that citizenship in a republic implies participation. That is all very well for a compact city-state, but it gives little guidance for our age. Our task is to define the sort of participation that is prudent and practical in a complex and continental republic. To Jefferson, the key was localism.

In 1809 he rode out of Washington a week after Madison was inaugurated, never to return. Seven years later he was still strong in his faith in decentralization: "As Cato, then, concluded every speech with the words 'Carthago delenda est,'* so do I every opinion, with the injunction, 'divide the counties into wards.' "[17] One can sympathize with Jefferson's yearning for centrifugal forces, but one can not deny the centripetal tendency of American history since—actually, even

* Carthage must be destroyed.

during—Jefferson's day. (President Jefferson's Louisiana Purchase, and the Embargo Act and its enforcing legislation, were early manifestations of the flow of power to the central government, however much Jefferson believed or pretended otherwise.) But this does not mean that we must meekly abandon participation as a value importantly implied by citizenship. One function of term limitation is to inscribe in fundamental law and infuse throughout political practice this sentiment: The essential act of republicanism—lawmaking in a representative institution—is not work that requires such a long apprenticeship that most citizens are effectively excluded from the pool of talent from which lawmakers can be drawn. Lawmaking is not the arcane province of a clerisy of experts and specialists whose ranks are open only to people prepared to commit substantial portions of their adult lives.

Term limitation covering 535 seats in the national legislature will affect only the minute fraction of the American public that will serve in those seats. But if term limitation is inscribed as a constitutional value it will perform, as law frequently does, an expressive and affirming function. It will express an idea central to the civic culture of republicanism (of the American, if not necessarily the Burkean, variety). The idea is that representation is not a function beyond the capacities of any reasonably educated and attentive citizen. Term limitation will affirm the democratic faith in the broad diffusion in the public of the talents necessary for the conduct of the public's business. Term limitation does not rest on the assumption that (as Lenin said but did not believe) any cook can run the state. However, term limitation does say, moderately and usefully, that democracy does not depend on any indispensable people.

The genius of American society, nicely distilled in Jefferson's idea of "natural aristocracy," is in the belief that the meritorious should rule but that merit can be found, or nurtured, in every social rank. And the merit of the public—of the nation itself—can be nurtured by the normal working of the institutions of self-government, especially the central institution of representation, Congress.

Many Americans reflexively flinch from the idea of government nurturing virtue. According to the instinctive notions of most Americans, politics generally should faithfully reflect, not seek to modify, the citizens' sentiments or characters. Americans have a bluff, commonsense belief that a government that has a hard enough time delivering the mail and patching potholes can not be expected to bring off anything as subtle and complex as moral improvement. Besides, even if government could do it, government should not do it, because soulcraft is incompatible with freedom. The boldness of the American experiment in liberal democracy is precisely this: Liberty is to be protected primarily by institutional arrangements rather than by reliance on the nurturing of virtue, either among the masses or in some saving elite.

However, although that is the primary reliance, it is not the only one. Virtue, too, is requisite. And the workings of the institutions of popular government are themselves supposed to nurture some of the virtues that their proper working presupposes.

The importance of the philosophy of classical republicanism in the American founding means that America's intellectual and moral origins and are not exclusively in modernity, not just in the liberalism that founds liberty on individualism, rights and materialism. America also arises from the ancient republicanism that stressed the fulfillment of man's political nature through political participation. But not through just any participation. It should be participation in the governance of a polity that nurtures what it presupposes, a modicum of public virtue. This virtue is a tendency to prefer the public good to personal interests; it is a readiness to define the public good as more than an aggregation of private interests.

Prior to the American—more precisely, the Madisonian—revolution in democratic theory, most political philosophers thought that a successful democracy needed a certain quantity of a particular quality. The quality was called virtue. And a sufficient supply of this quality could flourish only in a polity conducive to it. That meant a small polity. Only in a small, face-to-face society would there be sufficient homogeneity to avoid factions, which were presumed to be the bane of democracy.

However, a republic that is continental in scope and commercial in nature must welcome a multiplicity of factions. They make the machinery of government move, and their countervailing forces prevent it from moving to tyranny. This scheme of governance contrasts with the classic notion of a compact republic relying on virtue—both the virtue of the many who select the few that govern, and the virtue of the few.

The Madisonian scheme had, for the thoughtful statesmen who devised it, the intellectual charm of elegance and ingenuity. It also satisfied their rigorous realism. A system that relies on the physics of interestedness—that treats politics as a field of low but steady, predictable and manageable forces—is a system free from the inherently uncertain reliance on virtue. It is a system that will not count overmuch on virtue, either of the people or of the representatives the people select.

Not overmuch, but somewhat. America's Founders sought safety in both sociological and institutional factors. The sociological factors included diversity of factions and extensive territory. Two of the institutional factors were the constitutional principles of separation of powers and federalism. However, the Founders also counted on another constitutional factor to make democracy not only safe but a force for the steady, constant improvement of the nation's character. This third factor was supposed to be the conspicuous—and hence elevating—practice of deliberative democracy in Congress. Hence the Constitution itself was supposed to be, and should be seen to be, a moralizing force. Its dignity and its suitability as an object of veneration are partly a product of this grave function.

No sensible person lightly suggests amending it. Still, the Founders, by including the amending provisions, contemplated changes. And, anyway, the Constitution's meaning and force have been considerably changed by the nation's political and social evolution—sometimes seamless, sometimes with abrupt ruptures—during two centuries. In his history of Reconstruction, Eric Foner writes that it was fitting that as Congress debated a vast expansion of federal power "in February 1867, the last surviving veteran of the American Revolution died. For like the Revolution, Reconstruction was an era when the foundations of public life were thrown open for discussion."[18] It would be excessive to suggest that America in the 1990s stands at such a potentially critical pivot in its history, when the nature of the regime itself is at issue, and the structure of the regime seems malleable. However, it is not too much to say that for the first time since the New Deal, political debates about practical measures are raising questions concerning the essential nature of American republicanism.

These questions were at issue in the birth of our party system, in the controversy between Jefferson and Hamilton. There is an elegant memorial in Washington to Jefferson, but none to Hamilton. However, if you seek Hamilton's monument, look around. You are living in it. We honor Jefferson, but live in Hamilton's country, a mighty industrial nation with a strong central government. Questions about how republicanism should be understood were again—were still—at issue in 1861, when the nation was torn by the "irrepressible conflict" about its nature. Four years of that conflict gave the national government a giant shove toward supremacy but also toward a strength that has proven to be problematic. "On the eve of the Civil War . . . one could live out one's life without ever encountering an official representative of national authority."[19] Since the Civil War, and especially since the New Deal, the federal government has been woven into the fabric of daily life.

The 1932 presidential election inaugurated the modern era of American politics. What began then was only dimly perceived and only vaguely planned, but it was nothing less than a fundamental change in the relationship of the citizen to the central government. Ever since, Americans have been getting what they manifestly have wanted, a federal government taking responsibility for the nation's aggregate economic output, and for myriad lesser questions of distributive justice and social amelioration.

However, six decades have passed since the New Deal began to be improvised and Americans are not happy with the political process that has evolved in conjunction with the kind of government they have requested. Term limitation is an attempt, by a limited, surgical revision of the rules of representation, to restore a balance, a temperateness and—let us not flinch from the word—a virtue that has been lost from public life.

CHAPTER 4

"Like A Strong Wind": Love of Country and Respect for Congress

T he decade of the 1990s is a propitious moment for attempting such a restoration. Changes in the world have restored the nation to something like normality. It is not a mere coincidence, and it is fortuitous, that the rapid rise of interest in term limitation has coincided with the end of the Cold War. The sudden dissolution of that conflict, and the stepping-down from the hair-trigger world that conflict produced, should change the way Americans think about the presidency, and hence the way they think about Congress.

The Cold War was a just war, and perhaps the most important war ever waged. What was at stake was nothing less

than Western Civilization and its hard-won understanding of
the proper relation of the individual to the state. But like all
wars, the Cold War absorbed human energies, physical and
intellectual, that could have been more humanely used in a less
threatening environment. And one of the most regrettable aspects of the Cold War was its distorting impact on American
government. It deepened the fixation on the presidency that
various other factors, such as the mass media, have helped to
produce. The Cold War, and the national security state it ne-
cessitated, put nine presidents, from Truman through Bush,
front-and-center on a brightly-lit stage of constant drama. Day
and night, year-round, the president was shadowed by the
military aide carrying the "football," the satchel containing the
nuclear launch codes. It was a riveting sight, morning, noon
and night.

The Cold War and television arrived simultaneously. Since
the invention of broadcasting, the presidency has become especially prominent, and people tend to equate prominence with
power. But the presidency remains an inherently, meaning
constitutionally, weak office. A president can do little on his
own, except exhort the country and, by moving it, move Congress. That is one reason why most of the time, under most
presidents, there has been congressional ascendancy. There
have been ten strong presidents (Washington, Jefferson, Jackson, Polk, Lincoln, the two Roosevelts, Wilson, Lyndon
Johnson and Reagan). But the system of checks and balances
has generally been tilted toward the legislative branch.

The argument for presidential ascendancy is that the president is the only officer of government capable of eliciting a
national mandate or advancing national strategies for domestic
and international affairs. On the other hand, perhaps it is for-
tunate that presidential ascendancy requires a rare combination of political circumstances and personal capacities.
Considering the run of presidents, it is arguable that there is

generally more wisdom in Congress, collectively, than in the individual in the Oval Office at any moment. That individual has been the focus of expectations (for "leadership," "vision" and so on) that are bound to produce, more often than not, disappointment.

When Senator Tim Wirth, the Colorado Democrat, enumerated the reasons for his dismay about, and departure from, Washington, prominent among those reasons was George Bush. Wirth described Bush as a "leader [who] refuses to lead, who does not seem to have a sense of where he wants the country to go, and whose lack of direction in turn pervades the whole government."[1] When did Americans start talking, and thinking, like that? Since when has it been normal for Americans to think that the weightlessness of a particular president must "pervade the whole government"? Why is it that an emptiness in the Oval Office must echo throughout Washington? How came we to a point where the country is considered condemned to stasis, even to entropy in its government, if one person, the president, happens to be, as many presidents have been and are apt to be, flimsy?

The answer to those questions is bound up with the evolution of the "rhetorical presidency" sketched earlier. But note well this: Wirth's lacerating assessment of George Bush is also a severe commentary on the condition of Congress. That condition is partly a result of the rise of presidential government in the sprawling administrative state that defies close congressional oversight. The outline of a new status of the presidency, and of Congress, began to become clear in 1933. Then Congress began to experience the eclipse that is inevitable when the presidency is seen as the sun around which all else in political life should orbit. Since 1933—the onset of the New Deal, which meant a fundamentally new relationship between citizens and the federal government—Congress, especially its liberal bloc, has tried to have its cake and eat it, too. It has wanted to

construct a large, solicitous government, omnipresent and omniprovident, but it also has wanted to exercise control over
that government. However, it is an iron law of social life that
as government grows, legislative control contracts. This is so
because many of the "laws" Congress passes actually are less
laws than mere expressions of sentiments, values or goals.

A law is a substantive rule that regulates private conduct
or directs the operations of government. Today many laws are,
effectively, written in the executive branch. For example, in
the early 1970s Congress expressed the sentiment that there
should be no discrimination on the basis of sex in education.
What precisely did Congress mean? Congress meant almost
nothing with any precision. But regulation-writers in the bow-
els of the bureaucracy set about saying what Congress might
have said if Congress had had the time, energy, inclination and
courage. The result was a thick web of rules. And one result of
those rules was the brief but memorable ruling that an Arizona
high school could not have a father-son sports banquet. That
ruling caused the president and Congress to trip over one another in the rush to say that no one had meant to mean that.

Congress can influence the writing of regulations by mon-
itoring (or hectoring) the bureaucracy, and by holding hearings
and extracting promises from cabinet secretaries and those
who really run the government, the secretaries' underlings. In
a pinch, Congress can even make its intentions clear and bind-
ing by actually legislating—by passing a law that is more than
a sentiment. Still, the fact remains that Congress, by its own
actions—paradoxically, by its energy in mandating energetic
government—has pushed itself to the periphery. The federal
machinery can, indeed generally must, run without the close
supervision of the mechanic that put it together.

The marginalizing of Congress, and the consequent de-moralization of many of its best members, is not just a result of the rise of the presidency and the sprawl of the modern state. Congress's steep descent in the hierarchy of American government is also a result of legislative careerism. Careerism makes professional legislators content, even eager, for Congress to sag into a secondary role in governance. This means a small role for leadership understood as it should be in a republic. That is, a small role for the public exercise of deliberative judgment by representatives reasoning together at a constitutional distance from the represented. And it leaves the nation primarily reliant on leadership as it has been understood in connection with the presidency since Woodrow Wilson redefined that office. That is leadership understood in terms of charismatic, visionary, rhetorical acts of inspiration and (to use Wilson's word) "interpretation."

Furthermore, when Congress is marginalized—when it marginalizes itself—there comes into play a third and particularly problematic kind of leadership. When Congress recedes into the background of governance, courts are apt to rush into the foreground. The result is a proliferation of lawyers, a multiplication of rights, a decline in the rule of law and a further decline of representative institutions, especially of Congress.

In 1991 Vice President Dan Quayle, addressing the American Bar Association convention, suggested that something is amiss when America has 70 percent of the world's lawyers. It has almost 800,000 of them, one for every 311 citizens. Responding to Quayle, a law professor said, "We have a lot of lawyers because we have a lot of rights. . . . That's democracy. That's equality . . . we have environmental rights . . . discrimination rights . . . consumer rights . . . safety rights . . ." Can there be too many rights? Yes, when every social problem is presented as a clash of rights, and all advocacy is couched in the language of rights. The costs of these habits are calculated in a timely book, *Rights Talk: The Impoverishment of Political Discourse*, by Mary Ann Glendon, a professor of law at Harvard University.[2]

Until the 1950s, she notes, the focus of constitutional law was not on personal rights as the bulwark of liberty. Rather, it was on the structure of our political regime—the allocation of powers among the federal government's branches and between the federal and state governments. The strong tradition was that great controversies should be settled in representative political institutions, not in courts, unless the Constitution's text clearly indicated otherwise. But literary theories ("deconstruction" and all that) have been imported into jurisprudence to "prove" that all texts are of indeterminate meaning, and political theories have stigmatized tradition as oppressive. This has emancipated the discretion of judges and has licensed social reformers to prefer litigation, with its promise of quick and sweeping victory, over the slow, incremental progress of persuasion and legislation. Thus federal judges, egged on by academic admirers, have been running schools, prisons, hospitals and other things, always in the name of an expanding menu of rights.

Not only is America exceptionally lawyer-ridden, but lawyers' roles here are exceptionally adversarial. Courtroom law talk, Glendon notes, proceeds from a premise inimical to civil discourse: that two theses pushed to extremes will enable a third party to determine the truth. Our political discourse is so saturated with rights talk—the Supreme Court has even defined citizenship as "the right to have rights"—that the tributaries of nonlegal rhetoric are drying up. There is excessive concentration on two polarities of social life—the individual and the state—and insufficient attention to civil society's intermediary institutions, which Glendon calls "communities of memory and mutual aid."[3] They mediate the relation of the citizen to public power and are seedbeds of personal and civic virtue.

The exaggerated absoluteness of the American dialect of rights talk implies that Americans are too childish or volatile to be trusted to respect rights that are subject to reasonable limitations. Our hard-edged rights talk slights the grammar of cooperative living and also slights the art of building coalitions by achieving compromises. The language of rights—universal, inalienable, inviolable rights—leaves no room for compromise. As Glendon says, "The winner takes all and the loser has to get out of town. The conversation is over."[4] Rights talk, she warns, reinforces an all-too-human failing that also is encouraged by the language of psychotherapy, the tendency to place the self at the center of the moral universe. Prodigality in the bestowing of the label "right" is a tactic to give specious dignity to unbridled desires. It multiplies occasions for civic discord and leads to indignation about the inescapable limits inherent in life in society.

The linguistic and conceptual deficiencies of rights talk in our law-saturated society result in the portrayal of Americans as solitary wanderers in a land of strangers, throwing out aggressive rights claims, like sharp elbows, in an endless jostling for social space. This picture does not do justice to American sociability. And, over time, it damages that sociability. Glendon believes that what distinguishes American law is not its "individualism" but its view of what the individual is—a lonely rights-bearer, a self-determining creature unencumbered by duties and unconnected to the community.

By neglecting the social dimension of personhood and by exalting autonomy, rights talk creates a climate of callousness toward the very young, the severely ill and disabled and the frail elderly. So, for example, a poor and unmarried pregnant woman has a glistening "privacy right" to seek an abortion, but she has precious little claim on the community's compassion. ("You've got your right, don't bother us further.") Glendon believes it is telling that in Europe, where the abortion right is less sweeping, community provision for pregnant women and unwed mothers is more generous.

The romance of rights involves the belief that the high road to social justice can be paved by court decisions won by swashbuckling litigators, lone eagles like other American heroes—Lindbergh, Gary Cooper in *High Noon*. This modern version of a familiar American icon now serves a class interest. Glendon notes that America's agenda-shaping elites are apt to prefer to pursue social change through courts rather than through legislatures. The language of law and the mores of litigation are congenial to "members of the knowledge class that now predominates in government, political parties, corporations, universities, and the mass media."[5] They are geographically and socially mobile, with only attenuated ties, if any, to the little platoons that give an enriching, softening texture to the lives of most Americans. These elites are remote from the slow, organic processes of mass persuasion that are the essence of democracy. And Glendon says this remoteness reinforces the vanity of that class: "Their common attitude that the educated are better equipped to govern than the masses finds its institutional expression in a disdain for ordinary politics and the legislative process, and a preference for extending the authority of courts, the branch of government to which they have the easiest access."[6]

Behind the rights talk lurks a class prejudice in favor of minting fresh rights to fuel judicial activism. Shrill rhetoric about individual and, increasingly, group rights is drowning out other styles of discourse, including talk about the community's interest (not, please, "community rights"). Regarding rights, too many people subscribe to Mae West's theory that too much of a good thing is wonderful. In fact, too much rights talk is both a cause and an effect of the eclipse of legislatures.

The rise of the career legislator is another reason for the rise of judicial activism in a climate of rights talk. This is so because legislative careerism begets in legislators an unsavory prudence, which in turn begets the impulse to solve society's problems by judicial fiats rather than political deliberation. Therefore term limits for legislators would help to limit the imperial judiciary.

⤚⤙   ⤚⤙

One can not, of course, be sure that a Congress composed of noncareerists will more forthrightly deal with the sort of difficult problems that, in a democracy, should be dealt with by representative and deliberative institutions. But surely term limits will increase the likelihood that Congress will reclaim its role as the center of American government. This will mean putting both the courts and the presidency where they belong, which is more toward the periphery of political life. Critics who say that term limitation will make Congress a bewildered and deferential handmaiden of the presidency are missing a point. A Congress whose members are cured of careerism will be less risk-averse and more vigorous. Such a Congress will not only leave courts less latitude to act as legislatures, it will more readily risk challenging the president, whoever he is, as the definer of the nation's political agenda.

A career legislator is not only risk-averse, he or she lives by a perverse ethic that eliminates—indeed proscribes—any moral misgivings about the policy of avoiding politically risky decisions. This ethic is usually unspoken, even unconscious, so thoroughly is it part of the moral universe of the careerist. But one of this country's archetypal careerists, Lyndon Johnson, did state the ethic succinctly.

In his memoir of his years as senior domestic policy aide to President Johnson, Joseph A. Califano, Jr., recalls Johnson's short-lived plan to merge the departments of Labor and Commerce. George Meany, then head of the AFL-CIO, at first endorsed the idea. However, it met with unexpectedly fierce opposition from other members of the AFL-CIO Executive Council. Johnson had the entire Council to the White House for lunch and cajoling, but not even that could soften the opposition. Califano writes:

> At that point I urged the President to call Meany on his commitment and press the AFL-CIO president to come out publicly for the merger. Johnson turned to me, teacher to student, and said: not only would he not do that, but he didn't want anyone ever to know that Meany had committed to him. "It's just like a member of Congress," Johnson added. "You can't ever ask a man to do something that will jeopardize his job."[7]

That notion seems self-evidently true to people who are thoroughly socialized, as Johnson was, to the values and mentality of the political careerist. But it is wrong. Its premise is that elective office is a job like almost any other. The careerist mentality that Johnson expressed gives no recognition to the fact that someone elected to look after the public interest is necessarily operating in a complex and demanding moral matrix, a context different from the moral decision-making environment that most people operate in during their workaday lives. Carpenters and professors, plumbers and dentists, mechanics and stockbrokers, most people, in fact, may occasionally face moments in their work when they have a moral duty to do something that puts at risk their immediate material interests. But they almost never, if ever, face a dilemma in which it is their duty to put in jeopardy their ability to continue their profession. Elective politicians do face just such dilemmas. They are supposed to be thinking about more than the problem of prospering in their profession.

Many of the professions—law, medicine, business, journalism—are considered genuine professions in part because they have codes of professional ethics. The ethics of these professions are often taught as part of the professional education in law, medical, business and journalism schools at the postgraduate level. Electoral politics is not a profession for which one qualifies by acquiring formal credentials from such institutions. Still, politics has, nonetheless, professional ethics. Some are codified, such as those concerning conflicts of interest. Other parts of the professional ethics of politics can not be formally stated other than in propositions of considerable generality. However, ethical propositions that are general are not for that reason trivial. And surely the core of the professional ethic of a politician in representative government is this:

There are occasions when what the public interest demands, the public dislikes. On such occasions, the public interest conflicts with the personal interest the politician has in remaining in office. Still, what serves the public interest should be done, even if doing it will jeopardize his or her job. This points to an obvious merit of term limitation. If the legislator's job is not—if it can not be—a lifetime career, less is risked when risks are taken. So it will be easier under term limits for representatives to exercise the independent judgment that is the essence of leadership, properly understood, in a deliberative democracy.

By giving this book the title "Restoration," I mean to stress my conviction that term limits are a fundamentally conservative reform. But by "conservative" I emphatically do not mean that the reform will serve, or should be supported because it will serve, this or that portion of today's conservative agenda. I—and, I suspect, a good many others—would be hard-put to say with much precision what that agenda includes in the 1990s. Abroad, the world has changed at a pace without precedent in

human history. Domestically, as conservatism has prospered it
has brought many kinds of people into its tent and become a
pluralistic persuasion. That is the fate, and hardly a sad one, of
fighting faiths that win: They lose their hard, cutting ideological edge.

No one can know that term limits will serve "the conservative agenda," whatever that might be. Neither can anyone
say with certainty that term limits would help or hinder the
liberal agenda, whatever that is in the 1990s. In any case, such
partisan political calculations have no legitimate place in debates about constitutional change. Let me repeat here a credo
with which I began this book. There is a kind of scorched-
earth, pillage-and-burn conservatism that loathes government.
Those who subscribe to this unlovely faith have enjoyed watching as public esteem for government in general, and especially
for Congress, has plummeted. That is not my kind of conservatism. No American who loves the nation can like seeing the
central institutions of American democracy being degraded and
despised. Patriotism properly understood simply is not compatible with contempt for the institutions that put American
democracy on display.

When I call term limits a "conservative" reform I mean
only that the reform is a way of recapturing valuable aspects of
our civic life that have been lost, or have become diluted and
attenuated. The object is to restore a healthier relationship
between the citizen and the government. At bottom, the case
for term limits rests on the belief that such limits will help
Americans become reacquainted with the ideas and practices of
republicanism as that idea was understood by the most reflective members of this Republic's founding generation. This requires restoring the status, and hence the competence, of
Congress. Given the nature of modern government, such restoration requires breaking the dynamic of careerism. Term
limits will break it. Limits are required to institutionalize

healthy competition in the political market, just as antitrust intervention in economic markets can serve the values of a basically free market economy.

Politics in a free society is a free market. Not a perfect one, of course. The political market, like any market, has institutions, rules, customs, and mores that shape freedom the way a river's banks shape the river. But it would make no sense to say that a river does not run free because it has banks. Without banks, it could not be a river. Without institutions, rules, customs and mores, there can not be politics. The political market has, as most markets do, various frictions, information shortages and costs, barriers to the entry of new competitors, and other imperfections. Still, the American political market is remarkably responsive to public demands.

That's the problem. The political market usually reflects, almost immediately and remarkably faithfully, the desires of the American public. For many years now those desires have come in an incoherent clump that was certain to produce what we now have: fiscal shambles, government paralysis and public surliness.

Americans suffer from—although more serious suffering will be done by coming generations—what psychologists call "cognitive dissonance." They hold in their minds, simultaneously and with equal fervor and sincerity, flatly incompatible ideas and desires. They demand limited government, low taxes—and generous provision of public services that mirror an expanding menu of "rights." Political scientists diagnose the electorate as being ideologically conservative and operationally liberal. When voters describe themselves, Jeffersonian cadences come trippingly from their tongues: That government is best that governs least, and so on. But when speaking about practical measures rather than ideological stances, the voters prove themselves ravenous for government on a scale not even Hamilton could have imagined, let alone countenanced.

Because the public mind is addled, the accurate representation of it through the political market seems zany. It is. So, let us change the terms of competition and the nature of the competitors in the political market by instituting term limits. Term limits are a free choice to change the structure of political choice. Enacting term limits is an exercise of popular sovereignty in order to make a small excision from the sweep of popular sovereignty. It is a decision by the majority to limit, a little bit, pure majority rule.

In the politics of a temperate and orderly society, no principle can be absolute and untrammeled. However, in a republic, one of the most solemn and general principles is that majorities shall rule. The rub is this: Not every majority—not even every majority produced and expressed in conformity with the due processes and civilities of a republic—is wise. Still, the basic republican principle is not that only wise majorities shall rule. Hence much unwisdom must be permitted to become law. Therefore, the test of the craftsmanship of those who frame constitutions is their ability to institutionalize, in ways compatible with majority rule, the probability that majorities will be reasonable. Notice the restrained language: probability, not certainty. This is a moderate aspiration, this pursuit of a healthy "aptitude and tendency."

The unhealthy tendency that today requires constitutional correction is the distortion of government and the demotion of Congress in the regime. That distortion and that demotion have been produced by legislative careerism predicated on constant abuse of the power of the purse. Two centuries ago John Randolph, an often dyspeptic and eventually insane Virginian, was both a representative and a senator. He warned his colleagues against "the most delicious of privileges," that of spending other people's money. The exuberant enjoyment of that privilege is, unfortunately, another American continuity. It has brought the nation to a crisis of confidence about its governance.

No one should be surprised that many people who think federal spending is too high favor term limits as a means of changing the "culture of spending" in Congress. They believe, not unreasonably, that this culture is directly related to the reelection imperatives of career legislators. My position is somewhat different. I agree that such a culture exists on Capitol Hill and is seriously harmful to the nation's health. But I do not believe that a sound reason for advocating term limits—a reason intellectually sound and politically neutral—is that limits would reduce aggregate spending. Limits might not do that. Anyway, a better reason for term limits is that they would conduce to more reasonable spending patterns at whatever level of aggregate spending Congress favors. Term limits might result in spending levels lower than they otherwise would be. However, it is arguable that term limits would not and should not have that effect. Indeed, my hunch is that a Congress reformed by term limits would be more inclined than today's Congress to spend the large sums necessary for long-term national vigor. A reformed Congress would be less inclined to fund so many projects because they are conducive to legislators' electoral successes in the short-term political cycle.

It is possible, and I believe probable, that a reformed Congress would enjoy a reformed relationship with the electorate. A Congress purged of careerism would beget an electorate purged of its virulent cynicism about politicians, a cynicism born of suspicion about politicians' motives. From such a healthier relationship would come a greater willingness of citizens to trust government prudently to dispense the assets they have given up through taxation. This, in turn, would translate into a diminution of the taxaphobia that today is America's strongest—it sometimes seems to be the only strong—political passion.

It is hardly mysterious why in the 1990s taxaphobia is America's most widely shared political passion. Taxaphobia is, at bottom, a judgment on government's competence, a judg-

ment against government's worthiness to be trusted to exercise discretion over citizens' resources. Taxaphobia burgeoned
in the aftermath of the Great Society initiatives that quickly
came to be perceived as having promised much more than they
could deliver; after Vietnam and Watergate called into question not only government's competence but also its good motives; after the oil shocks and the Iranian hostage crisis of the
1970s gave Americans the sense that the government was increasingly impotent when challenged to mitigate the forces
buffeting the nation; after the inflation of the Carter years
radicalized the middle class by convincing its members that
government was benefiting from the inflation it caused—benefiting because inflation imposed a steady, surreptitious tax
increase (this was before Reagan indexed the tax code) by
floating people into higher tax brackets.

Taxaphobia exploded onto the political agenda in June,
1978, when Californians, as is their wont, took lawmaking into
their own hands, passing Proposition 13 to limit property taxes.
It was a dozen years and a straight line from Proposition 13 to
1990 and Proposition 140, imposing term limits on California's
state legislators. In 1990 Californians re-sent to the political
class the message of 1978: We don't trust you.

In the autumn of 1990 Willie Brown, Speaker of the California Assembly, led a ferocious but unavailing fight against
the drive that imposed, by popular initiative, term limits on
him and his colleagues in both houses of that state's legislature.
Seven months later, during a national television interview concerning California's mounting and interlocking crises (fiscal,
educational, infrastructure), Brown said:

> Well, we have literally covered up the sins and the problems
> over the last 12 or 13 years. Most of us were addicted to the idea
> of never raising anybody's taxes so we could get re-elected and
> in the process, the infrastructure went in the toilet, the schools
> just about went out of business or are just about out of business.
> One after another, you're seeing districts go bankrupt.[8]

Brown's theory clearly is that legislative careerism caused in-sufficient public expenditure. If he is right, then it certainly is arguable that term limits, by making it easier for the public to respect legislatures, would bolster the public confidence that must exist before there will be increased tolerance of public expenditures.

In this regard it is noteworthy that even during the re-cession years of 1990 and 1991, voters approved more than 60 percent of state and local bond issues that were on ballots. They approved almost all of the issues that pertained to trans-portation and pollution control.[9] This pattern reflects the po-litical mood: dedicated revenues—those that can not be spent at the discretion of the discredited political class—are apt to be approved by taxpayers who are taxaphobic when asked to put more resources at the disposal of incumbent politicians who are free to spend for incumbency-protection purposes.

The pattern of expenditure produced by legislative career-ism—a pattern politically comprehensible but socially and eco-nomically irrational—leads directly to large deficits. They are the incumbent's best friend because they buy present bene-fits—and votes—by burdening future voters. Deficits, when they are as large and systemic as they have become in the 1990s, reduce to insignificance the government's range of move-ment. The budget becomes increasingly swallowed by entitle-ment programs, interest payments and pork. (Actually, interest payments are, and hence the deficit itself is, a kind of entitlement program—or perhaps pork—for wealthy purchas-ers of Treasury bills.) The paralysis of government means that the pleasure serious people can derive from government ser-vice—the pleasure of getting things done—is less and less at-tainable. So the people who continue to be interested in serving in Congress are apt to be the unserious.

Notice how much the government's parlous fiscal condi-tion, and hence Washington's mental world, has changed in a quarter of a century. Senator Pat Moynihan recalls that for fifteen months beginning in 1969 the Nixon administration, in which he was the president's domestic policy adviser, fiercely debated establishing a guaranteed annual income. The debate concerned practicalities and ethics—but not costs. "The subject of cost," he says, "scarcely arose." Later, Moynihan published a 559-page book on the episode. He devoted just thirty-four lines—lines, not pages—to the subject of costs. Back then "it was simply a given" that "the money could be found" for any defensible idea.[10] A government that operates on that assumption eventually finds itself in a very different situation: No matter how good an idea is, there is no money for it.

When that happens, the politicians to whom ideas are important find congressional service sterile. They look elsewhere for satisfactions suitable to serious people. And Congress becomes, increasingly, a playpen for the unserious. There is, alas, a steady supply of the unserious.

In May, 1992, after Representative Vin Weber, the Minnesota Republican, then thirty-nine, had announced his decision not to run again, he spoke about a kind of person who might be coming to Congress in large numbers in 1993. Weber, speaking with the candor of someone liberated from legislative careerism, said he had been reading the campaign literature of a lot of Republican candidates and had found much of it depressing. It consisted of promises not to cash checks at the House bank that no longer exists, and promises not to eat in the House restaurant or use the House gym or barbershop, and promises to give Capitol Hill parking places to the homeless. What we will have, said Weber, is a lot of out-of-shape, unkempt congressmen with balanced checkbooks. To which one can only say: But, of course. Republican careerists are indistinguishable from Democratic careerists. Of course they do not promise to do anything important. They are clawing their way to Congress not to do something, but to be something: career legislators. To that end they will do almost anything to stay on the safe side of public opinion. But only almost anything. There is, you see, the obnoxious fact that the public wants term limits.

Throughout this century Americans have become steadily better educated (or at least more schooled, which is not the same thing), as well as better informed (or at least offered a richer menu of journalism) and more articulate (or at least more assertive). They certainly have become more skillful at what the First Amendment calls petitioning for redress of grievances. They have become less docile, less deferential, less tolerant of governance that displeases them. The methods of transmuting their grievances into pressures, methods ranging from opinion measurement to direct mail solicitations to lobbying organizations, have imparted fresh saliency to political discussion, have added velocity to political events and have increased the plasticity of America's political agenda.

It is therefore notable, although not at all surprising, that the issue of term limits is a conspicuous exception to the general tendency of the political class to tumble all over itself in its haste to satisfy strong public desires. On the issue of term limits a substantial American majority is adamantly opposed by the vast majority of legislators. Of course there have been, and are, exceptions.

Readers of Robert Caro's biography of Lyndon Johnson have met a man who deserves a wee footnote in the history of the term limitation movement.[11] He was W. (for Wilbert) Lee "Pass the Biscuits, Pappy" O'Daniel, who began his rise in Texas as a radio announcer and flour salesman for Light Crust Flour of Fort Worth. He wrote country and western songs such as "The Boy Who Never Grew Too Old to Comb His Mother's Hair," and he was especially gifted at writing songs in praise of Texas ("Beautiful, Beautiful Texas," "Sons of the Alamo"), even though he began cranking out such songs shortly after he arrived from Kansas. He was often confused about basic Texas facts (such as the difference between the Battle of San Jacinto and the Alamo), but never mind. By 1938 he was selling his own brand of flour and buying Fort Worth real estate (this barefoot boy had a business college degree) and had more listeners than anyone else on Texas radio.

On Palm Sunday, 1938, he told his listeners that a blind man had asked him to run for governor, and he asked his listeners to write to tell him whether or not he should. Write they did, 54,449 of them, and all but three said he should run. The three said he shouldn't because he was too good for the job. On his Mother's Day broadcast he said:

> Good morning, ladies and gentlemen, and hello there, boys and girls. This is Lee O'Daniel speaking. This is Mother's Day from a sentimental standpoint only. Tired, forlorn, disappointed, and destitute Texas mothers several months ago thought they saw Mother's Day breaking in the East—but the golden glint preceding sunrise faded and faded again and again until today perhaps the practical Mother's Day is more obscure than ever before. But from the Texas plains and hills and valleys came a little breeze wafting on its crest more than 54,000 voices of one accord—we want W. Lee O'Daniel for governor of Texas. Why that avalanche of mail? Surely each of every one of you 54,000 folks could not have known that W. Lee O'Daniel is an only living son of one of those tired, forlorn, disappointed, and destitute mothers—a son who had played at that widowed mother's skirts, while during each day and way into the darkness of the nights she washed the dirt and grime from the clothes of the wealthy on an old worn-out washboard—for the paltry pittance of twenty-five cents per day—and that by that honest drudgery she provided corn bread and beans for her children which she had brought back with her from the Valley of the Shadow of Death.[12]

Professional politicians did not take seriously the man who said his only platform was the Ten Commandments. They called him a joke. A few months later they called him Governor.

In 1941 Governor O'Daniel ran for the Senate. He won, beating, among others, Representative Lyndon Johnson. O'Daniel won largely because a lot of people wanted him out of Austin and in Washington, where they thought he could do less harm. But by 1947 his "popularity had been rapidly eroding because of his buffoonery on the Senate floor, and because of reports of his profiteering in Washington real estate."[13]

In 1947, when Congress was debating the Twenty-second Amendment to the Constitution, imposing a two-term limit on presidents, O'Daniel showed that he had an appetite for political Alamos—lonely and losing fights. He proposed limiting all elective officials to a single term of six years. His proposal lost, 82–1.

I have paused to tell the story of "Pappy" O'Daniel even though it may hinder the argument for term limitation. I have done so for two reasons. First, in the let-the-chips-fall-where-they-may spirit of ruthless full disclosure, we who favor term limitation should acknowledge that our side has had, and still has, some supporters who are, shall we say, imperfect exemplars of deliberative democracy. Second, perhaps you have to be, as O'Daniel was, a bit loopy to be able to force the issue of term limits onto the floor of either house of Congress. That 82–1 vote forty-five years ago was the first and, so far, the last time the Senate ever voted on the subject. The full House has never had even one vote on term limitation, which is instructive.

Today poll after poll reveals lopsided majorities, usually of at least 75 percent, in favor of term limits. Can you think of anything else that more than 75 percent of Americans favor but that has never even been a voting issue on the floor of that House chamber outside of which is inscribed the motto, "Here the people govern"? Today politicians who pledge to be "responsive," and who, regarding almost everything else, would not tarry about supplying what more than 75 percent of the public demand, are, for once, slow. More than slow, they are obdurate. They are unwilling even to put term limits before the states' legislatures in a proposed constitutional amendment.

In the summer of 1992 the House Judiciary Committee had custody of such an amendment. And there the amendment languished, securely bottled up by Chairman Jack Brooks, a Texas Democrat then in his fortieth year in the House. Still, some members persevered with an attempt to pry the amendment loose from the Committee's grip by means of a discharge petition. The attempt was doomed but not pointless. Such a petition requires the signatures of a majority of House members, 218. Such petitions rarely succeed. In the last sixty years about five hundred of them have been filed, but only forty-three have succeeded. The last successful one was in 1990. It brought to the floor a proposed constitutional amendment to require balanced budgets. That amendment failed by just seven votes, thereby setting the stage for the showdown over such an amendment in June, 1992, when it failed by nine votes. During that summer, candidates for House seats all across the nation were committing themselves to support term limits. Thus the Congress that convenes in January, 1993, will have many more members eager to, or at least obligated to, sign a discharge petition for a term limits amendment.

Of course the fact that a candidate gives his word does not guarantee that he will keep his word when careerism is at stake. In June, 1992, more than the nine-vote margin of defeat for the balanced budget amendment (the vote was 280 to 153 in favor of it but short of the two-thirds required for constitutional amendments) was provided by a dozen Democrats who did not just say they supported the amendment, they even put their names on it as co-sponsors—and then voted against it.

Balanced budget and term limit amendments are related, for two reasons. Deficit spending is integral to legislative careerism. And both amendments are attempts to improve government's "aptitude and tendency" for reasonableness. In the summer of 1992 a mixture of cringing opportunism and moral seriousness combined (large political events often result from such an alloy of motives) to cause Congress to take seriously, and nearly pass, a balanced budget amendment.

One reason it did not pass is that the routinization of deficit spending on a huge scale is one of the kindest things incumbents have ever done for themselves. There was a time—before 1980—when Republicans excoriated Democrats for adhering to Harry Hopkins's formulation for political prosperity: Tax and tax, spend and spend, elect and elect. Then the Republicans buckled down to the business of coming up with something even more pernicious. They did. It is the system of borrow and borrow, spend and spend, elect and elect. Harry Hopkins's formula involved the distressing unpleasantness of arguing about how the incidence of taxation should fall on society as it consumes the goods and services that government supplies. However, under the "borrow and borrow" formula, the political class gets to duck that politically dangerous debate. It gets to charge the public just 80 cents for every dollar of government services delivered. The rest of the costs are borrowed, and the bill is sent to the future.

That is why what Speaker Tom Foley casually said one day in April, 1992, would have sent shivers down the city of Washington's spine, if it had one. Foley predicted the end of civilization, as that city has known and loved it. He predicted—mistakenly—that Congress would, within a few months, pass a balanced budget amendment. His prediction came as Congress was preparing the fiscal 1993 budget. In it gross interest costs, which in fiscal 1980 were just $74 billion, were projected to be $315 billion. In fiscal 1993 interest—the rental of money—would be the largest single federal expenditure.

Discerning conservatives know that huge deficits make big government cheap for current consumers of its services, thereby reducing resistance to the growth of government. Sentient liberals recognize that huge deficits involve regressive transfer payments: We are transferring $315 billion from taxpayers to buyers of Treasury bills—generally rich individuals and institutions—in America and places like Tokyo and Riyadh.

A balanced budget amendment would serve Congress's institutional interests by requiring the president to propose a balanced budget, something neither Reagan nor Bush has come close to doing. Thus the amendment would end the tiresome presidential posturing—"Only Congress can spend money"—that places on Congress exclusive blame for deficits. In fact, in the states as well as in Washington, executive branches generally determine the level of spending, and legislatures merely modify—and not very much—spending patterns.

Some people predict that a balanced budget amendment would be used as an excuse for large tax increases. That is possible but, given today's taxaphobia, not likely. Other people predict that an amendment would result in cuts in program X, Y or Z. Such predictions are implicit confessions that if Congress were ever made to enforce priorities, then X, Y or Z would be deemed dispensable. When $400 billion deficits are permitted, marginal, even frivolous programs get funded because costs can be shoved onto future generations. Furthermore, as was seen in the argument about public broadcasting, when deficits reach that size, a perverse dynamic takes hold: The size of the deficit becomes a reason for not resisting attempts to make it even bigger. Every program that costs just a few billion dollars (remember Everett Dirksen's celebrated jest: "A billion here, a billion there—pretty soon it adds up to real money") is rationalized on the ground that it does not add appreciably to the existing Mount Everest of debt.

It would be wrong to make support for a constitutional amendment change contingent on guesses about particular short-term policy consequences. A sufficient reason for a bal-

anced budget amendment is to impose, on both the legislative
and executive branches, a regime of constitutionally compelled
choices. It would be an abuse of the Constitution to constitu-
tionalize a particular economic doctrine. It would, for example,
be an abuse to require that taxes be no more than some particular portion of Gross National Product, or that revenues rise
only in some stipulated relation to the growth of the economy.
However, proscribing deficits is different, because deficits are
political and moral events, not merely economic events. A balanced budget amendment would do something of constitutional
significance: It would protect important rights of an unrepre-
sented group, in this case the unborn generations that must
bear the burden of the debts. The amendment would block a
form of confiscation of property—taxation without representation.

The Constitution is fundamental law and should indeed
deal only with fundamental questions. But as Jefferson made
clear in a letter to Madison in 1789, the question of public debt
does implicate fundamental values:

> The question, whether one generation of men has a right to bind
> another . . . is a question of such consequences, as not only to
> merit decision, but place also among the fundamental principles
> of every government. . . . I set out on this ground, which I
> suppose to be self-evident, that the *earth belongs in usufruct to
> the living*; that the dead have neither powers nor rights over
> it. . . . Then, no man can, by *natural right*, oblige the lands he
> occupied, or the persons who succeed him in that occupation, to
> the payment of debts contracted by him. For if he could, he
> might during his own life, eat up the usufruct of the lands for
> several generations to come; and then the lands would belong to
> the dead, and not to the living, which is the reverse of our
> principle. What is true of every member of the society, individ-
> ually, is true of them all collectively. . . . Turn this subject in
> your mind, my dear Sir, and particularly as to the power of

contracting debts, and develop it with that cogent logic which is
so peculiarly yours. . . . At first blush it may be laughed at, as
the dream of a theorist; but examination will prove it to be solid
and salutary. It would furnish matter for a fine preamble to our
first law for appropriating the public revenue. . . . No nation
can make a declaration against the validity of long-contracted
debts, so disinterestedly as we, since we do not owe a shilling
which will not be paid, principal and interest, by the measures
you have taken, within the time of our own lives.[14] [Emphasis in
original]

The ethics of public finance and long-term public investment
are more complicated and less "self-evident" than Jefferson
thought. He did not do justice, at least in that letter, to the
organic nature of society and its continuous identity through
the seamless flow of the generations. Still, his moral instinct is
clearly sound regarding an activity as grossly and, yes, self-
evidently immoral as the current scale of deficit spending for
the pleasure of the living and the convenience of the incumbent
politicians.

But even though a balanced budget amendment would now
be wise, ratifying it would not be a pleasant task for sensible
people. Such people have a proper disinclination to alter the
nation's fundamental law. One reason for such a disinclination
is that every time the Constitution is amended, resistance to
further amendments is diminished. We do not want to become
promiscuous amenders. Let the French be the ones with a
constitution that libraries file with the periodicals. However,
because there are today parallel movements pressing for balanced budget and term limitation amendments—movements
reinforcing one another—it is important to note this: If we
already had term limits, we would be much less likely to need,
or to see such pressure for, a balanced budget amendment.

Consider one of the most sophisticated arguments for a
balanced budget amendment, the argument made by William

A. Niskanen.[15] Between his years teaching economics at Berkeley and UCLA, and his current service as head of the Cato Institute in Washington, Niskanen was a member of President Reagan's Council of Economic Advisers (1981–85). So his theory has been shaped by the searing experience of watching Washington's practices. Also, his argument derives much of its considerable power from his knowledge of the pedigrees of the issues and arguments involved. He knows that they divided Jefferson and Madison from Hamilton, and hence are part of a fault line running through much of American history.

Niskanen begins his justification of a balanced budget amendment by noting that for the first fourteen decades of this Republic—until the New Deal—the general growth of government and federal budget discipline were regulated by two understandings. One was a particular conception of the Constitution, the other was a particular idea of fiscal morality. The first understanding was that spending was constitutional only when done in the exercise of powers specifically enumerated under Article I, Section 8 of the Constitution, the provisions concerning Congress's powers. (Readers will note that we are here revisiting an issue touched on in Chapter 1, concerning Thomas Jefferson and the road bill and Representative Patricia Schroeder and midnight basketball.) The second understanding, which Niskanen calls an "informal rule," was that government could properly borrow only during recessions and wars. Niskanen argues that the coming of the New Deal meant the final passing of the old order, which he calls "the fiscal constitution."

Under the old order Congress could spend pursuant to "only 18 rather narrowly defined powers, only a few of which—such as the powers to 'establish Post Offices and post roads, raise and support Armies, and to provide and maintain a Navy'—involve the potential for substantial expenditures."[16] Niskanen's view of constitutional law may strike many readers

as of merely antiquarian interest. History has long since settled the constitutional question in the Hamiltonians' favor by
making the language of Section 8's first clause vastly elastic
and hence completely permissive. That language, which gives
Congress the power to act for "the general welfare," has become a loophole large enough for Leviathan to stride through.
Leviathan has done so.

And, truth be told, even Niskanen's heroes, Jefferson and
Madison, contributed to this. In December, 1816, Representative John C. Calhoun, soon to become the foremost paladin of
states' rights and bitter foe of federal supremacy, introduced a
bill for "internal improvements"—roads and canals, princi-
pally—to be paid for by the federal government. Calhoun knew
that wealthy states, such as New York, with its Erie and
Champlain Canals, could finance their own improvements.
Without federal help, the South would stagnate. However,
President Madison, although a Virginian, would have none of
it. He wrote:

> I am not unaware of the great importance of roads and canals
> and the improved navigation of water courses, and that a power
> in the National Legislature to provide for them might be exer-
> cised with signal advantage to the general prosperity. But see-
> ing that such a power is not expressly given by the Constitution,
> and believing that it cannot be deduced from any part of it
> without an inadmissable latitude of construction and a reliance
> on insufficient precedents . . . .[17]

This veto message, sent to Congress on March 3, 1817, was
Madison's last official act as president. It was more obviously
principled than wise. History judges it harshly, as to both its
consequences and its constitutional premises. As the historian
Herbert Agar wrote, "One cannot help feeling that he was
performing an act of purification, rather than of statesmanship,
that he was burning a little incense at the altar of the lost

cause."[18] Certainly the cause—a federal government limited by strict construction of the Constitution's enumerated powers—was well on the way to being lost, and Madison had been an early participant in the losing of it. He had been Secretary of State when President Jefferson—another devotee of strict construction of those enumerated powers—leapt to accomplish the Louisiana Purchase, for which there was not a shred of power "expressly given by the Constitution." And Madison was in Jefferson's Cabinet when the Embargo Act and its enforcing legislation (which hurt the South as much as Calhoun's bill would have helped it) made a mockery of Madison's and Jefferson's doctrine of enumerated powers. Still, Madison vetoed Calhoun's bill and the South was shoved a little further in the direction of retarded development and increased alienation.

And the war came. With it came the rise in Washington of the strong, energetic, modern government that has now provoked many thoughtful people like Niskanen to favor a balanced budget amendment.

However, the power of Niskanen's argument does not depend on acceptance of his interpretation of Article I, Section 8, Clause 1. Neither does it depend on his belief that a constitutional (actually, an anticonstitutional) revolution was effected in 1936 when the Supreme Court stated that "the power of Congress to authorize expenditure of public moneys for public purposes is not limited by the direct grants of legislative power found in the Constitution."[19] Niskanen acutely notes that as late as the Eisenhower administration there was still at least rhetorical deference to the doctrine of enumerated powers. For example, the legislation that led to the Interstate Highway System was titled the National Defense Highway Transportation Act (1954). And the federal government's first major education program, providing loans for college students, was called the National Defense Education Act (1958). But, says Niskanen, by the time of the Johnson administration the doctrine of enumerated powers "no longer commanded even rhetorical deference."

What is indisputable is the fact that in the last half-century, because of changed political and cultural as well as constitutional ideas, the federal government has become hyperactive and has permeated American life. Niskanen says a balanced budget amendment would restore the constitutional values trampled since the overthrow of the strict construction of Congress's enumerated powers. The Constitution's substantive limits on the purposes for which Congress may spend, and the old political culture's "informal rule" about borrowing, have both been abandoned. Therefore, Niskanen says, a balanced budget amendment, imposing more constraining rules on the voting that affects budget totals, is a conservative means to achieve a traditional end: limited government.

There are two basic ways to limit a government that is based on popular sovereignty. One is by a constitution that authorizes government to exercise its powers by simple majority rule but enumerates only a narrow range of powers. The other way is to grant government a broad range of purposes, and all the powers necessary thereto, but to require supermajorities for particularly important decisions. Niskanen believes that because we have abandoned strict construction of enumerated powers, the correct road back to the constitutional goal of limited government is an amendment requiring votes of two-thirds of the membership of both houses of Congress to raise the debt ceiling or to impose a new tax or raise an existing one.

The dissolution of political, cultural and constitutional restraints on Congress obviously has served the interests of legislative careerists. They have a permanent, inherent vocational incentive to borrow to finance current expenditures. Niskanen and I agree about that but have opposite positions regarding balanced budget and term limitation amendments. I believe that a balanced budget amendment is a dubious idea whose time, alas, has come. And it has come because term limitation, a good idea, has not yet come. Niskanen believes that a balanced budget amendment is a shining reaffirmation and restoration of the original "fiscal constitution" that was overthrown by the overthrow of the strict construction of the enumerated powers of Congress. He believes that if the proper doctrine of enumerated powers were still adhered to, there would be far less scope for legislators to use the modern state to perpetuate their careers. Therefore, term limitation would be unnecessary.

Perhaps. His position is defensible. It also is of mainly academic interest, because the doctrine of enumerated powers is as dead as a doornail. The modern state is a sprawling, palpitating fact, and here to stay. A balanced budget amendment may moderate its growth somewhat but will not cause it to stop growing, let alone to contract. (Bet on the survival, whatever the Constitution requires, of the honey and peanut and wool subsidies.) So although a balanced budget amendment can be justified sufficiently on moral and prudential grounds, it would not by itself sufficiently inhibit the practice of bending modern government to the service of careerism. For that, term limitation is required.

∽　∾

Wherever one looks, one finds senators and representatives testifying, consciously or unwittingly, to the value of term limits, or at least to the values that term limits would serve. For example, before Howard Baker of Tennessee retired from the Senate at the end of his third term in 1984, he became embroiled in one of the then-recurring spats about congressional pay. Bone-weary of this particular unpleasantness and dismayed by the trajectory of life in the national legislature,

Baker proposed that senators be paid just $36,000, in seven monthly installments, January through July. If the Senate loiters longer, he said, let senators receive only a small per diem. (Similar thoughts have occurred in another political culture. "One must not become too obsessed with Westminster. We used to run an empire with a parliament that sat for five months of the year, rising as the grouse season started and not coming back until the pheasants had been finished off.")[20] Baker's proposal, the act of a good but exasperated senator, was sincerely made. Baker had long said that no one should be a professional legislator. Legislators, he said, should be farmers, merchants, teachers, mechanics, lawyers. The citizen-legislator should be a legislator secondarily and temporarily. Otherwise a legislator will lose contact with life as it is lived by those he or she is supposed to represent. George McGovern did.

For many years McGovern was one of Senator Baker's colleagues. When, in 1981, McGovern left the Senate and joined the ranks of the represented, he had an epiphany. He had been a veteran of government (two terms in the House and two years as Director of Food for Peace) before he served eighteen years in the Senate. After he was defeated in 1980, his various retirement activities included operating—briefly—a hotel in Connecticut. That business venture failed. No disgrace attaches to such failure. The attrition rate among new small businesses is always high. What made McGovern's experience notable was what he said about it: "I wish that someone had told me about the problems of running a business. I have to pay taxes, meet a payroll—I wish I had had a better sense of what it took to do that when I was in Washington."[21]

Many Americans wish that a lot of legislators had a better sense of American life, and particularly of what it is like to be on the receiving end of the high-minded laws and regulations that gush like a cataract from Washington. Term limits, guaranteeing a steady rotation of offices, would help. They would make it impossible for anyone to come to Congress counting on a long career there. Therefore term limits would increase the likelihood that people would come to Congress from established careers, with significant experience in the private sector. Furthermore, term limits would increase the likelihood that people who come to Congress would anticipate returning to careers in the private sector and therefore would, as they legislate, think about what it is like to live under the laws they make.

In March, 1992, Representative John Paul Hammerschmidt, an Arkansas Republican, announced that he would not seek reelection to a seat he had held, usually without serious challenge, since 1966. (Once, in 1974, he had to exert himself to spank a whippersnapper fresh from Yale Law School: Bill Clinton.) Hammerschmidt, seventy years old in May, 1992, said, "I'd just like a little time in the other world." Such plain language expressed a thought that had become oppressive to many members of Congress and to scores of millions of Americans, including those Bay Area commuters who in 1991 were being warned by billboards about the sinister congressional "they." The thought—and the truth—is that elective office has become another world, inhabited by professionals preoccupied with staying in it. And it is no longer as much fun as it once was.

When, in 1952, the young Barry Goldwater allowed himself to be enticed into politics, he quipped, "It ain't for life and it might be fun." A healthy spirit, that. What is not healthy is that more and more people bring to politics a grim, desperate craving for careers in Congress—this at a time when life in Congress has become, according to much testimony, dreary. In fact, we are today in the presence of a large and dismal paradox: The paralysis of government and the demoralization of those responsible for governing intensify legislative careerism.

It is difficult to determine just when and why the federal government began to grind to something like a stall. Some people say the turning point was the 1966 congressional elections. The 1964 anti-Goldwater landslide had shattered the congressional coalition of Republicans and conservative Democrats that prevented liberal presidents from exercising hegemony over the federal government. For two years, 1965 and 1966, years that Lyndon Johnson made the most of, there was a liberal legislating majority. It was the first such majority since 1938, when the liberal majority put in place by the 1932 election was shattered by the reaction against the New Deal radicalism symbolized by FDR's plan to "pack" the Supreme Court.

Or perhaps the paralysis of government began to set in in 1973, with the oil shocks that presaged an era of slow growth—of the economy and of government revenues. Or perhaps the paralysis began with—indeed, was supposed to begin with—the Reagan tax cuts, which (so goes the theory) were designed to produce paralyzing deficits.

Whatever.

In any case, for some while now government has seemed impotent, for many reasons, three of which are especially important. One is that government has not satisfactorily performed its most fundamental functions of guaranteeing domestic tranquility and providing the rudimentary prerequisites for the general welfare. Americans want to assume that their children can walk down safe streets to efficient schools. They can not assume that. A second reason government now seems impotent is its fiscal condition. Without entering the hot debate about the assignment of blame, the indisputable fact is that the government is out of money. Which is to say, it is "out of money" in the Washington way: Its supply of money is limited by its willingness and ability to borrow. A third reason for the government's perceived paralysis is intellectual. Many of

America's most serious problems, such as the soaring cost and maldistribution of health care and the social regression of the urban underclass, are intractable simply because we do not understand them and do not know what to do next.

Now, the paradox about governmental paralysis is this: As government has sunk into stasis, the job satisfactions of elective office have shrunk. But as a result of that shrinkage, the energies of competitive political people, energies now finding scant outlet in governance, are being channeled into the business of staying in the business, no matter how sterile the job has become. Careerism has become a career in itself, an endless season of running for reelection. Frantic fundraising is perpetual. The legislative calendar is cluttered with measures that are brought to the floor only to get opponents to vote for or against this or that provision, all for the purpose of building a record useful in negative campaigning, the most effective form of campaigning in an era of cynicism about impotent government and political careerism.

Government paralysis, which is partly produced by legislative careerism and is conducive to such careerism, produces, over time, a larger and larger class of officeholders who are content to be holders of an office. For such a person, happiness, and even a sense of identity, depend on retaining an iron hold on office. Defeat means not just oblivion but a kind of annihilation. Thus such a person will bring to the business of seeking reelection the energy that desperation generates.

Does "annihilation" seem too strong? In April, 1992, when Representative Vin Weber, the Minnesota Republican, announced his decision not to seek reelection, his decision was influenced by political difficulties—hardly insurmountable— arising from his overdrafts at the House bank. But Weber, one of Congress's most admired young members, was moved primarily by other considerations, including the fact that he could conceive of other things to do with his life. "A lot of my colleagues worrying about defeat say they can't possibly imagine doing anything else."[22]

It has become a bleak axiom of contemporary politics: The white-hot, single-minded, whole-hearted devotion to politics that brings success in election after election should be a disqualification from politics. It has often been said (first, I believe, by the columnist David Broder) that anyone who will put himself or herself through the years of agonies and indignities associated with winning a presidential nomination is obviously the kind of obsessive and imbalanced person who should be kept a long distance from presidential power. Certainly any politician who "can't possibly imagine doing anything else" besides politics should be required to do something else.

This brings us to another paradox, this one double-edged. People who cling to congressional seats in this current season of despair prove by their clinging that they are deriving satisfaction from the wrong sorts of things. And many of the people now deciding voluntarily to leave the national legislature prove by their decisions that they are the kind of people we might wish would stay.

One such is Representative Ray McGrath, a New York Republican from Long Island. When in June, 1992, McGrath, then fifty, became the eleventh member of the thirty-six member Ways and Means Committee to decide against seeking re-election, he said: "About six weeks ago, after a series of town meetings, I sat in a plane on the runway at La Guardia Airport for three hours while my son's first birthday party went on without me. . . . I have decided that I would rather be at my sons' Little League games than throwing out the first ball in ten other communities."[23]

Earlier, in April, 1992, Senator Tim Wirth, a Colorado Democrat, was in his eighteenth year in Washington, having served twelve years in the House and all but ten months of the sixth year of a Senate term. Then he announced his decision not to seek a second term. He gave a number of reasons for the decision.[24] One was the nation's "attention-deficit," which Wirth said was caused, in part, by sensation-seeking and trivializing journalism that is failing to fulfill its role as "the crucial intermediary between government and the governed." A second reason Wirth gave was dissatisfaction with the working of the Senate. He found the Senate just as petty and partisan and just as much in the grip of pandemic careerism as the House had been when he was there. This second reason was directly related to a third. It was the paralyzing power—a negative and barren power to block change, not a creative power—of intense and well-financed single-issue interests. Wirth was leaving the Senate because he had become convinced he could contribute more to America's betterment, and could find more fulfillment, somewhere other than in the national government.

At the end of the press conference at which Wirth announced his decision not to seek a second term, he was approached by a reporter who asked "if I was sick." This was, Wirth thought, an encoded inquiry about the possibility that he had AIDS. Another journalist "wanted to know—again with the microphones off—whether a 'financial scandal' was about to break over my head."[25] These two questions came from journalists in the grip of crackpot realism, journalists so dogmatically skeptical that they can not see a simple truth even when it is being announced in clear language. Such journalists are so vain about their monopoly of virtue and their role as auditors of public hygiene that they assume that the "real" story is always hidden, always "behind" what people say, always something secret and shameful. Wirth's ostensibly "tough-minded" and "worldly" questioners (as they no doubt think of themselves) revealed the soft-headed parochialism of Washington in the age of careerism among professional politicians. Many journalists considered Wirth's words unconvincing, even unintelligible. Those journalists share the values and world view of the professional politicians they cover. For these journalists, as for the political class they so much resemble, being in Washington, not getting anything particular accomplished in Washington, is the point of life. To these journalists, Wirth's ability—no, his eagerness—to walk away from this circumscribed world was, strictly speaking, incredible.

However, there are wisps of evidence that healthier attitudes are sprouting here and there, like tufts of grass growing in cracks in concrete. It is devoutly to be hoped, if not confidently predicted, that historians will someday say that an epochal change in American politics began not with the many retirements announced in 1992 but with one resignation effected in June, 1991. Representative Bill Gray of Philadelphia, third-ranking Democratic leader in the House and the highest ranking black in the history of the House, might have become Speaker, in time. And he had time. He was just fifty years old in the summer of 1991. But there were, he thought, better uses for his time. He resigned to become head of the United Negro College Fund.

Washington—or, more precisely, the city's predominantly white political and media sliver—was uncomprehending and aghast. Many liberals were particularly dismayed by this instance of self-determination by a black man.

Gray's decision, which gestated for two years, involved a mix of motives. True, he can make more money as a private citizen (and he has a handicapped child for whose future he must provide). However, Gray also knows that not just political empowerment but social development—particularly enlargement of the black middle class—is the crucial challenge for the black community. In this, Congress can be at most marginally important. Given the surge of their enrollments—up 17 percent in four years, twice the college average nationally— the forty-one colleges served by the UNCF may educate close to 1 million students in the next decade. The students range

from needy inner-city and rural blacks, who for cultural reasons do not test well but who are college material, to upper-
middle-class blacks seeking an intensely black experience—the
Huxtable children from *The Bill Cosby Show*. Gray, a preacher
who values pastoral duties more than political duties, is a
former teacher whose father was president of two black colleges. His career change, as an affirmation of fresh starts and
of education, is quintessentially American.

So, too, was his decision to stride purposefully away from
the prospect of a lifetime in national politics. His retirement
from the House displayed an admirable sense of proportion
about the importance of politics, and of himself. His decision
proclaimed that although politics is important, it is not all-
important. And his decision made clear that he did not have
delusions of indispensability. From Philadelphia, as from the
rest of the American population, will come other people quite
capable of conducting the people's business. We can count on
that, because America's population is (in the late Eric Hoffer's
splendid phrase) lumpy with talent.

Lumpy enough that the nation need not tremble at the
prospect of political turbulence producing unusually high rates
of turnover in the membership of Congress. As this is being
written, in the summer of 1992, Washington is expecting—
queasily expecting—the 1992 elections to produce as many as
120 new members of the House. That would be the largest
freshman class in six decades, since the 165 freshmen elected in
1932. The wave of retirements that washed through Congress
prior to the 1992 elections, and perhaps a significant number of
defeats of incumbents in the elections (do not bet much on
this), may temporarily drain some of the steam from the term
limits movement. Some people may conclude that the era of
careerism and invincible incumbents has passed, permanently,
and therefore formal limits are unnecessary. Such a conclusion
would be mistaken, for several reasons.

First, the fundamental factors that underlie the power of incumbents to protect their incumbency are unchanged and, given elemental political realities, are not about to be significantly changed in the foreseeable future. Those factors include the many subsidizing and regulating activities of modern government, activities that enable incumbents to curry favor with constituents and cause constituents to place high value on an incumbent's seniority.

Second, the concatenation of events and circumstances that produced 1992's unusually large number of departures from Congress prior to the 1992 elections was peculiar and is not apt to be repeated soon or often. Those events and circumstances included redistricting that forced some incumbents to run in substantially new districts and even to run against other incumbents; the longest recession since the Depression; and the House bank debacle (and, by the way, the cocaine-selling in the House post office), which came after scandals that caused the resignations of a Speaker (Jim Wright) and a Democratic Whip (Tony Coelho).

And there was one more thing, a provision in the law that made 1992 the last year in which members could retire and convert to private use money raised for campaign spending. As of July, 1992, thirty-nine retiring members were eligible to pocket, collectively $10.2 million, or an average of $260,000 apiece.[26] At least twenty-eight of the thirty-nine said they planned to donate the money to their parties or to charities. In the past, some members who made such pledges did not fulfill them. (A question: How many years does it take the average American family to save $260,000? A clue: In 1989 the median American approaching retirement age had assets—including a house—worth $91,000; adding the capitalized value of pension and Social Security entitlements, the total rose to around $200,000.)[27]

We can not count on and should not wish for regular recurrences of such disagreeable episodes to churn Congress's membership. And if churning is good, what is bad about making it regular, systematic and orderly? Furthermore, the fact that many opponents of term limits can placidly anticipate such a substantial turnover of Congress's membership undercuts one familiar argument against term limits. The argument is that we dare not drain the reservoir of expertise and institutional memory lest . . . but wait.

Lest what, precisely? Lest we have bad government? We have got bad government by the bushel. Of course things can always be made worse. But how probable is it that a Congress operating under term limits will do worse than the Congress that has collaborated with the production of $400 billion deficits, the savings and loan debacle, and many other policy wrecks, and has driven away in despair many of its best members?

Consider a baseball analogy. In 1988 the Baltimore Orioles (on whose board of directors I sit) were dreadful. They were somewhat like today's Congress—expensive and incompetent. They lost their first twenty-one games, a record, and went on to lose a total of 107. After the season the Orioles' management had a thought: Hey, we can lose 107 games with inexpensive rookies. The 1989 Orioles were major league baseball's youngest team and had the smallest payroll and came within a few October pitches in Toronto of winning the American League East.

Increasingly, the principal argument against term limits turns out to be a somewhat serpentine assertion. It is that limits would be both harmful and redundant—harmful because rotation depletes the reservoir of wisdom, and redundant because there already is a healthily high amount of rotation. Tom Foley, the Speaker of the House of Representatives, arrived on Capitol Hill (actually arrived there for a second time; he had previously been an aide to Senator Henry Jackson) in 1965. He was part of the bumper crop of new congressmen produced by the anti-Goldwater tide. By 1992 Foley was fond—rather too fond—of noting that 93 percent of the members of the House had arrived since he did, that 81 percent had arrived since the thunderous post-Watergate election of 1974, and that 55 percent had come since Reagan rode into town in 1981.[28] However, a more pertinent number is this: Of the 1,692 congressmen who have sat since 1955, when Democratic control of the House began, 35.7 percent of the members, or 604 congressmen, have served seven terms or more. Of the current members of the 102d Congress (1991–92), 37.5 percent are already in at least their seventh term.[29] In the last four elections (1984–90) the turnover in the House due to death, retirement or—much the least important cause—defeat averaged about 10 percent per election.

Much of the turnover comes not from the defeat of incumbents in competitive elections but from the voluntary departure of members who despair of enjoying useful service in a Congress geared to the service of careerism. The leadership of Congress—the ruling class that runs the committees and subcommittees that are the primary instruments for self-promotion—has not been changed nearly as much as Foley's numbers lead people to believe. Systematic changing by term limits would make serious service possible more quickly than it now is. Hence term limits would make Congress more attractive to serious people. In 1991 the economists W. Robert Reed of the University of Oklahoma and D. Eric Schansberg of Indiana University at New Albany argued that term limitations, while eliminating the possibility of long careers, would increase access to leadership positions. Representatives would be eligible for leadership positions much sooner than at present. "Currently," they said, "it takes sixteen years to reach the 80th percentile of seniority." On the basis of certain assumptions about how many members serving under term limitations will choose to serve the maximum permissible number of terms, and how many will die or be defeated, Reed and Schansberg calculated that under a six-term limit the time required to reach the 80th percentile would be cut in half, to eight years.[30]

Some opponents of term limits say that limits are a recipe for institutionalizing ignorance. They say that if all congressional careers are short, no one will have time to master the subtleties and mysteries of the government's vast and increasing penetration of society, a penetration carried out by subsidies, taxation and regulation. But that argument tends to turn around and bite its authors, as follows: If government now is so omnipresent (because it strives to be omniprovident) and so arcane that it makes a permanent legislative class indispensable, that is less an argument in favor of such a class than it is an argument against that kind of government. It is an argument for pruning the government's claims to omnicompetence. It is an argument for curtailing government's intrusiveness at least enough so that the supervision of the government can be entrusted to the oversight of intelligent lay people. Or amateurs. Sometimes called citizens.

Critics of term limitation worry that compulsory rotation of offices will mean that a substantial number of representatives and senators will always be looking ahead to their next employment. This, say the critics, means, at best, that these legislators will be distracted from the public business, and it may mean that they will be corrupted by the temptation to use their last years in power to ingratiate themselves with potential employers. Both of these possibilities are, well, possible. But the critics must confront a question: Would such corruption be worse—morally more reprehensible, and more injurious to the public weal—than legislative careerism has proved to be? Careerism, after all, is the legislator's constant surrender—with an easy conscience—to the temptation to use every year in power to ingratiate himself with all the factions useful to his permanent incumbency.

Also, people who would come to Congress under term limits would be less susceptible than cynics think to the temptation to misuse their congressional service to court future employers. After all, people who will choose to spend a necessarily limited span of time in Congress are apt to come from serious careers and will want to return to them. Furthermore, the political incentive for private interests to hire politically influential people from the ranks of ex-congressmen will be radically reduced by the term limits that will swell those ranks. Think about it. One reason ex-legislators are hired by private interests today is to take advantage of their relationships with ex-colleagues who remain in Congress. But term limits will guarantee that those relationships are short-lived. Those ex-colleagues will soon be ex-congressmen.

Would term limits deplete the pool of talent from which we draw presidents? History, which is all we have to go by, says otherwise. Presidents are rarely launched from long legislative careers. How many people have become president after serving twelve or more consecutive years in the House or the Senate? Just three, and two became president by accident. The three are James Polk, Lyndon Johnson and Gerald Ford.

Unquestionably term limits would substantially increase the number of competitive congressional races. It is highly probable that this would lead to increased rates of voting. People are apt to vote at the end of campaigns that they have been talking and arguing about. They are more apt to talk and argue about campaigns when the outcomes are in doubt. Every four years the presidency provides the electorate with an election to argue about. Congress could be a much more prolific producer of wholesome arguments. Every four years Congress offers voters 936 elections—two elections of the 435 members of the House and elections of two-thirds of the one hundred senators. Term limits, by reducing the number of incumbents running, would increase the number of competitive races and would thereby enliven the nation's civic conversation.

Nevertheless, critics of term limits are especially numerous among political scientists. Mark Petracca, in the role of an anthropologist studying a tribe of which he is a member,[31] notes that his fellow political scientists often couch their opposition to term limits in shrill language, and their arguments often lack the circumspection that should characterize scholarly disputation. He thinks there are six reasons for this peculiarly intense opposition.

First, political scientists have been involved, as advisers and advocates, in promoting the professionalization of state legislatures. Long legislative careers are ingredients of that professionalization. Second, the theory of democracy adopted by mainstream political scientists clashes with the classical republican ideals espoused by many advocates of term limits. Since World War II many democratic theorists have stressed stability and efficiency rather than participation and the development of civic virtue as the primary criteria for judging the success of democracy. Third, most political scientists are skeptical about term limits because most voters are not. This is not necessarily a mistake by the political scientists. They know much about the dynamics of public opinion and therefore they know that folly often is popular. But it is a bit dogmatic to insist, as some intellectuals are inclined to do, that only folly can enjoy the support of more than 75 percent of the people. Fourth, a theme of modern political science has been the need to conserve leadership, a resource that is scarce relative to the public's need to be led. (Remember the third reason.) Political scientists believe that the public support for term limits involves, simultaneously, excessive optimism and excessive pessimism. That is, supporters of term limits supposedly believe that potentially high-caliber leaders are more plentiful than they actually are. And supporters of term limits also believe that today's leadership class is worse than it is.

Furthermore, many political scientists regard term limits as an attack on their status as professionals. The assumption that political knowledge is cumulative and that there can be a science of politics leads political scientists to put a premium on experience, longevity, specialization and experts. And it leads political scientists to dismay about "amateurs." Finally, plain partisanship explains some of the opposition of political scientists to term limits. Their profession is more liberal than the national political culture. Their profession partakes of the general academic culture. And political scientists have a vocational inclination to think of government as a comprehensible, manageable instrument. That belief is—or until recently was— characteristic of contemporary liberalism.

The academic culture, which is inhospitable to term limits, is an important tone-setting portion of what Irving Kristol calls "the new class."[32] It consists of people, often well-schooled and upper-middle-class, who have a keen desire for political power. They also have a firm conviction that they are especially qualified to exercise power in the national interest, which they are especially qualified to define. This class practices "supply-side politics." Their political entrepreneurship creates a demand for the programs they supply. These people produce government services, which then generate a demand for the defense and enlargement of the services. This demand becomes incarnate in permanent interest groups. And, says Kristol, because the intervention of government in society "involves large numbers of accomplices—sometimes whole professions or institutions—it creates a substantial political base for itself."[33] Lawyers, lobbyists and consultants who specialize in dealing with legislatures, regulatory agencies, bureaucracies and public opinion management are in professions that expand as government expands. So there is a symbiotic and mutually aggrandizing relationship between government and the interest groups that government's activities generate.

The professionalization of politics by a class of career legislators inclines a society such as ours toward a particular notion of social health. Such a society comes to measure its health in terms of governmental activity. It particularly measures social health in terms of the scope and inclusiveness of government entitlements and other benefits. Not surprisingly, public officials are apt to define the public good with reference to what they dispense. Doing so suits the professional interest of the professionals, and it also reflects the socialization of them by long service in the dispensing institutions. This is not to say the professionals are cynical. On the contrary, it is their ingenuousness that is dismaying.

The fact that the professionalization of politics has encouraged a notion of social health more congenial to liberals than to conservatives, is another reason why term limitation, an antidote to professionalization, is often characterized as a conservative measure. And, alas, many people advocating term limits do so because they think limits will serve the immediate political advantage of the Republican Party. They expect term limits to produce, quickly, a decline in the number of Democrats in Congress. That expectation is at best dubious and probably is wrong. And whether or not the people who have that expectation are correct, they are bringing the term limitation movement into disrepute. Their argument for term limits is intellectually trivial and violates the morality that should control consideration of constitutional amendments.

Now, term limitation is the right thing to do even if some supporters of term limits have unworthy reasons for wanting to do it. In T. S. Eliot's "Murder in the Cathedral," a play about the assassination of Thomas Becket, Thomas says:

The last temptation is the greatest treason:
To do the right thing for the wrong reason.[34]

That ethic is too fastidious for the untidy world of politics. It is
particularly inapposite for the politics of our large, complex democracy. Here decisions are made by coalitions, and therefore
necessarily reflect mixed motives. Any reform movement is apt
to include people with different motives, some more worthy and
reasonable than others. There are apt to be unreasonable and
unworthy components even of coalitions supporting the most
admirable reforms. In the movements that advanced abolition
of slavery, trust-busting and repeal of prohibition, the altruism
of individuals mingled with the self-interest of factions, and
lofty theory was tangled with low passions. Thus it should come
as no surprise that the movement for term limits contains dis-
cordant voices. Any serious political movement, and certainly
any movement as large as one must be to effect constitutional
change, will be a composite of factions.

The faction that today advocates term limits simply in the
hope of wresting control of Congress from Democrats is apt to
be disappointed. One can, of course, understand why this faction feels aggrieved and impatient. The 1992 House elections
will be the thirtieth since the Democrats' almost unbroken domination of the House began in 1930. Since then the Republicans
have wrested control of the House only twice, and for only two
years each time (1947–49, 1953–55).[35] In that sixty-two-year
period, party control of the British House of Commons has
changed seven times. When the 102d Congress convened in
January, 1991, it had six members—Roemer of Indiana, Nus-
sle of Iowa, Swett of New Hampshire, Andrews of New Jersey, Santorum of Pennsylvania and Molinari of New York—
who were not even born when the Republicans last had a House
majority. That fact may have stirred melancholy thoughts in
two senior Republican members.

Robert Michel of Peoria, Illinois, and William Broomfield of Lake Orion, Michigan, were born a year apart (Michel in March, 1923, Broomfield in April, 1922) and arrived in Washington together as young freshmen congressmen in January, 1957. They were joining the Republican minority just two years after the Republicans had lost the majority status they had enjoyed for just two years, 1953–55. In 1957 Michel and Broomfield may well have thought: Not to worry. Republicans also had a majority 1947–49. So, in the normal course of things, our day will come again. They did not know that what they considered the normal course of things—pendular swings of the parties' fortunes—was not going to be the norm again for a very long time. In 1992, as Michel and Broomfield each completed their eighteenth terms, they were co-holders of a record: In the entire history of the Republic, no one else had served so long in Congress without ever being in the majority.[36] In 1993 Michel will have the record to himself. In 1992, Broomfield decided to call it quits.

Still, it can not be said too often: The fact that Republican exasperation is understandable does not dignify exasperation as a reason for enacting a constitutional amendment limiting congressional terms. Besides, it is unrealistic of Republicans to think that term limitations will solve their competitive problems. True, term limits will produce a steady supply of open seats—those not sought by incumbents. But Republican problems involve more than the incumbency advantages of Democrats.

Those advantages are, of course, substantial. Anyone who has read to this point in this book knows the most important advantage. It is modern government itself, with all its subsidizing and regulating powers. However, Norman Ornstein, a subtle and sympathetic student of Congress (and a vigorous opponent of term limits), rightly argues that the results of open seat elections strongly suggest that Republicans can not reasonably ascribe their long run of losses to the advantages enjoyed by Democratic incumbents. Since the 1954 election, which began the Democrats' long reign in the House, Republicans have won seventy-seven open elections for seats last held by Democrats. But in the same period Democrats have won 107 open seats last held by Republicans. So since 1954, Democrats have benefited from 58 percent of the total party turnovers in open seats.[37]

Furthermore, if incumbents' advantages were the only explanation for the Democrats' long domination of the House, Republicans should have prospered in special elections for seats that became open between election cycles, due to members' deaths or resignations. But in the 165 special elections from 1954 through 1991, Republicans have had a net gain of just one seat. Since the election of Ronald Reagan in 1980—since, that is, the moment when conservatives said that their hour had come 'round at last—there have been forty-two special elections, and Republicans have made a net gain of only one seat.

Republican anemia in congressional elections—anemia relative to Republican strength in presidential elections—is partly a consequence of the caliber of Republican candidates. And that caliber is in part a consequence of Republican successes in presidential elections. Ornstein rightly notes several things that have handicapped Republicans in their attempts to recruit high-caliber candidates. One is a vicious cycle: "Them that has, gets." The party that has a majority in Congress gets to offer enticements to potential candidates that are beyond the reach of the minority party—committee assignments, extra staff and other advantages. Second, the partisan culture favors Democrats. As Ornstein says, Democrats and Republicans tend to have different definitions of desirable careers and professional success. For the Republicans' "best and brightest, the careers of choice are business, commerce, or the professions. Politics, especially in Washington, is not high on the list. For Democrats, a career in politics or government is much more highly prized."[38] This is partly a function of philosophy. Conservatives who hanker to "get Washington out of our lives" are not apt to be eager to get into a Washington life.

Furthermore the multiplication since the 1970s of financial-disclosure and conflict-of-interest requirements are especially burdensome for persons whose lives and finances are especially complicated. This affects both parties, but Republicans, who tend to turn more to business executives and entrepreneurs when recruiting candidates, are affected more.[39] And then there is the Republican handicap of Republican success. Republicans have done so well in presidential politics that Republicans who are interested in public service often have an alternative to running for elective office. They can serve in the executive branch, which is a culture more akin to the corporate world than is the culture of Congress. Finally, as Ornstein says, "the longer a party holds the White House, the worse it does in Congress."[40] It is not clear why this is so. Perhaps Americans do instinctively treat Congress as a flywheel to control the executive. But whatever the reason, the stark fact is that since the Civil War "every party has left the White House with fewer members of Congress than it had when it entered."[41]

Leaving aside (far aside, where it belongs) the possibility—which is slight—of quick partisan advantage, it might at first seem strange for a conservative to champion term limits. The reform is undeniably radical. In fact, its radicalism is what recommends it. But modern conservatism, properly understood, from Edmund Burke on, has preached wariness and skepticism about radicalism generally. Conservatives do not merely take seriously the law of unintended consequences, they often are conservatives largely because of it and all that it intimates about political life. That law says that the unintended consequences of any substantial change of social policy are apt to be larger than, and contrary to, the intended consequences. The more radical the policy, the more surely and severely the law applies.

Furthermore, one of the certain results of term limitations will be undeniably unfortunate. Term limits unquestionably will truncate some great careers. It is, Lord knows, not the case that all long careers are great, but many great careers are long. Eliminating long careers is not a cost I consider trivial. The person I have most admired in my twenty-two years in Washington was Henry M. "Scoop" Jackson, the Democratic senator from the state of Washington, who died at age seventy-one on September 1, 1983. He came to the House of Representatives in January, 1941, five months before I was born. He moved to the Senate side of the Capitol in 1952. If there had been term limits of the sort most commonly discussed, limiting senators to two terms (and House members to six), he would have been gone from the Senate by the end of 1964, long before I came to Washington in 1970.*

So, term limitation, like any other reform, will be only a mixed blessing. The question is: How mixed? Are the benefits apt to be larger and more long-lasting than the costs? For the many reasons given in the preceding pages, I think the answer is clearly yes. In the 1990s the country will, I think, say so too, if given a chance.

* Term limits restricting House members to six consecutive terms and Senators to two consecutive terms would not have interfered with the careers enjoyed by two members of "The Great Triumvirate" of the first half of the nineteenth century. John C. Calhoun served sixteen years in the Senate (in two non-consecutive terms of eleven and five years) and another six in the House. Henry Clay served a total of sixteen years in the Senate in four separate stays of one, one, eleven and three years, and eleven years in the House in three nonconsecutive terms of three, six and two years. Daniel Webster served a total of eight years in two nonconsecutive stints in the House (four years representing New Hampshire and four representing Massachusetts), but he served nineteen years in two nonconsecutive stays in the Senate, one of them extending fourteen years.

The first important test of the term limitation movement came in 1990, in California, where one-ninth of the American electorate lives. California voters passed term limits for the state legislature. The movement's second important test came in 1991, in Washington State. There the movement fell short in a 54–46 percent vote. However, the movement could take considerable satisfaction from coming as close as it did in Washington State, considering the political context and some strategic mistakes.

The Washington State term limit initiative seemed punitive and mean-spirited because it would have applied retroactively to the congressional delegation. That is, the terms that members had already served would have counted against the twelve-consecutive-years-of-service limit that the new law would have imposed. This was especially important to Washingtonians because their delegation includes Speaker Tom Foley. He is much-loved and very valuable for a state that has profited substantially from the seniority of its national legislators. (Scattered all across the state there is evidence of the effectiveness of "the gold dust twins," Warren Magnuson and Henry Jackson, who between them served sixty-seven years and eight months in the Senate.)

There were several other reasons why Washington State was an unpromising place to make a conspicuous early test case for term limits. In Washington, as in most Western states, the federal government is in some ways much more important than it is elsewhere. Begin with three of the most basic elements of existence—land, water and power, both electrical and political. The federal government owns 28.9 percent of the land in the State of Washington. You are startled? The federal governments owns substantial percentages of the lands of many Western states: Nevada 82.2, Alaska 67.8, Utah 63.7, Idaho 62.5, California 60.9, Wyoming 48.7, Oregon 48.1, Arizona 43.3, New Mexico 33.1, Montana 27.7. (East of the Mississippi, the highest federal ownership in a state is 13.6 percent of West Virginia. The federal government owns 27.8 percent of the District of Columbia.) Furthermore, Washington, like other Western states, has a huge stake in federal policy decisions regarding water, including the generation of electricity by water. So it was reasonable for Washingtonians to worry about what price they might pay by acting alone to limit the terms of their congressional delegation. Opponents said that acting alone would be a foolhardy act of unilateral disarmament in the unending competition for "clout."

After the voting, the high-powered media team that had been hired by opponents of term limits wrote that the people who hired them knew they "could not win this initiative on the basis of the pros and cons of congressional term limits alone. In order to win [they] would have to shift the debate . . . to the consequences of Washington state losing its congressional clout."[42] In this argument, California—or, more precisely, Californiaphobia—played a crucial role. As Mindy Cameron of the *Seattle Times* said: "California was very much painted as the bogeyman. The thrust of the anti-term limit campaign was to say that if it passed, within three years we would lose all of our incumbents and, thus, our clout in Congress. California would then be free to, willy-nilly, drain the Columbia [river], raise our power rates, and undermine our whole economy."[43]

It is a tad paranoid for Washingtonians to think that Californians harbor all these dark designs, and it is preposterous to believe that only Washington's representatives and senators, like so many Horatios at the bridge, stand between Washington State and a pillaging California. But preposterousness can work in politics, and it did work this time. Term limits lost in Washington State by an eight-point margin and a *Seattle Times* exit poll showed that 16 percent of those voting against term limits did so because they feared the state's loss of congressional power. However, 15 percent of those who voted against term limits said they would favor term limits if they were imposed nationwide. That is, they objected not to term limits but to Washington State's opting out of the seniority sweepstakes.[44]

Another reason the Washington State term limit initiative failed, and perhaps should have, is constitutional. Although this is an unsettled area of constitutional law, the preponderant weight of constitutional argument may be against the possibility of limiting congressional terms by state law. And even if limitation by state law is constitutionally possible, it might be more proper to achieve limitation by constitutional amendment.

Article I, Section 4, Clause I of the Constitution stipulates that states have the authority to set "the times, places, and manner of holding elections for senators and representatives," but also that Congress "may at any time by law make or alter such regulations." Does the power of states to make time, place, and manner decisions about elections encompass a power to restrict the class of persons eligible to seek House or Senate seats? That is what term limitation would do. It would add a qualification to those qualifications enumerated in the Constitution. Term limitation would say that no person may run who has served a specific number of consecutive terms.

There is language in some Supreme Court rulings that encourages the belief that the Court would affirm the power of states to enact term limits for their U.S. senators and representatives. Courts do have a tradition of deference toward measures that states adopt to enhance the openness of their electoral processes. And the Supreme Court as constituted in the 1990s is apt to be particularly deferential toward a state's decision to impose term limits on the persons elected from that state to the federal legislature.

However, advocates of term limitation want to be careful not to argue as though the virtue of their end justifies shortcuts as to means. They do not want to appear more ingenious than ingenuous in trying to achieve term limits without getting into the properly rigorous process of amending the Constitution. Besides, the supposed shortcut—fifty decisions by states in favor of term limits—might not turn out to be shorter than the process of amending the Constitution. That process is not usually as protracted as many people think.

Let us leave aside that ludicrous aberration, the 27th Amendment, which was proposed by James Madison in 1789 and was not finally ratified by the requisite number of states until 1992. Were Congress not invertebrate in 1992, it would have declared the amendment invalid because proper ratification requires *contemporaneous* consent of Congress and three-quarters of the states. But, then, if Congress were not invertebrate, this trivial amendment concerning congressional pay raises would not have been pushed to ratification by the indignation aroused by recent congressional slipperiness regarding pay raises.

The average length of time required for ratification of the other twenty-six constitutional amendments has been just one year, eight months and one week. The average time for amendments passed in this century has been one year and six months. The longest time required for ratification in this century was the three years and eleven months required to ratify the Twenty-second Amendment, which in 1951 imposed a two-term limit on the presidency. The shortest time required for ratification was the three months it took the states in 1971 to ratify the Twenty-sixth Amendment lowering the voting age to eighteen.[45]

Advocates of term limits should cheerfully face the fact that they are caught in the cleft stick of their own logic. If term limitation is not important, then it is much more trouble than it is worth. On the other hand, if term limitation is as important as its proponents insist it is, then perhaps they should want to achieve it by constitutional amendment. Perhaps they should make the constitutional amendment process an advertisement for the seriousness of the stakes. All proper arguments for term limits demonstrate that matters of fundamental importance—fundamental values—are at issue in the controversy. Therefore, it may be proper for these matters to be addressed in the fundamental law of the land. Advocates of term limits correctly insist that their reform would improve the way representative institutions are constituted. That is a reason for acting through the constituting document—the Constitution.

The term limits movement should adopt a three-track strategy. It should continue with attempts to get individual states to limit the terms of members of the U.S. House and Senate. Such measures may indeed turn out to be deemed proper in the judgment that ultimately matters most, that of the Supreme Court. Certainly the term limits movement is not obligated to assume a particular answer—one adverse to its interests—to a still-open constitutional question. However, the term limits movement also should simultaneously campaign for state limitations on the terms of state legislators and for a constitutional amendment limiting members of the national legislature. Progress regarding the former will increase the probability of success regarding the latter. This is so for reasons pertaining to ambition and legitimacy.

The ambitions of state legislators can be harnessed to help the cause of term limits for U.S. senators and representatives. As more and more state legislators are brought under term limits, those who want to prolong their sojourn in politics will need to find other offices to seek. Compulsory rotation of congressional offices will clear the ground of entrenched incumbents. So term limits for Congress will be attractive to those state legislators who are themselves forced by term limits to make an "up or out" choice—moving up to other offices or out of politics.

The imposition of term limits on state legislatures also will impart momentum to term limits for Congress because limits will become associated with legitimacy. The legitimacy of Congress as currently constituted will come to seem attenuated if Congress never permits a forthright debate and national choice on term limits.

Watch the states. Term limits will come from them to Congress. Here is how. More and more states will pass term limits for state legislatures. California, Colorado and Oklahoma already have them. Limits for state legislators will be on at least nine and perhaps fifteen state ballots this year. Furthermore, in close House and Senate races, more and more candidates will seek an edge by endorsing limits. Soon many U.S. representatives and senators will be committed to sending to state legislatures a constitutional amendment limiting terms. All state legislators, especially those whose terms are limited, will rush to ratify a reform that will unclog the political system and open higher offices to competition.

The best members of Congress, such as Representative Willis Gradison, a Republican from Cincinnati, may come to regard it as a requirement of honor to send forth such an amendment, even if they do not necessarily favor it. Describing himself as "an opponent of term limits who is re-examining his position," Gradison says:

> We have to decide if we really trust the people. If we do, the Congress will eventually submit a constitutional amendment for congressional term limitations to the states with or without recommendation—and then abide by the results. To continue the present situation could well lead to the Congress being one of a diminished number of legislative bodies in the country without term limits, and yet afraid to let the people decide if they want limits for the Congress.
>
> In my view this would only intensify the feeling that the Congress is out of touch. But worse still, it further undermines the sense of legitimacy of our actions without which represen-

tative government could be viewed as a mere slogan used by those whose overriding concern is maintaining power, not serving the public.[46]

Term limitation will take time. Constitutional change should. But it is coming. Since the first Congress met in 1789, 10,600 Constitutional amendments have been tossed into the legislative hopper. Only twenty-seven have been adopted. And ten of them—the Bill of Rights—came from the first Congress in a package that had essentially been promised during the states' debates over ratification of the Constitution. Americans' reverence for the Constitution disposes them toward healthy conservatism: If it is not necessary to change, it is necessary not to change. And any attempt to demonstrate such necessity must surmount the healthy skepticism of a nation that also is conservative in believing that the Constitution should be touched to address only serious problems of governance. However, today's problems, and especially the overarching problem of the crisis of confidence in government's competence and motives, are of constitutional dimension.

Our Constitution is not beyond the reach of majorities, but it is beyond the reach of slender majorities, and beyond the quick reach of even sizable majorities that are evanescent. To change the Constitution you need a substantial majority with staying power. Such power should be the product of serious ideas. Term limitation is grounded in serious ideas, such as deliberative democracy and classical republicanism.

❧ ❧

In the famous first paragraph of the first of the Federalist Papers, Alexander Hamilton said that Americans, "by their conduct and example," will decide whether government by "reflection and choice" shall supplant government by "accident

and force."[47] Since that was written the world has turned many
times, and many democracies have been born. America's sense
of uniqueness, and hence of mission, has been somewhat diminished by this multiplication of democracies.

It has been diminished, but not extinguished. Ours is the
oldest democracy and remains much the most important. By
virtue of our relative antiquity, our example carries special
saliency. And because of the material power we possess,
which we have from time to time been called upon to deploy
in defense of democracy, we feel, and are, more implicated
than any other nation in the world's political evolution.
Therefore how we do at the day-to-day business of democracy
matters. It matters mostly to us, but not only to us. The
world is watching.

It has been watching American democracy since 1776.
Friends of popular sovereignty held their breath between 1861
and 1865. For two centuries American history has been the
most important drama the world has known. And there is
heartening evidence that Americans have a quickening sense of
just how dramatic it is.

At the dawn of this decade many millions of Americans
shared an extraordinary experience. The sharing was done in
the modern manner of a wired nation, via television. The experience was public television's presentation of Ken Burns's
eight-part series on the Civil War. It was a profoundly moving
immersion in the event that was the hinge of our history. Viewers came away from Burns's masterpiece feeling that they had
passed through a fiery furnace, and that their citizenship was,
like tempered steel, stronger because of it.

For many viewers, the most memorable moment was in
the first episode, when the narrator read portions of the letter
written by Major Sullivan Ballou of the 2nd Rhode Island to his
wife, a week before the first battle of Bull Run. Here are those
portions:

July 14, 1861

Camp Clark, Washington

My very dear Sarah:

The indications are very strong that we shall move in a few days—perhaps tomorrow. Lest I should not be able to write again, I feel impelled to write a few lines that may fall under your eye when I shall be no more. . . .

I have no misgivings about, or lack of confidence in the cause in which I am engaged, and my courage does not halt or falter. I know how strongly American Civilization now leans on the triumph of the Government, and how great a debt we owe to those who went before us through the blood and sufferings of the Revolution. And I am willing—perfectly willing—to lay down all my joys in this life, to help maintain this Government, and to pay that debt. . . .

Sarah my love for you is deathless, it seems to bind me with mighty cables that nothing but Omnipotence could break; and yet my love of Country comes over me like a strong wind and bears me unresistibly on with all these chains to the battle field.

The memories of the blissful moments I have spent with you come creeping over me, and I feel most gratified to God and to you that I have enjoyed them so long. And hard it is for me to give them up and burn to ashes the hopes of future years, when, God willing, we might still have lived and loved together, and seen our sons grown up to honorable manhood, around us. I have, I know, but few and small claims upon Divine Providence, but something whispers to me—perhaps it is the wafted prayer of my little Edgar, that I shall return to my loved ones unharmed. If I do not my dear Sarah, never forget how much I love you, and when my last breath escapes me on the battle field, it will whisper your name. Forgive my many faults, and the many pains I have caused you. How thoughtless and foolish I have often times been! How gladly would I wash out with my tears every little spot upon your happiness. . . .

But, O Sarah! if the dead can come back to this earth and flit unseen around those they loved, I shall always be near you;

in the gladdest days and in the darkest nights . . . always, al-
ways, and if there be a soft breeze upon your cheek, it shall be
my breath, as the cool air fans your throbbing temple, it shall be
my spirit passing by. Sarah do not mourn me dead; think I am
gone and wait for thee, for we shall meet again. . . .[48]

Seven days after Sullivan Ballou wrote this letter he was killed at the first battle of Bull Run.

I began this book with some words spoken long ago, by American soldiers at the surrender of Charleston. Those words—"Long live Congress!"—suggest how much the American mind has changed—has soured—regarding what should be a glory of our Republic, the national government's great institution of representation and deliberation. I shall end the same way, by calling attention to some words that are especially revealing because they were written so unself-consciously. The words of the soldier in 1861, like the words of the soldier in 1779, have a spirit and resonance about our nation's government that may seem strange to us. This is, for us, a misfortune.

The sweet power of Major Ballou's love letter derives, in part, from the fact that he professes two loves—for Sarah and for the United States. And he expresses the latter love in direct references to the government. The letter may have struck an especially deep chord among Americans in the 1990s precisely because its language of love for America's government seemed, in the 1990s, so sharply, and sadly, anachronistic: "I know how strongly American Civilization now leans on the triumph of the Government. . . . And I am willing—perfectly willing—to lay down all my joys in this life, to help maintain this Government. . . ."

Fondly do we hope that American civilization will never again be in the kind of crucible it was in between April, 1861, and April, 1865. Nevertheless, American civilization still leans on the success of the government. Our national life is still the world's preeminent drama of popular sovereignty. Nowadays Americans are not asked to lay down the joys of life to help maintain the government. However, the demands of civic duty, although much lighter than those borne by Major Ballou, are not negligible. They all serve the goal of making self-government shine. Fulfillment of that goal ultimately depends on each citizen's governance of his or her civic self. Americans must restrain themselves, heeding the exhortation of the third verse of "America the Beautiful" to "confirm thy soul in self-control." Americans must be less demanding of government. They must give to government more constitutional space in which to think, more social distance to facilitate deliberation about the future. And Americans must resolve especially to seek a more reserved and respectful relationship with the First Branch of government, Congress.

Term limitation is a measured, moderate and—let it be said—loving step toward such a restoration.

Notes

Introduction

1. Robert Middlekauff, *The Glorious Cause: The American Revolution, 1763–1789* (New York: Oxford University Press, 1982), pp. 448–49.
2. Constitutional Convention, *The Debates in the Federal Convention of 1787*, p. 34, as cited in Sula P. Richardson, CRS, *Congressional Tenure: A Review of Efforts to Limit House and Senate Service* (Washington, D.C.: Congressional Research Service, 1989), p. 3.
3. Abraham Lincoln, *The Collected Works of Abraham Lincoln*, Roy P. Basler, ed. (New Brunswick, N.J.: Rutgers University Press, 1953), vol. IV, p. 190.

CHAPTER 1.   From Bristol to Cobb County

1. Robert V. Remini, *Henry Clay: Statesman for the Union* (New York: W. W. Norton, 1991), p. 45.

2. Stephen B. Oates, *With Malice Toward None: The Life of Abraham Lincoln* (New York: Penguin Books, 1977), p. 230.

3. William S. McFeely, *Grant: A Biography* (New York: W. W. Norton, 1981), p. 286.

4. Phil Duncan, "CQ Roundtable: Defending Congress, the Institution," *Congressional Quarterly*, November 30, 1991, vol. 49, no. 48, p. 3554.

5. Brooke A. Masters, "Federal Program Subsidizes Flights to Homestead Resort," *Washington Post*, November 19, 1991, pp. A1, A7.

6. *Ibid.*, p. A7.

7. Jonathan Rauch, "The Golden Fleece," *National Journal*, May 18, 1991, pp. 1168–71.

8. *Ibid.*, p. 1169.

9. *Ibid.*, p. 1170.

10. *Ibid.*, p. 1168.

11. Morton M. Kondracke, "Pennsylvania Avenue: Caught Between Old Politics and New, Clinton Gets Stung," *Roll Call*, June 25, 1992, p. 6.

12. *Kansas City Star*, "Failing The Grade," a special report originally published December 8–14, 1991.

13. James Bovard, "Bush Protection," *The New Republic*, January 20, 1992, p. 9.

14. *Ibid.*, p. 9.

15. David Hess, "Yes, W. Va., there is a Santa Claus," *Philadelphia Inquirer*, August 9, 1991, p. 21A.

16. Daniel Patrick Moynihan, from a speech "If We Can Build Saudi Arabia Can We Not Rebuild America?" the Robert C. Weinberg Fund Lecture, American Planning Association, at the University Club, New York City, June 18, 1983, p. 4.

17. John A. Byrne, "The Flap over Executive Pay," *Business Week*, May 6, 1991, p. 90.

18. Charles E. Shepard, "Perks, Privileges and Power in a Nonprofit World," *Washington Post*, February 16, 1992, p. A1.

19. Dennis Barbagello, "As I See It: Redistricting Eliminates State Senate Candidate," *Greensburg Tribune-Review*, November 17, 1991, p. A4.

20. Robert D. Popper, letter to the author, June 9, 1992.

21. Eric Foner, *Reconstruction: America's Unfinished Revolution 1863–1877* (New York: Harper & Row, 1988), p. 590.

22. Susan B. Glasser, "Disillusioned with the Money Chase, Eckart Makes Surprise Decision to End Hill Career," *Roll Call*, October 3, 1991, p. 16.

23. Dennis Eckart, interviewed by George F. Will, November 5, 1991.

24. Statement of The Honorable Dennis E. Eckart, September 30, 1991.

25. Eckart interview with author, November 5, 1991.

26. *Ibid.*

27. *Ibid.*

28. Representative Donald J. Pease, interview with author, November 6, 1991.

29. *Ibid.*

30. *Ibid.*

31. Willie Stargell, quoted in Thomas Boswell, *How Life Imitates the World Series: An Inquiry into the Game* (Garden City, N.Y.: Doubleday, 1982), p. 247.

32. Representative Donald J. Pease, "Guest Observer: Why I've Decided to Leave Congress After Next Year," *Roll Call*, October 21, 1991, p. 5.

33. *Ibid.*

34. Nelson W. Polsby, "Congress Bashing for Beginners," *The Public Interest*, no. 100 (Summer 1990), p. 21.

35. Richard Shapiro and Maria Touya, *1990 U.S. House of Representatives Employment Practices: A Study of Staff Salary, Tenure and Demographics* (Washington, D.C.: Congressional Management Foundation, 1990), p. 7.

36. David Twenhafel, *1991 U.S. Senate Employment Practices: A Study of Staff Salary, Tenure, Demographics and Benefits* (Washington, D.C.: Congressional Management Foundation, 1991), p. 17.

37. James Madison, *The Federalist*, Jacob E. Cooke, ed. (Middletown, Conn.: Wesleyan University Press, 1961), No. 52, p. 355.

38. *Ibid.*, No. 53, p. 362.

39. James L. Payne, "The Congressional Brainwashing Machine," *The Public Interest*, no. 100 (Summer 1990), p. 13.

40. *Ibid.*, p. 5.

41. *Ibid.*, p. 5, emphasis in the original.

42. *Ibid.*, p. 6.

43. *Ibid.*, p. 7.

44. *Ibid.*, p. 12.

45. Colleen Cordes and Jack Goodman, "Congress Earmarked a Record $684 Million for Non-Competitive Projects on Campuses," *The Chronicle of Higher Education*, vol. 38, no. 32 (April 15, 1992), pp. A1, A26, A31–36.

46. *Ibid.*

47. *Ibid.*

48. Senator Albert Gore, Jr., *Congressional Record—Senate*, March 3, 1992, S 2648.

49. Sharon Percy Rockefeller, "An Answer to George Will's Answer," *Washington Post*, May 15, 1992, p. A25.

50. Dr. Laurence Jarvik, Backgrounder: The Heritage Foundation, "Making Public Television Public," # 873, January 18, 1992.

51. Walter Goodman, "TV VIEW: Pull The Plug on PBS?" *New York Times*, March 22, 1992, p. H33.

52. Andrew Ferguson, "POINT OF VIEW/Not With My Money: With So Many Alternatives On the Air, Does Public TV Still Deserve a Handout? *The Washingtonian Magazine*, July, 1990, p. 64.

53. Sharon Percy Rockefeller, "Big Bird: Someone Didn't Do His Homework," *Washington Post*, April 29, 1992.

54. *Ibid.*

55. *Ibid.*

56. *Ibid.*

57. Bill Moyers, as a guest on *NIGHTLINE: Conservatives Trying to Kill Off Public Broadcasting*, ABC Television, May 12, 1992; see page eight of transcript for show # 2862.

58. Robert J. Samuelson, "Special Pleading for Public TV," *Washington Post*, May 27, 1992, p. A19.

59. *Ibid.*

60. *Ibid.*

61. *Congressional Record—Senate*, June 3, 1992, S 7472 Rollcall Vote No. 114 Leg.

62. Aristotle, cited in Garrett Ward Sheldon, *The Political Philosophy of Thomas Jefferson* (Baltimore: Johns Hopkins University Press, 1991), p. 90.

63. *Ibid.*

64. Trudy Pearce, *Term Limitation: The Return to a Citizen Legislature* (Langley, Va.: U.S. Term Limits Foundation, 1991), p. 18.

65. Norman J. Ornstein, Thomas E. Mann and Michael J. Malbin, *Vital Statistics on Congress 1991–1992* (Washington, D.C.:

American Enterprise Institute/Congressional Quarterly, 1992), Table 1–6, pp. 19–20.

66. *Ibid.*, Table 1–7, p. 21.

67. David C. Huckabee, *CRS Report for Congress: Re-election Rates of House Incumbents, 1790–1988* (Washington, D.C.: Congressional Research Service, 1989), p. 2.

68. *Ibid.*, pp. 5–13.

69. Inter-University Consortium for Political and Social Research and Carroll McKibbin, ROSTER OF UNITED STATES CONGRESSIONAL OFFICEHOLDERS AND BIOGRAPHICAL CHARACTERISTICS OF MEMBERS OF THE UNITED STATES CONGRESS, 1789–1991; MERGED DATA (computer file), 8th ICPSR ed. (Ann Arbor, Mich.: Inter-University Consortium for Political and Social Research, producer and distributor, 1991).

70. Inter-University Consortium for Political and Social Research and Carroll McKibbin, ROSTER OF UNITED STATES CONGRESSIONAL OFFICEHOLDERS AND BIOGRAPHICAL CHARACTERISTICS OF MEMBERS OF THE UNITED STATES CONGRESS, 1789–1991; MERGED DATA (Computer file), 8th ICPSR ed. (Ann Arbor, Mich.: Inter-University Consortium for Political and Social Research, producer and distributor, 1991).

71. David C. Huckabee, *CRS Report for Congress: Re-election Rates of Senate Incumbents, 1790–1988* (Washington, D.C.: Congressional Research Service, 1990), Summary.

72. *Ibid.* (1990), p. 2.

73. Ornstein, Mann and Malbin, *Vital Statistics*, Table 2–2, p. 49.

74. *Ibid.*, Table 2–7, p. 58, and Table 2–8, p. 59.

75. Samuel Kernell, "Toward Understanding 19th Century Congressional Careers: Ambition, Competition, and Rotation," *American Journal of Political Science*, vol. 21 (November 4, 1977), pp. 669–93.

76. *Ibid.*, pp. 691–92.

77. *Ibid.*, p. 674.

78. *Ibid.*

79. William Dean Howells, *Indian Summer* (New York: Vintage Books/The Library of America, 1990), p. 11.

80. Kernell, p. 671.

81. Woodrow Wilson, *Congressional Government: A Study in American Politics* (Boston: Houghton, Mifflin, 1900), p. 324.

82. Everett Carll Ladd, "Public Opinion and the Congress Problem," *The Public Interest,* no. 100 (Summer 1990), pp. 60–61.
83. John L. Jackley, *Hill Rat: Blowing the Lid Off Congress* (Washington, D.C.: Regnery Gateway, 1992), p. 47.
84. *Roll Call,* June 25, 1992, p. 4.
85. William Booth, "The House Bank Aftermath, Georgia: Hatcher Still Plays to Peanut Gallery," *Washington Post,* April 19, 1992, p. A1.
86. *Ibid.*
87. Peter Applebome, "Gingrich Tries to Avoid Heat of Voter Outrage He Fanned," *New York Times,* April 18, 1992, p. 1.
88. Edmund Burke, Speech of October 13, 1774, *Burke's Politics: Selected Writings and Speeches of Edmund Burke on Reform, Revolution and War,* Ross J. S. Hoffman and Paul Levack, eds. (New York: Knopf, 1949), pp. 114–17.

CHAPTER 2.   The Recovery of Deliberative Democracy

1. Edmund Cody Burnett, *The Continental Congress* (New York: W. W. Norton, 1964), p. 605, as cited by Sula P. Richardson, *CRS Report for Congress: Congressional Tenure—A Review of Efforts to Limit House and Senate Service* (Washington, D.C.: Congressional Research Service, Library of Congress, September 13, 1989), pp. 2–3.
2. The Committee's *Report,* in the writing of Roger Sherman, Papers of the Continental Congress, No. 23, Folio 247, as cited in Richardson, *CRS Report,* pp. 2–3.
3. Harvey C. Mansfield, Jr., *America's Constitutional Soul* (Baltimore: Johns Hopkins University Press, 1991), p. 8.
4. Alexander Hamilton, *The Federalist,* No. 68, Jacob E. Cooke, ed. (Middletown, Conn.: Wesleyan University Press, 1961), p. 461.
5. James Madison, *The Federalist,* No. 10, Jacob E. Cooke, ed. (Middletown, Conn.: Wesleyan University Press, 1961), p. 62.
6. Mansfield, *America's Constitutional Soul,* p. 68.
7. *Ibid.,* p. 140.
8. Madison, *Federalist* No. 51, p. 349.
9. Mansfield, *America's Constitutional Soul,* p. 182.
10. Alexis de Tocqueville, *Democracy in America,* Phillips Bradley, ed. (New York: Knopf, 1963), vol. II, part IV, chapter 6, p. 317, as cited in Mansfield, *America's Constitutional Soul,* p. 177.
11. Mansfield, *America's Constitutional Soul,* p. 5.
12. *Ibid.,* p. 3.

13. Constitution of the State of Massachusetts, Declaration of Rights, Article VIII, cited by Mark P. Petracca, "Rotation in Office: The Massachusetts Commitment," in his comments prepared for submission to the State of Massachusetts Legislative Hearing on Term Limitation Amendment (#H4000), March 25, 1992.

14. John Adams, quoted in *ibid.*

15. Elbridge Gerry, quoted in *ibid.*

16. Article VIII, Declaration of Rights, Constitution of the State of Massachusetts, quoted in *ibid.*

17. Joseph M. Bessette, "Is Congress a Deliberative Body?" presented at Thomas P. O'Neill, Jr., Symposium on the U.S. Congress, Boston College, 1981, in Dennis Hale, ed., *The United States Congress* (New Brunswick, N.J.: Transaction Books, 1983), p. 11.

18. *Ibid.*, p. 9.

19. *Ibid.*

20. Charles A. Vanik, "Congress Is Deliberative: Compared to What?" presented at O'Neill Symposium on U.S. Congress, in Hale, ed., *United States Congress*, p. 16.

21. *Ibid.*

22. *Ibid.*, p. 17.

23. *Ibid.*, p. 18.

24. *Ibid.*

25. *Ibid.*

26. Madison, *Federalist* No. 57, p. 386.

27. Madison, *Federalist* No. 63, p. 425.

28. *Ibid.*

29. *Ibid.*

30. Hamilton, *Federalist* No. 71, pp. 482–83.

31. *Ibid.*

32. Mansfield, *America's Constitutional Soul*, p. 148.

33. *Ibid.*, p. 174.

34. Tocqueville, *Democracy in America*, vol. II, part IV, chapter 7, p. 325.

35. Jeffrey K. Tulis, *The Rhetorical Presidency* (Princeton, N.J: Princeton University Press, 1987).

36. *Ibid.*, Table 3.1, "Presidential Tours and Other Popular Communication, before the Twentieth Century," p. 64.

37. U.S. Senate, *Proceedings in the Trial of Andrew Johnson* (Washington, D.C., 1869) 1, 4, 5–6, as cited in *ibid.*, p. 91.

38. Tulis, *Rhetorical Presidency*, p. 63.

39. *Ibid.*, key to Table 3.2, "Purposes of Popular Presidential Rhetoric," p. 66.

40. Benjamin Harrison, *Speeches of Benjamin Harrison*, comp. Charles Hedges (New York: U.S. Book Co., 1892), pp. 383, 469, 495, cited in *ibid.*, p. 86.

41. Tulis, *Rhetorical Presidency*, p. 87.

42. *Ibid.*, p. 102.

43. Woodrow Wilson, "Leaderless Government," address before the Virginia Bar Association, August 4, 1897, cited in *ibid.*, p. 117.

44. Cited in *ibid.*, p. 125.

45. Cited in *ibid.*, p. 129.

46. *Ibid.*, p. 27.

47. *Ibid.*, p. 130.

48. *Ibid.*, p. 31.

49. *Ibid.*, p. 14.

50. *Ibid.*, p. 26.

51. Woodrow Wilson, "Abraham Lincoln: A Man of the People," in Baker and Dodd, eds., *College and State*, 2:94–95. See also idem, "A Memorandum on Leadership, May 5, 1902," in *The Papers of Woodrow Wilson*, ed. Arthur S. Link (Princeton, N.J.: Princeton University Press, 1966–), vol. 12, p. 365, cited in *ibid.*, n. 33, p. 135.

52. Link, *Wilson Papers*, vol. 27, p. 150, cited in *ibid.*, footnote on pp. 135–36.

53. Mark P. Petracca, "The Professionalization of American Politics: Representational Consequences and a Principled Response," prepared for submission to the *California Political Review*, March 12, 1991; revised September 17, 1991.

54. Mansfield, *America's Constitutional Soul*, p. 16.

55. *Ibid.*, p. 156.

56. Joseph M. Bessette, "Deliberative Democracy: The Majority Principle in Republican Government," in Robert A. Goldwin and William A. Schambra, eds., *How Democratic Is the Constitution?* (Washington, D.C.: American Enterprise Institute, 1980), pp. 102–16.

57. Aristotle, "Politics," *The Basic Works of Aristotle*, Richard McKeon, ed. (New York: Random House, 1941), book 1, chapter 2, p. 1129.

58. Susan B. Glasser, "Traxler Makes 52," *Roll Call*, vol. 37, no. 83, May 4, 1992, pp. 1, 25.

59. Susan B. Glasser, "Broomfield Out: Congress 'Intolerable,' " *Roll Call*, vol. 37, no. 80 (April 23, 1992), pp. 1, 55, 56.
60. The Hon. John C. Danforth, *Congressional Record—Senate*, March 26, 1992, p. S-4305.

CHAPTER 3.   The Revival of Classic Republicanism

1. James Thomas Flexner, *George Washington in the American Revolution, 1775–1783* (Boston: Little, Brown, 1967, 1968), p. 535.
2. *Ibid.*, p. 526.
3. William Shakespeare, *Troilus and Cressida*, I, iii, 109.
4. John Maynard Keynes, *The General Theory of Employment, Interest and Money*, bk. VI, ch. 24, as cited in *The Macmillan Dictionary of Quotations* (New York: Macmillan Publishing Company, 1987), p. 176.
5. *Ibid.*
6. Garrett Ward Sheldon, *The Political Philosophy of Thomas Jefferson* (Baltimore: Johns Hopkins University Press, 1991).
7. Louis Hartz, *The Liberal Tradition in America* (New York: Harcourt Brace, 1955), p. 140, cited in *ibid.*, p. 4.
8. Sheldon, *Political Philosophy of Jefferson*, p. 5.
9. J. G. A. Pocock, *The Machiavellian Moment* (Princeton, N.J.: Princeton University Press, 1969), cited in *ibid.*, p. 5.
10. Forrest McDonald, *Alexander Hamilton: A Biography* (New York: W. W. Norton, 1979), p. 4.
11. Noble E. Cunningham, Jr., *In Pursuit of Reason: The Life of Thomas Jefferson* (Baton Rouge: Louisiana State University Press, 1987), p. 314.
12. *Ibid.*, p. 314, and note 37 on p. 394.
13. Bernard Bailyn, *The Ideological Origins of the American Revolution* (Cambridge, Mass.: Harvard University Press, 1967), pp. 24–25, cited in Sheldon, *Political Philosophy of Jefferson*, p. 149.
14. Thomas Jefferson to Joseph C. Cabell, February 2, 1816, cited in Sheldon, *Political Philosophy of Jefferson*, p. 85.
15. *Ibid.*
16. Thomas Jefferson, *The Anas*, pp. 1208, 1246, cited in Sheldon, *Political Philosophy of Jefferson*, p. 91.
17. Jefferson, letter to Joseph C. Cabell, February 2, 1816, *The Life and Selected Writings of Thomas Jefferson*, Adrienne Koch and William Peden, eds. (New York: Modern Library/Random House, 1944), p. 662.
18. Eric Foner, *Reconstruction: America's Unfinished Revolution*

1863–1877 (New York: Perennial Library/Harper & Row, 1989), p. 278.

19. *Ibid.*, p. 23.

CHAPTER 4. "Like a Strong Wind"

1. Timothy E. Wirth, "Time for a New Crew in Washington," *Washington Post*, May 12, 1992, p. A19.

2. Mary Ann Glendon, *Rights Talk: The Impoverishment of Political Discourse* (New York: Free Press, 1991).

3. *Ibid.*, p. 3.

4. *Ibid.*, p. 9.

5. *Ibid.*, p. 177.

6. *Ibid.*, p. 178.

7. Joseph A. Califano, Jr., *The Triumph and Tragedy of Lyndon Johnson: The White House Years* (New York: Simon & Schuster, 1991), p. 185.

8. *This Week with David Brinkley*, July 21, 1991, Program no. 508. Copyright © 1991 American Broadcasting Companies.

9. Joseph Spiers, "Do Americans Pay Enough Taxes?" *Fortune*, June 1, 1992, p. 68.

10. Daniel Patrick Moynihan, *Social Science and Social Policy: A Case Study of Overreaching* (New Haven, Yale University Conference on Sociological Visions, April 5, 1992), p. 15.

11. Robert A. Caro, *The Years of Lyndon Johnson: The Path to Power* (New York: Knopf, 1986), pp. 695–701.

12. *Ibid.*, p. 700.

13. Robert A. Caro, *The Years of Lyndon Johnson: Means of Ascent* (New York: Knopf, 1990), p. 141.

14. Thomas Jefferson, *The Life and Selected Writings of Thomas Jefferson*, ed. by Adrienne Koch and William Peden (New York: The Modern Library, 1944), pp. 488–93. Emphasis in original.

15. William A. Niskanen, testimony to the House Budget Committee, Washington, D.C., April 29, 1992.

16. *Ibid.*

17. James Madison, cited by Herbert Agar, *The Price of Union* (Boston: Houghton Mifflin, 1966), p. 184.

18. *Ibid.*

19. *United States* v. *Butler*, 297 U.S. 1 (1936).

20. Simon Heffer, "Politics: Some Helpful Suggestions About How Best to Use the People's Mandate," *The Spectator*, April 25, 1992, p. 6.

21. John H. Fund, "Making the Case for Term Limits," *Chicago Tribune*, December 16, 1990, p. 3.

22. Vin Weber, "Asides," *Wall Street Journal*, April 10, 1992, p. A16.

23. Susan B. Glasser, "McGrath's Retirement Brings Ways & Means Departures to 11 of 36," *Roll Call*, June 11, 1992, p. 16.

24. Timothy E. Wirth, "Time for a New Crew in Washington," *Washington Post*, May 12, 1992, Editorial Page.

25. *Ibid.*

26. Martin Tolchin, "33 Retirees in House Are Eligible for $8.6 Million," *New York Times*, June 7, 1992, p. A22; "Inside Congress: Congressional Departures," *Congressional Quarterly Weekly Report*, June 27, 1992, vol. 50, no. 26, p. 1859.

27. Michael Barone, "On Politics: The New 'Save Our Wealth' Voters," *U.S. News & World Report*, June 22, 1992, p. 45.

28. Norman Ornstein, "The Permanent Democratic Congress," *The Public Interest* (Washington, D.C.: National Affairs, Inc., 1990), no. 100 (Summer 1990), p. 32.

29. D. Eric Schansberg, from a paper, "Moving Out of the House: Analysis of Congressional Quits," Texas A&M University, College Station, June 1992.

30. W. Robert Reed and D. Eric Schansberg, from a paper, "An Analysis of the Impact of Congressional Term Limits, Texas A&M University, College Station, July 1991.

31. Mark P. Petracca, "Why Do Political Scientists Oppose Term Limits?" *Cato Institute Briefing Papers* (Washington, D.C., 1992), no. 14, February 18, 1992.

32. Irving Kristol, "On Corporate Capitalism in America," in *Reflections of a Neoconservative: Looking Back, Looking Ahead* (New York: Basic Books, 1983), p. 211.

33. Irving Kristol, "The Cultural Revolution and the Capitalist Future," *The American Enterprise*, vol. 3, no. 2 (March–April 1992), pp. 42–51.

34. T. S. Eliot, *Murder in the Cathedral* (New York: Harcourt Brace 1935), p. 44.

35. *Guide to U.S. Elections*, 2d Edition (Washington, D.C.: Congressional Quarterly, Inc. 1985), p. 111.

36. Ornstein, "Permanent Democratic Congress," p. 25.

37. *Ibid.*, p. 29.

38. *Ibid.*, p. 37.

39. *Ibid.*

40. *Ibid.*, p. 39.
41. *Ibid.*
42. *Campaign Magazine*, February 1992, cited in "The Term Limit Outlook Series: Handling the Clout Issue—The Lessons of Washington State" (Washington, D.C.: U.S. Term Limits, April 1992), no. 1, p. 2.
43. Mindy Cameron, *Seattle Times*, in an interview with the *Orange County Register*, cited in *ibid.*, pp. 6–7.
44. *Ibid.*, pp. 7–8.
45. Harold W. Stanley and Richard G. Niemi, *Vital Statistics on American Politics* (Washington, D.C.: CQ Press, 1990), Table 1–3, p. 16; David Huckabee, Library of Congress, Congressional Research Service.
46. Representative Willis D. Gradison, Jr., *Congressional Record—House*, vol. 137, no. 163 (November 6, 1991).
47. Alexander Hamilton, *The Federalist*, Jacob E. Cooke, ed. (Middletown, Conn.: Wesleyan University Press, 1961), No. 1, p. 3.
48. Geoffrey C. Ward, *The Civil War: An Illustrated History*, based on a documentary filmscript by Geoffrey C. Ward, Ric Burns, and Ken Burns (New York: Knopf, 1990), pp. 82–83.

Acknowledgments

et again thanks are owed to Erwin Glikes and the others who make The Free Press a pleasure to work with. In my office Dusa Gyllensvard, Mary Moschler and Gail Thorin again proved themselves to be the Ruth, Gehrig and Dimaggio of book production.

Index